The Objects of Social Science

The Objects of
Social Science

ELEONORA MONTUSCHI

continuum
LONDON • NEW YORK

Continuum
The Tower Building, 11 York Road, London, SE1 7NX
370 Lexington Avenue, New York, NY 10017-6503

First published 2003

British Library Cataloguing-in-Publication Data
A catalogue record for this book is available from the British Library.

ISBN: 0–8264–6634–6 (hardback), 0–8264–6635–4 (paperback)

Typeset in Times New Roman by RefineCatch Limited, Bungay, Suffolk
Printed and bound in Great Britain by
Biddles Ltd, Guildford and King's Lynn

Contents

Preface

The roots of this book are the lectures and seminars in the philosophy of the social sciences I have been giving in the last few years at the London School of Economics, and previously at Oxford. The book also elaborates on work I contributed to a series of seminars on the epistemology of the social sciences at the University of Pavia between 1995 and 1998.[1]

Though trained in the philosophy of science, I have always found social science a rich, often intriguing domain of investigation, and a fertile reservoir for philosophical analysis. In looking at both the natural and the social sciences, I find especially the differences in their epistemologies and in their ontologies instructive. Among other things, they ultimately offer clues as to how a large number of controversial issues in both domains of inquiry could be thought anew. Objectivity is one such issue.

By focusing on objectivity, this book will serve a double purpose. On one side, it will draw attention to the various procedures, methods, forms of description and of classification of objects used in social scientific inquiry. On the other, it will help reflect on the theoretical, methodological, or more generally philosophical queries posed by the practice of social science. The book can be read, by and large, as an introduction to the philosophy of social science aimed at those (including philosophers) who are interested in what goes on in the social sciences. In line with this approach, objectivity will not be treated, nor identified as an ideal, or a predefined standard. It will rather be analysed as the result of a specific type of activity, namely social scientific practice.

A few words on the structure of this book might prove useful. The introductory chapter is meant to provide a general survey of some of the main issues raised by the quest for objectivity in social science, and to indicate the contexts in which these issues have been discussed and analysed in the philosophical literature on social science. The expert reader might simply want to use it as a reminder of

---

[1] I used part of this work to write Part III of Borutti, S., *Filosofia delle scienze umane. Le categorie dell'Antropologia e della Sociologia*, Milan: B. Mondadori, 1999.

the main issues. The beginner will find in it an overview of some relevant topics, together with bibliographical suggestions for where these topics are discussed. What both categories of readers will find in it, nonetheless, will be a rationale as to how to read the chapters to come.

The chapters in the book investigate the ways in which specific social sciences deal with the objects of their own research, and their goal is to solicit reflection on how the objectivity of social scientific research depends on the ways in which these objects are identified, and on what questions are being asked of them. Each chapter will offer some background information concerning the 'disciplinary' field of inquiry under investigation, and the history of its methodological debates; some detailed analysis of case studies and illustrations of the objects of inquiry; and a selection of bibliographical aids, alongside the quoted references, for those who are interested in finding out more.

The choice of social sciences in this book is by no means complete. Indeed, it was not meant to be so. The idea was to give examples (and I used examples which were more familiar to me), not to offer an encyclopaedia of social scientific objects. I hope that the limited selection presented in this book will encourage readers to come up with their own, further examples.

Separating out 'objects' by reference to the different 'sciences' which deal with them is a controversial move. The distinctions among disciplines today are not so clear-cut, and it is often the case that more than one such science is put to use in the analysis of the same social phenomenon. In fact, the emphasis given in the book on the complexity of social scientific objects is a way to point up the fact that these objects are multifaceted, and that they can be approached from many different angles. Despite there being problems about demarcation, in what follows I will nonetheless distinguish the objects of social inquiry by referring to the kinds of activity the practitioners of a discipline identify themselves with. This of course does not exclude that a practitioner within a discipline may make use of methods and procedures from other disciplines.

There are several people I am grateful to: colleagues and friends who discussed, read, commented, disagreed, advised on this book, and encouraged or showed interest in its completion. I would also like to thank the social scientists and the philosophers who, over the last few years, came to speak at my seminars and invited me to speak at theirs. I hope none of them will be too disappointed in seeing what I made of what I learnt from them. Here is a no doubt incomplete list out of the categories of people I just mentioned: Gareth Williams, Sophie Weeks, Orly Shenker, Simon Schaffer, Andy Pratt, Marcello Pera, William Outhwaite, Steven Lukes, Tony Lawson, Colin Howson, Rom Harré, Adrian Haddock, Ian Hacking, George Gaskell, Johannes Fabian,

John Dupré, Nancy Cartwright, David Bloor, Silvana Borutti, Barry Barnes, Rita Astuti.

For helping with the editing, I thank Robert Northcott. For their insightful comments, I thank two anonymous referees. Last but not least, I am indebted to my students, for asking me all sorts of questions and for keeping me critical of what I know.

Places are as important as people, in writing a book. In writing mine, I have been lucky enough to be part of, and to be able to enjoy the friendly and stimulating atmosphere of the Centre for Philosophy of Natural and Social Science at LSE.

On a more personal note, I am grateful to Alistair Morley, for having kept me entertained and well fed all along.

I dedicate this book to the memory of my parents, Giacomo and Ada Montuschi. And to Jack.

London
6 July 2002

Introduction: Objectivity, Science and Social Science

1. A SKEWED COMPARISON

An old and often revisited question is still lingering on in contemporary philosophical debates concerning the social sciences: can we attain 'objective' knowledge of the social world? For a series of reasons, which are partly methodological and partly historical, this question goes hand in hand with another question: is knowledge of the social 'scientific'? By taking these two questions as germane, the objectivity of social scientific knowledge has been treated as a normative issue.[1] A paradigm of objective knowledge is fixed – i.e. natural science – and by claiming that there is only one way to be objective (the way of natural science), social scientific knowledge then becomes objective only if it follows the method and procedures of natural science. 'Being scientific' – according to the model of science purportedly instantiated by natural science – is treated as the ideal to be emulated by any discipline that seeks to produce reliable information about its object of inquiry. 'Scientific knowledge', on this view, is considered to be the highest ranked type of knowledge which a field of inquiry should aim at.[2]

The history of social science is full of examples which reflect the adoption of this normative attitude. We have been told that history is 'objective' when its explanations comply with what a scientific explanation looks like, that is a logical inference from a law (together with initial conditions) to the occurrence of individual events. Why did the French Revolution occur? Because the conjunction of a series of events necessarily led to the revolution, as it would lead to a revolution every time a similar conjunction historically occurs. Similarly, we have been told that anthropological or sociological understanding is 'objective' only if we can treat anthropological and sociological findings as 'facts', or 'data' to be generalized by means of universal laws. For example, anthropology widely made use, in the nineteenth century, of the so-called comparative method. This method relied, on the one hand, on the existence of recurrent traits and features across different cultures, and on the other, on the formulation of explanatory laws of human/social development.

However, the history of social science is also a history of endless readjustments of the protocols of natural, 'real' science, in order to let them meet the specific needs of, and comply with the features belonging to, social scientific practice. It was clear from the start that social scientific inquiry was for a series of reasons at odds with those protocols. Curiously, but not surprisingly, from this comparison with natural science, it was social science which was to emerge with a remarkable 'inferiority complex'. I say 'not surprisingly' because the reasons given to explain why social science cannot comply with natural science, or why its results cannot be objective, are reasons traditionally developed from within the paradigm of objective knowledge purportedly offered by natural science. It is as if social science was forced into fighting a battle which it had no chance of winning.[3]

For example, the often-rehearsed argument that, in order to reach objective (i.e. factual) conclusions, a scientist is to keep his personal values at bay, is usually said to score differently in the case of either natural or social science. In the latter case, unlike the former, values often also appear as part of the conclusions of the social scientist's arguments. This is an indication that such conclusions are reached not *despite* but rather *by means of* value-laden claims, as are laid out in the premises.[4] For instance, imagine a natural scientist who puts forward the hypothesis that the earth is surrounded by a radiation belt of a certain kind.[5] In support of his hypothesis, he appeals firstly to some relevant observational data; secondly, to some pre-established theories, through which those data have been reliably interpreted; and finally, he invokes some value judgements, such as 'it is good to ascertain truth'. Clearly, the latter is logically irrelevant to the acceptance or rejection of the hypothesis. On the other hand, imagine, in support of the hypothesis that different races are intellectually unequal, that some intelligence theorist were to adduce (1) evidence coming from IQ tests performed on different racial groups, showing racially consistent differences in scores; (2) some theory about the genetic, inherent basis of human intelligence; (3) some racially motivated belief against certain groups of people. In this case, it might well be that (3) is as involved in reaching the conclusion that a certain race is more intelligent than another as (1) and (2) are. Even more worryingly, it might be that (3) informs and encourages a certain reading of the results offered by purportedly 'objective' measurement.[6] Of course, the objective credentials of the conclusion reached on the basis of such 'evidence' appear rather questionable.

Similar queries emerge from assessing the different role played in either the natural or social domain by other potentially interfering factors. This is the case, for example, with the argument that any science is pursued within the limits of particular *contexts* (social, cultural, historical), and that the results of science are then to be understood within the limits of these contexts.

In the 1930s, Mannheim put forward a rather radical view.[7] As Mary Hesse explains in her 1976 essay,[8] Mannheim supports two rather controversial theses. The first consists of two theories of ideology – one particular, and one total. According to the former, ideology is a form of distortion of reality by means of a set of biased beliefs. Particular ideologies are detrimental to any objective assessment of some reality, and need to be eliminated. A typical example is the self-interested ideological views held by the ruling classes, as pictured by Marx's theory of capitalism. However, interest-driven beliefs are not the prerogative of the ruling classes, Mannheim argues. Also the ruled classes, and their spokesmen have their own ideologies, as well as an interest in seeing their ideologies prevail. This brings Mannheim to shift from the particular to the total theory of ideology: there is no set of beliefs in a society, which is not subservient to some social party or group. The result, then, is that any criticism of some particular ideology cannot but come from another particular ideology, and therefore it is itself socially determined.

If this is the situation, then Mannheim falls victim to a contradiction created by his own first thesis. If all beliefs are ideologically determined – or, to use a more recent terminology, 'essentially contested'[9] – then there is no way to distinguish between distorting/distorted beliefs and reality. Objectivity becomes a meaningless standard, as well as a purposeless goal. He then introduces a second thesis. As Hesse reminds us, Mannheim claims that natural science, mathematics and logic are excluded from the total/particular ideology thesis, by assuming that 'in these areas at least we can preserve the distinction between the body of true and grounded beliefs equated to knowledge on the one hand, and false belief or error on the other'.[10] The fact that such a distinction does not work for the social domain of inquiry might be taken to be an indication of the endemic limits and specific problems of the latter. It is interesting that, in order to rescue his first thesis from its fatal impasse, Mannheim is prepared to make social science pay the worst price.

In the 1960s, Lakatos eloquently explained the role played by contextual factors on both the discovery of scientific facts and on the genesis of theories in the natural domain. Contextual factors, he argued, are only 'external' influences on the genesis of scientific theories, and they acquire weight only in the explanation of 'pathological' or rationally/scientifically deviant beliefs. Scientific theories can be judged independently of contextual factors (or 'internally'), and a good methodology should be able to explain theories and the discovery of the facts to which they refer without any substantial recourse to context-dependent factors – in particular, without any recourse to sociological-type explanations. Lakatos's distinction between 'internal' and 'external' factors was aimed both at banning (or minimizing) social analysis from the realm of objective justification and at depriving social scientific investigation itself of any value, credential, and efficacy.[11]

A further example of how purportedly interfering factors promote objectivity-preserving strategies, which might not work so well for social science as they do for natural science, is provided by that complex of arguments built on the claim that facts are socially 'constructed'. The reasons put forward against social constructionist viewpoints normally aim at making it more difficult to accept that natural, rather than social, facts are constructed.[12] Natural facts cannot be socially constructed if, for instance, we want to avoid falling prey to the absurd thought that the world of nature cannot exist without human beings creating it; or that there is no way to distinguish between facts (an order of reality independent, though not 'resistant to', human intervention) and beliefs about facts (a man-dependent reality). It is sometimes even argued that natural facts must exist in a non man-made reality if we want to be able to explain the successes of science. Interestingly, the same reasons do not appear so crucial, nor so devastating, in assessing the purportedly not-constructed nature of social facts. Is it incoherent to claim that in the absence of human beings there are no social facts? Is it as controversial to claim that, say, a political leader exists because somebody (one or many) believes that he/she exists, as it is to claim that molecules exist because a scientist believes that they exist? Even the 'success' of social science can hardly be used as an indication that social science describes non-socially constructed facts, given that often the opposite view seems to hold (the actual lack of success of social science is used as evidence against the reality of its objects of investigation). Overall, what seems to be hard(er) to accept is that a constructivist metaphysics applied to scientific/natural facts would ultimately eliminate the idea of an objectively existing (as opposed to subjectively), external, independent world of natural objects, processes, etc., as a plausible referent for scientific inquiry. It is also hard to accept one consequence of such a move, namely that in the absence of that world as a referent, the so-called discoveries of science are subjective (as opposed to objective) events. It is not surprising, then, that the debates over constructivist issues happen to be at their harshest when natural science is put under scrutiny. The so-called 'science wars' are a testimony of how the 'invasion' of social/sociological viewpoints onto the grounds of natural science are received by a domain of inquiry (viz. natural science) both unsuitable and hostile to sociologically inclined scrutiny.[13]

Does then the comparison between natural and social science entail a biased view of what the objectivity of social scientific knowledge should amount to? Why should we believe that the only way to argue in favour of an objective social science is through a certain model of what scientific research should look like? Philosophers of science in the so-called post empiricist tradition showed that the model of 'being scientific' and 'being objective', as suggested by natural science, is flawed.[14] The orderly, methodological, rule-bound, value-free picture of natural science is a misrepresentation of what scientific research is in actual fact.

The picture, so it is claimed, hardly describes what science really is, or how it is conducted. Such a picture succeeds still less when prescribing what any discipline which aims at being objective (just like natural science) should imitate. This critique ended up denying that there are universal standards for being a science. As a consequence, normative connotations such as 'objective', 'rational', or 'true' lose their prescriptive power. It is a short step to making the boundaries between disciplines disappear. In the end, and at its most radical end, nothing is left to demarcate, in principle, science from any other practice of inquiry. Paradigmatic models of knowledge are part of the same fantasy picture. Methodologically prescriptive views of scientific knowledge were replaced by relativistic assessments of the local conditions under which knowledge is achieved, and of socially determined scientific beliefs.[15]

In some instances relativism is assimilated into strong forms of contextualism. Strong contextualism entails some form of *epistemological holism*, that is a view according to which the assessment of a belief depends on the support of the whole structure (context) of beliefs to which the one in question belongs. It also entails some form of *interpretivism*: to say that the assessment of a belief is contextual is to say that there is no direct descriptive relation between the belief and what it represents. Context wholly determines content (according to a selected and non-universal series of assumptions), and contextual representations cannot ever be mere (re)descriptions of independently existing states of affairs.

Epistemological holism plus interpretivism is often charged with sceptical consequences, as most famously exemplified by the so-called 'hermeneutic circle'.[16] The underlying argument runs as follows. Our knowledge claims are interpretations (rather than representations), since they depend on context. However, a context is itself interpretative (it depends on other interpretations). So, when we try to assess our knowledge claims, we ultimately rely on yet other interpretations, rather than on independent evidence. When this argument is made to work in the context of either natural or social science, normally the direct consequence is a denial of objectivity.[17] Interpretive knowledge – featured as indeterminate, partial, and perspectival – is taken to be the opposite of justified true belief. What the argument challenges, and ultimately denies, is that science can 'capture some feature independent of the activity itself', that is independent of the kind of activity (or social practice) that science is.[18]

However, these kinds of reaction still seem to proceed from the assumption that being scientific and being objective are the two sides of the same coin, to the effect that if we discredit one side, the other goes with it. Besides, this criticism, despite its devastating consequences for the methodological image of science, has left the common perception of the practice of science almost untouched. In fact, the successes of natural science in terms of prediction and measurement remain a good argument in favour of the objective value of its methods of inquiry.[19] While, on the one hand, we are offered ground evidence to question whether natural science is indeed a paradigm of objective knowledge, on the other, we are constantly confronted by the fact that the paradigmatic appeal of natural science endures almost undisturbed. This ambiguity of assessment deeply affects social science, which appears to be divided between a desire for emulation of 'proper' science and the awareness that such a desire lacks the very condition for its own fulfilment (i.e. a reliable image of what 'proper' science consists of).

The root of this ambiguity – as I see it – rests with the acceptance of the paradigmatic role of science, and with the normative attitude which such acceptance promotes. To remove such ambiguity, we should start, I believe, by questioning *what is meant to imitate what*, as regards the comparison between natural and social science. This means that a possible answer to this question is to be looked for, and framed on two levels. On the one level, we should expose the model of science which is normally adopted in talks of social scientific objectivity. On the other level, we are to figure out what model of knowledge is most pertinent to social scientific inquiry. Both lines of investigation have been addressed in the philosophical literature on social science.

2. WHAT MODEL OF SCIENCE FOR SOCIAL SCIENCE?

With regard to the first level of questioning, it has been pointed out that, traditionally, the paradigmatic model of science is *positivist*. Positivism is nowadays an abused term. There are many and various types of positivism, and not all positions labelled as 'positivist' share the same features (for example, positivism is often and mistakenly taken to be equivalent to empiricism).[20] There is nonetheless a common core underlying the variety of approaches falling under the label. The etymology of the term might offer some useful insight. The French term '*positif*' means 'based on facts or experience'. It was used by Comte (and by Saint-Simon before him) to refer to the 'scientific' stage reached by human knowledge, after evolving from more primitive stages, namely the 'theological' and the 'metaphysical'.[21] In the scientific or 'positive' stage, the exclusive source of all objective information (true knowledge) comes from observable experience, the only experience which can be logically and mathematically treated, as well as measured and predicted by science. Science is then about facts, and facts are observable or empirically identifiable. What guarantees the objectivity of knowledge claims is the accuracy of the representation of the factual features of the objects of scientific knowledge. Instrumental to achieve such accuracy is scientific method, which provides reliable guidelines to select those pieces of information that are meant to comply with facts and which, therefore, can enter the domain of objective knowledge. To select objective information entails eliminating all those factors (such as values, contextual features, human-dependent elements) which are deemed to interfere with purely factual knowledge.

If science, according to this picture, is the highest (most evolved) level of knowledge, then a positivistic philosophy must promote the extension of the scientific attitude and method to all those fields of inquiry which are yet immune from them. In Comte's days, scientific method had already been adopted by such mature disciplines as mathematics, astronomy and physics; whereas it was still absent from politics, ethics and economics. This is why such disciplines, Comte argued, appear to be full of prejudices, biases and superstitions. The task of a positive philosophy is that of unifying all the results of each science, and to make a joint use of those results in view of producing a real science of society – a science which Comte names 'social physics', or 'sociology'.

Comte's views were echoed, on the other side of the Channel, by J. S. Mill.[22] Mill entitled the part of his *System of Logic*, which deals with social issues, 'On the logic of the moral sciences'. He appeared to be confident that the domain of individuals and of social behaviour could be treated logically and scientifically. His confidence, nonetheless, did not entail that such a domain be endowed with a logic of its own: if we want to treat the social domain logically and scientifically, Mill claimed, we ought to make use of the inductive method, and we must discover empirical laws. Like Comte, Mill recommended the application of the same method and the same logic which already pertained to the natural sciences.[23]

Perhaps, one of the most famous illustrations of how scientific method is made to work in social science is provided by Durkheim's *Rules of Sociological Method*. Acting on Comte's and Mill's prescription that a science of society should adopt the same method as natural science, Durkheim laid down a detailed methodological strategy to achieve this aim.[24] The 'rules' of sociological method should, firstly, help in identifying social phenomena as factual referents (just like natural facts). This entails the elimination of all those factors which are deemed to interfere with such factual identification (evaluations, individual elements, ideological projections, subjective beliefs, etc.). By relying on the rules of sociological method, we will then be prevented from mistaking ideas (mental projections) of things for real 'things'. Secondly, and as prescribed by the rules of method, the so identified social facts are to be offered to sociological analysis in the same way as any natural 'facts' can be. In positivist style, this means that procedures such as measurement, testing, statistical analysis, nomological explanations, etc., can all be employed when accounting for social facts. The applicability of these procedures is, in its turn, an indication of a sufficient degree of objectivity in sociological inquiry.

However, and as suggested earlier, by looking at the history of the extension of scientific method into the realm of social scientific inquiry, a whole host of strictures are encountered, which might just point at the fact that such an extension is overall unjustified. In the specific case of Durkheim's view, for example, it has been pointed out that, were social science to comply with the dictates of scientific method, important aspects of the social domain of inquiry would be neglected or altogether eliminated. Real people and actions are substituted by typologies of individuals and classifications of acts and recurrent behaviour. This is because the latter are better and more easily amenable to empirical testing, statistical analysis and law-like generalization (i.e. to 'scientific' procedures). Social science becomes more preoccupied with turning social phenomena into *factual/empirical* occurrences (the best paradigm of which being that of natural facts), than with exploring what is specifically *social* about those occurrences. As we will discuss in more detail later, Durkheim's well-known study on suicide[25] in terms of the explanation of the 'rates of occurrences' of acts of suicide provides a good illustration of this.

An alternative tendency has developed in the literature on social science, whereby a different methodological strategy is endorsed. Rather than neutralizing potentially interfering factors for the sake of salvaging the positivistic ideal of objective/scientific knowledge, attempts are made to include such factors, and to make a constructive use of them, both in social inquiry and in the descriptions of its methods and results. Such a 'rescue operation', however, can only be undertaken by changing some essential features of the epistemological picture on the basis of which those factors are assessed. In other words, what is considered to be 'interfering' in the context of positivistic science is made to lose this negative connotation, and acquire a different meaning, by separating it from that context. The reasons, which traditionally conjured against the aptness of social science to comply with the paradigm of objective knowledge, can now be viewed as reasons to rethink both what that paradigm wrongly entailed and what any relevant analysis of 'objective' social scientific inquiry is to acknowledge.

3. WHAT MODEL OF KNOWLEDGE FOR SOCIAL SCIENCE?

We then come to the second level of questioning the comparison between natural and social science, namely how to figure out what model of knowledge is most pertinent to social scientific inquiry. As suggested above, in some literature this is pursued by trying to establish how factors such as values, contexts, and constructions can be included in a model of social scientific knowledge without necessarily detracting from the 'objectivity' of this model. In other words, the attempt is to find out whether an argument of the following form can be at all validated:

1) *if* values/constructions/contexts are part of knowledge claims in social science
2) *then* for objective claims to be possible in social science, those values/constructions/contexts should themselves give us reasons to believe so.

Some of the possible merits of following this alternative strategy were already envisaged, for example, by Weber and Myrdal. In their views, values in particular acquire a different role in social scientific inquiry from that which was traditionally attributed to them. In Weber, values are used to select our objects of inquiry. What we call 'reality', he argued, is constituted by a potentially infinite number of phenomena, and of features of phenomena. When we do scientific research we choose, from that number, only some phenomena and/or some features, namely those we have an interest in inquiring about. In making such a choice, we cannot count on strict criteria. What we use instead are values, which attribute significance to, and reveal our interest in, what we investigate. In other words, these values make certain phenomena (organized according to certain selected features) to be the 'objects' which are *relevant* for us to inquire about.[26] Nonetheless, once these objects are identified, values cease to play any role, according to Weber, and social scientific inquiry can be carried out in an empirical, causal, and nomological style.[27] For Myrdal, values permeate social scientific inquiries. More radically than Weber, he argues that they insinuate themselves into all stages of research, from premises to conclusions. It is then crucial to make them explicit, to expose their influence on the results achieved, and to analyse what part they play in reaching those results themselves. Values can, in fact, acquire a constructive role in social scientific inquiry by making us aware of the conditions under which the results of inquiry are achieved.[28] Myrdal goes even further, by claiming that we might want to choose deliberately our value-premises, and give them a '*strategically favourable* position'[29] in designing our research.

Though both still under the spell of a fact-value distinction, and driven by the urge to preserve the factual integrity of social scientific research, these two positions are interesting for our discussion here, as they mark a significant departure from the traditional epistemological picture underlying the positivistic model of science. Firstly, they deny that what we refer to as the 'object' of social inquiry is (must be) factual. It is rather what a series of conditions, intellectual categories or evaluational premises identifies as a particular object of knowledge.[30] Secondly, they amend the role of values, by reclassifying their meaning. Not all values are the same (i.e. subjective, unwarranted beliefs), not all values are biases, and not all biases are in principle detrimental to the way research is carried out and assessed. On one side, Weber separates out biases from cultural, socially shared values, and distinguishes between value-judgement (an ideologically entrenched and potentially distorting practice) from value-relevance (an epistemologically valuable and validated strategy of attributing meaning to the objects of research).[31] On the other side, Myrdal draws attention to the constructive relation between facts and values, and urges us to rethink the meaning of objectivity in social research by questioning the conditions (partly factual and partly evaluational) under which social scientific results are achieved: 'biases', he claims, 'are the unfortunate results of concealed valuations'.[32]

Both suggestions have been developed in more contemporary literature. For example, according to some feminist epistemologists, an adequate and more complete meaning of objectivity, both in natural and social science, is to include the evidence coming from the subjective side. Besides, any adequate assessment of what constitutes 'objectivity' needs to rely also on the evidence arising from this subjective side.[33] Against the view that objective knowledge is to exclude values, it has been suggested that no theory, explanation, or mode of inquiry is completely 'objective' if it eliminates subjective factors. A view of objectivity based on a rigid distinction between facts and values fails in its attempt at maximizing objectivity.[34] Firstly, it does not deliver the kind of objectivity it promises. While promoting techniques for eliminating values from the results of research, this view is not so well effective in policing over those values which are already included as a consequence of the choice of a particular way of conducting research. Secondly, it is too indiscriminate. It turns away from all values (interests, desires), without considering that not all values are the same, and not all of them have the same detrimental effects on the results of research. For instance, some values might prove crucial in 'mediating' between evidence and results of scientific inquiry. As argued by Longino, 'contextually located background assumptions play a role in confirmation as well as in discovery' and therefore 'scientific inquiry is . . ., at least in principle, permeable by values and interests superficially external to it.'[35] It is crucial to distinguish, according to Longino, among the different types of values and the various ways by, and levels on, which they affect the descriptions and interpretations of scientific data. A fruitful interplay occurs, she claims, between scientific knowledge and *cultural/social* values, to the point that the latter can be proved to have a specific role in shaping scientific knowledge. They can also be proved to have a role in keeping biases in check.[36] For such a role to be appreciated, however, a different view of what scientific knowledge amounts to, and of how it can be claimed to be 'objective', is necessary. It is Longino's view that scientific knowledge is a form of social knowledge, and consequently that objectivity, according to this view, becomes 'a function of community practices rather than . . . an attitude of individual researchers towards their material or a relation between representation and represented'.[37] The reference to community practices is meant to block the thought, not only in principle, that the inclusion of subjective assumptions in knowledge claims introduces an element of arbitrariness in those claims. Subjective experience undergoes the critical scrutiny and social, intersubjective control, as they are carried out in specific communities, as well as in the larger social context where communities belong.

A different assessment of the role of context has, then, also come to the fore, against the sceptical consequences of strong contextualist views. It has been pointed out that these views work only on the assumption that a context, or background, is taken to be a 'limit' on knowledge in the sense of being an obstacle, a constraint, or an impediment on the objective content or results of knowledge. However, this is not the only meaning that the concept of limit might have. Bohman, for example, provides a different assessment of the concept.[38] He believes that the limits imposed on knowledge claims by contexts can also work as 'enabling conditions' for those very claims. To illustrate his point, he makes use of an analogy. Compare two people who speak a foreign language. One is fluent, the other makes use of a phrase book. The latter is 'limited' in the number of things he can say and understand in a way that the former is not. The phrase-book speaker's conditions of expression and interpretation are determinate and fixed by the book. They are also material and specific (they refer to the particular sets of beliefs and skills the speaker acts under). The fluent speaker's conditions are variable, modifiable, and enabling. They are also formal and general (they abstract from specific cases, and can be transferred, reflectively, onto other, yet-to-be explored possibilities). The former conditions only tell us that the speaker is engaging himself with a particular language. They alone do not say anything about what is required of a speaker to become 'fluent' in the use of the language.

Similarly, a context – though unquestionably a constraining condition of knowledge – is not by itself strong enough to act as a negative, fixed limit on what can be known. Besides, it does not in principle prevent the content of an interpretation from being evaluated to some extent independently of the general context. This means that the limit provided by a context might allow for possibilities of knowledge to come to the fore, which are not necessarily to be judged by those constraints. As we will examine later,[39] ethnographic inquiry provides a good example of how knowledge of other forms of life, though 'limited' by socially contested categories of description, is not only possible but also 'enabled', and promoted by those very categories. Besides, the contextual standards for the evaluation of the knowledge so acquired might themselves call for additional criteria of evaluation, in order to be able to 'understand how it is that we understand understanding not our own.'[40]

Some form of contextualism must therefore be retained, but such form does not lead to sceptical conclusions as regards knowledge.[41] In particular, it does not support the view that the only alternative to objective knowledge (in the positivistic sense) is contextual indeterminacy. In order to avoid such an unfruitful alternative, once again the meaning of objectivity is revisited and amended. Bohman uses the expression 'reflective adjudication'[42] to refer to a form of 'conditioned' objectivity. Contextual knowledge can be 'objective' if it is 'capable of being intersubjectively warranted and publicly adjudicated'.[43] If the assumptions and conditions which collectively make contextual knowledge possible are public and social, then the testing of those conditions and assumptions guided by epistemic norms should also be so.

Finally, against the idea that objective facts cannot be socially constructed, it has, for example, been pointed out that it is crucial, firstly, to understand what we refer to when we say that fact X is constructed; and secondly, to investigate what the construction of specific categories of facts actually entails. As to the first query, we ought to acknowledge that objects, in either the natural or social domain, are classified in certain terms, and that these classifications (or kinds) are indeed socially constructed. As to the second, we must be able to see that natural classifications and human classifications are not constructed in the same way. There is a big difference between, say, quarks and child TV viewers (and criminals, women refugees, etc. etc.).[44] For Hacking, the former – though affected by what we say and know about them – do not act the way they do because they are aware of what we know and say about them. 'The classification "quark" is indifferent in the sense that calling a quark a quark makes no difference to the quark.'[45] Traditional natural sciences are about 'indifferent kinds': these are, to some extent, 'stationary targets' – which does not mean passive. Many of these kinds do rather extraordinary things when people act on them.[46] However, they do not know that they are doing those things, and they do not do any of those things because of the ways we classify them.

The situation appears to be different in the social domain of inquiry, where people always act 'under description', and they experience themselves in the world according to ongoing descriptions – that is, they perceive themselves as being people of certain kinds. Kinds of people are, for this reason, 'interactive kinds'.[47] Consequently, when people become the object of study of a social science, they interact with the ways they are classified by such science, and rethink the kind(s) by which they perceive themselves accordingly (or contrastively). There is a feedback, or 'looping' effect involved with classifying people, where 'self-conscious knowledge plays much of a role'.[48] *Kinds* of people may change, because the *people* classified as being of certain kinds might themselves change as a consequence of being so classified. The targeted referents of social scientific inquiries are, so to speak, on the move. Interaction stands for an active, bidirectional relation, which seems suitably to accommodate at the same time 'actors, agency and action'. In other words, it alerts us to 'the way in which the actors may become self-aware as being of a kind, if only because of being treated or institutionalized as of that kind, and so experiencing themselves in that way'.[49]

Quite rightly, Hacking reminds us that the social sciences are often under pressure to emulate the natural sciences, and 'produce true natural kinds of people'. However, for this to be possible, the social sciences have to endorse a certain epistemological picture (that there is 'an object to be searched out, the right kind, the kind that is true to nature, a fixed target'[50]) which simply proves inadequate in the social domain of inquiry. This is not to claim that the 'kinds' social science deals with can never be in any way 'indifferent'. For instance, an autistic child can be classified both interactively and indifferently: that is, a social classification does not exclude the possibility that the individual so classified is in some such pathological state. It does mean, though, that a social ontology exclusively informed by indifferent classifications will not do its job properly. It also, and most importantly, make us reflect on the way the objects of our classifications and the classifications themselves relate and conform to each other in specific instances of social 'constructions'.

What all these positions seem to show is that an inclusion of purportedly interfering factors does not necessarily detract from objectivity talk. It only requires that the conditions under which we can refer to the objectivity of our inquiries, beliefs, and descriptions are reviewed and made explicit. Such a task is to be undertaken, as far as I can see, along two parallel routes. Firstly, and as we infer from the perspectives just outlined, a revision of some basic epistemological vocabulary must be promoted. Secondly, and consequently, a reassessment of the actual concept of objectivity must be endorsed. If 'values', 'contexts' and 'constructions' are not bound to be equivalent to 'biases', 'constraints' and 'fictions', then nothing in principle prevents the concept of objectivity from being made value- and context-sensitive. Nothing also prevents, and in fact it seems to be advisable, that a careful reflection on what objects social scientific inquiry 'constructs' and, at the same time, tries to be objective about, is carried out.

4. WHAT MODEL OF OBJECT FOR SOCIAL SCIENCE?

Part of the philosophical literature on social science has taken special interest in modelling the object of social scientific inquiry, meaning that object which the social scientist tries to produce knowledge of. The type of inquiry suitable to social objects, it has been argued, depends on the types of objects this inquiry is concerned with. In particular, it has been claimed that these objects are *different* from natural objects, and that, as a consequence, knowing these kinds of objects requires either additional rules and categories of description, or specific procedures of analysis. These rules, categories and procedures can be found either in the context of a different model of science, or in that of a radically different model of social science.

Among those who addressed the specificity of social scientific objects in yet scientific terms are the critical realists. Mostly inspired by the views and arguments of R. Bhaskar,[51] the critical realists defend the specificity of the objects of social scientific inquiry by acknowledging their ontological differences from natural objects. However, the comparison between the two categories of objects, and the specific features which such comparison brings to light as regards social objects, do not detract from the possibility for these objects to be treated scientifically. What is only denied is that they can be treated as categories of *positivistic* scientific objects. In fact, the realists argue, the only relevant comparison between natural and social objects must be conducted on the basis of a realist model of scientific objects. According to this model, scientific objects are ontologically 'intransitive' (existing independently of our knowledge/ methods of inquiry) and unobservable (conceived in terms of generative mechanisms or structures, of which empirical, observable phenomena are only a manifestation). The difference between natural and social objects, vis-à-vis this model, consists of the type of independence they have from knowledge/ inquiry: it is total independence, in the case of the former; partial, in the case of the latter.

The partial independence of social objects that Bhaskar talks about manifests itself in various forms. Social objects, unlike natural ones, do not exist independently of the activities they govern (and also they cannot be identified independently of them empirically). For example, marriage does not exist outside the practice of people getting married. Social objects – unlike natural ones – do not exist independently of the agents' conceptions of what they are doing in their activities. Marriage exists because people believe in some form or other of an institution called 'marriage', and a 'marriage' is brought into reality by the belief that by pronouncing certain words in certain, socially sanctioned circumstances two people 'get married'. This also means that social objects are 'conceptualized in the experience of the agents concerned'[52] and since people's conceptualizations have a history, these objects are not immutable (marriage, like any other institution, can change over time). Finally, and more generally, it has to be acknowledged that the social sciences, unlike the natural sciences, are part of their own field of inquiry, in the sense that they are 'internal' with respect to their subject matter. This makes social scientific categorizations

self-referential, and the referents of social scientific inquiry themselves dependent on the processes which produce the knowledge of those very referents.

Nonetheless, partial independence is only taken to demonstrate that the
objects of social science are of a specific nature (i.e. social nature), not that they
do not constitute a category of scientific objects – and even less, that they cannot
be treated scientifically.[53]

Among those who use the specific nature of social scientific objects as evidence that these objects cannot be investigated by a 'science' are various categories of interpretivists. The interpretivist tradition, in its various forms and
arguments, ideally relates to the humanistic and historicistic tradition which
first developed in Germany, back in the nineteenth century.[54] A most famous
follower of this perspective in the Anglo-Saxon tradition was Peter Winch.
Winch put significant emphasis on the idea that social phenomena are 'complex', and on the fact that their complexity cannot be dealt with by scientific
analysis. He explicitly sets out his view against Mill's. Complexity is for Mill
directly proportional to the *number* of intervening/interfering factors, or 'local
conditions' in the context of which some phenomenon occurs and operates
(quantitative definition).[55] The weather, or the tides (and, by Mill's analogy,
human behaviour) are not, would not be, intrinsically irregular or unpredict-
able phenomena, if it were not for these interfering factors. The presence of the
latter, nonetheless, does not detract from the fact that regular laws still govern
them. They are additional factors which create an effect, or appearance of complexity, which must be, and can be, dealt with appropriately by scientific means
(e.g. by using statistical laws). By no means are they a constitutive part of the
phenomena themselves.[56]

F or Winch, this view might perhaps well apply to natural phenomena, but the
'complexity' of social objects is quite different. The equivalent of the local conditions, or additional variables in Mill's view, are actually (to be treated as)
intrinsic, definitional features of social phenomena in Winch's idea of social
science. Complexity does not depend at all on numbers, but rather on the *kinds*
of features which constitutively and qualitatively define the very object of social
inquiry. More precisely, social objects are complex not because they comprise
more variables than natural objects, but rather because they include special and
characteristic traits (concepts, meanings, rules) which are irrelevant to the definition and analysis of natural phenomena. So, in the end, for Winch what we
perceive as complexity is, in actual fact, to be treated as a symptom of a *difference
in kind* (qualitative difference). What Winch really wants to establish is the
irreducible diversity of the object of social inquiry, and his revisited idea of complexity is used instrumentally to that end. From here (and perhaps far too
quickly), Winch draws the conclusion that difference in kind cannot but entail
an 'incompatibility' thesis, that is the view that the scheme of concepts involved

in explaining human society has nothing to do with that used in natural science. The very notion of human society is not an empirical one, and therefore it cannot be analysed by means of scientific concepts. Notions such as meaning, rule and reason, rather than fact, law and cause are to be employed to understand the object of social science, that is to understand human behaviour and action.[57]

Both views (the realist and the interpretivist) seem themselves to work normatively. They prescribe what features the object of social science must possess in order to qualify for what is taken to be the correct mode of inquiry. If social objects can be shown to be a variation of scientific objects, then they can be analysed by means of the same (similar) methods of natural science. If social objects cannot be shown to be a qualified form of natural objects, then an interpretivist method of inquiry only can be resorted to, in order to deal with them (and to the exclusion of any scientific method).

I endorse the criticism of the positivist picture of science, which both views put forward. In fact, I believe it is important to question whether there are ways to divorce the idea of objectivity from that specific ideal/model of 'being scientific', in order to explore what meaning the word 'objective' might have when social scientific knowledge is under scrutiny. I also support the idea of the 'specificity' of the object of social scientific knowledge, as emerging from both views. Indeed, the complexity of such an object is to be singled out, and dealt with accordingly. However, it is part of my view that it is the context of the actual practice of social science which ultimately reveals the way(s) to depict the relation between objects and our methods of inquiry. It is in such practice that we find the types of questions which orient our research, and offer a frame to the results we look for. It is such practice which might, then, also suggest a rethinking of the idea of 'objectivity' outside the strictures imposed by the adoption of a (any) normative/paradigmatic view. It seems to me that before speculating about the 'ought' of social science, it might be worthwhile assessing the 'is' of both social and natural science. That is to say, a descriptive task appears to be in order, before embarking on any prescriptive enterprise concerning the status of social science, and the 'objective' value of social scientific knowledge. Fixing a model of social object (scientific or philosophical, under some description or other) seems to go in the opposite direction to that of acknowledging the multifaceted identity of that object, and to that of subscribing to the variety of possible lines of questioning as regards such identity. If an idea of the 'complexity' of the object of social scientific inquiry is to be taken seriously, a plural description of that object in the context of the widest array of methods of description is to be pursued.

Nelson Goodman once talked of 'relevant kinds',[58] and brought our attention to the 'world-making' activity of selecting and organizing our classifications and categorizations. It is this activity that for him determines what we take to be the world. How does such activity take place? According to Searle, in the case of social reality there is a unified logic, underlying the construction of social (institutional) facts. Such logic can be summarized by the formula 'X counts as Y in C'.[59] The formula expresses the principle by which some function or meaning can be imposed on some thing (X) in a certain context (C) and, within this context, the thing in question becomes what the function or meaning *represents* that thing to be (Y).[60] The principle expressed by the formula works as a *constitutive rule* for social facts. It makes it possible for social objects to exist; it creates classes of entities (money, property, political offices) which did not, and could not, otherwise exist. The acceptance of this principle or rule, Searle claims, does not make us surrender to a nominalist, or even worse, 'social constructivist' position.[61] There is more to social *reality* than *social* reality. As can be inferred from the logical formula above, 'Y exists in C iff X'. In other words, social reality, according to Searle, is to be viewed as part of the physical environment, and social facts as existing 'on top of' brute facts (broadly identifed). The ontology of the social world is part of a general, basic ontology, which includes physical, chemical and biological elements, but which still cannot be reduced to any of those elements.[62] The ontology of the social world can only exist as a consequence of the attribution of social functions and constitutive meanings to the objects belonging to its domain. Attaching functions or meanings to objects, which are not intrinsic to the physics of these very objects, is possible because it is a collective and public practice (which is itself rooted, according to Searle, in humans' innate capacity for co-operative behaviour, or 'collective intentionality'), and because it is sustained by collective recognition. Back to the logical formula above ('X counts as Y in C'), we can now further infer from it that 'X counts as Y iff C', that is the practice of making an X a Y by assigning a function and/or a meaning to X belongs in a network of practices which are ultimately responsible for the intelligibility of that practice, and for its successful performance (as a socially acknowledged practice).

However, classifications and categorizations are not only part of the shared experience of a community. They can also be modified, as well as invented anew. Social science is one of the activities engaged in such a task. Hacking's concept of interactive kind allows us to reflect on 'the complex ways in which a kind can be made and molded',[63] by appealing, rather than to the discovery of an underlying logic, to the actual description of how this moulding occurs in practice. Kinds are formed within 'matrices', and a 'matrix' comprises many and very different types of elements.[64] Quite interestingly, among the elements of a matrix, we might also find scientific concepts. This does not turn interactive kinds into indifferent ones, to follow Hacking's distinction as mentioned above.[65] It does though allow for questions of a scientific nature to be formulated about these kinds, while keeping in mind that the use of a scientific concept does not necessarily add objectivity to the classification in question, merely by virtue of the concept being scientific. This also means that there is no general theory of kind-making, and no single story to recount.[66] Even the acceptance of a unified logic of kind-making does not entail the conclusion that the 'complex' object of social inquiry can be captured by one method of classification – either empirical or conceptual, or critical-realist. It seems as if both methodological unification (as prescribed by naturalistic perspectives), and methodological incompatibility (as recommended by anti-naturalistic or interpretivist ones) are wrong turnings in social science. Or at least, more prudently, we might want to suggest that before any normative choice of analysis is made, a description of the various modes of construction of such complex objects should be undertaken for each individual case.

In the chapters to follow, samples from various social sciences will be presented and explored, with the aim of illustrating how the complexity of social objects of investigation opens up a series of important questions regarding the objectivity of the theories and methods of inquiry which relate/refer to these objects. To attribute complexity to social scientific objects does not simply amount to acknowledging that such objects are partly natural and partly interpretative (and that, therefore, can be treated both scientifically and philosophically). More interestingly, the idea of a multifaceted identity makes us focus on the possible levels and/or angles from which these purported objects are questioned and analysed. In other words, with social scientific objects it is not so much a matter of *combining* natural and interpretative features, in view of a more *complete* description of their identity. It is rather a matter of knowing at what level, or from what angle we formulate our questions about them. In this context, trying to establish the objectivity of our analyses is to some extent dependent on what has been questioned, and on how questions are formulated, rather than on whether our analyses are able to represent, reproduce, or correspond to (according to some pre-established set of rules) an independently identified object. A matrix is not the same as a complete description.

Does it make any sense to pursue 'objectivity' in the analysis of these complex objects? Can we ever claim that we are able to offer objective analyses (theories, explanations, classifications) when the objects we investigate are only 'partially' formulated? As a preliminary to answering these questions, we ought to look into the very meaning of the term 'objective'. Objectivity is an idea with a very long history – a history of change, both in meaning and value.[67] In particular, modern objectivity is a 'layered' concept, made up of disparate components, each of which has a history and a conceptually specific identity.[68] To use social constructionist language, 'objectivity' is itself a socially constructed idea, and so its meaning is not immutable. Nonetheless, even if objectivity is a construction in the sense suggested, and its meaning can be constructed in several, alternative ways, depending on context and circumstances, we might still want to be able to use the idea – for instance, to be able to assess whether a classification is 'object-ive', or whether it can be analysed 'objectively' – at least according to one or some of those meanings. This leads us right back to standing questions such as what meaning of objectivity we might want to make use of in certain circum-stances, or why one meaning (and not another) appears to be more/most suit-able, etc. etc. In this Introduction, two options have been envisaged, which stand at the opposite poles of an ideal spectrum.

A first option is to 'borrow' a meaning of objectivity from the natural domain of inquiry, namely a relation of perfect, or best fit between an object and a classification (an extensional relation), and make use of it in social science. I have presented reasons not to bet on the success of this strategy, at least in the case of social science. A second option is based on a different strategy, or line of questioning. What is here asked is not (or perhaps not just) whether there is a class of objects which fits a certain classification, but rather whether a classifica-tion is so construed that a class of purported objects becomes significantly recognizable by means of it (intensionally). I find this second option more fruit-ful, and part of the task of this book will be that of illustrating why. As a pre-liminary to the task ahead, I will spend a few conclusive words on clarifying the meaning of the very term 'object', as it is used in this book, in the context of objectivity talk.

There is an everyday meaning of 'object', which equates objects with things. However, 'object' is also a philosophical word, and one with not a very long philosophical history. The idea of objects as separate from, or opposed to, sub-jects, as well as the connotation of 'objective' as used to refer either to the property of some state of affairs, or to whatever activity is able to reproduce faithfully such a state, both appear only with modern philosophy.[69] In particu-lar, the modern philosophical idea of object makes sense only in contrastive terms: some thing is an object only for someone (a subject) who stands opposite to it, and is aware of being in such a position. In philosophical terms, taking this position allows the subject 'to know' the object (to know that the object is other, or apart from himself, and to know what this 'something other' is). Notoriously, modern philosophy agonizes over the issue of how reliable the means employed by the subject are (ideas, representations, etc.) to attain true, reliable knowledge of the object. Kant gives an interesting twist to this story, by making us reflect on the fact that objects, as we predispose ourselves to know them, do not pre-exist our capacity for organizing them in specific, coherent configurations. This is not to say that objects (= things) are just ideas, but that the very idea of an object only makes sense on the assumption of a regulative (or configurative) mind. Objects of knowledge are not created as far as their reality is concerned, but as far as their forms are. Despite the changing history of the epistemological assessment of these forms,[70] the underlying epistemological framework for the identification of what counts as a Kantian 'object' of inquiry remains fundamentally the same. Objects are not ontologically 'given'. They are rather made 'possible' by the conceptual forms furnished by the intellect (or by its culture-sensitive categories, in a more contemporary assessement). These forms, rather than experience *per se*, are the necessary conditions of objective knowledge. Ultimately, to be 'objective', within a Kantian context, ceases to mean 'to correspond to a given object, existing externally to the mind'. It means, instead, to be constructed out of the external world according to the rules of the intellect (or the rules of a social community and of its epistemic standards), which allow for the constitution of objects. Knowledge is objective not because it produces perfect (best) representations of the objects of experience, but rather because it reveals the conditions which lead to the constitution of the objects of (= out of) experience.

How is this meaning of the term 'object' relevant to understanding the second option concerning how to frame the problem of objectivity in the social scientific domain? According to this option, any talk of the objectivity of social scientific investigation must start from studying the way in which phenomena in the social domain (people, behaviour, actions) become 'objects' of social scientific inquiry by being classified in certain ways, in specific contexts, and under some descriptive conditions. There are no 'children TV watchers' as a 'class' of individuals out in the real world; there are only children who watch television. The class or kind turns the latter into a specific object of analysis, out of a series of individuals behaving in some ways, which the kind classifies as similar. To find an alternative to the methodological prescription 'no objectivity without science', we must start from an understanding of the constructive procedures of classification, both empirical and conceptual, of the objects of social scientific inquiry. It is then to the analysis of this variegated domain of objects that I will now turn.

CHAPTER I

Anthropological Objects

1. FROM POSITIVISM TO INTERPRETIVISM

Anthropology emerged at the same time as sociology, in the nineteenth century, in an intellectual milieu dominated by positivism and evolutionism. Under the influence of evolutionism, the archaeological discoveries in the first half of the nineteenth century were used as evidence that in ancient times the European lived in primitive conditions supposedly similar to those of contemporary so-called 'savages'. Therefore, these 'savages' were believed to be the last surviving representatives of an archaic stage of the development of humans. Such a stage was to be superseded by more developed ones, the ultimate model being the civilized Victorian individual. He was considered to be the representative of the *positive*, final stage of evolution.

Under the influence of positivism, the method for analysing the diversity of these stages of human development, and of particular cultures and societies, was the comparative method. Given that cultures and societies were believed to belong to the same, grand evolutionary picture, they could be described in such a way that similar traits and conditions were brought up, and systematized by means of general laws. In 1871, for example, the British anthropologist Edward Tylor put forward a theory of culture which was both evolutionistic and universalistic. He defined culture as 'that complex whole which includes knowledge, belief, art, morals, law, custom and any other capability and habits acquired by man as a member of society.'[1] Given that all peoples possess a culture, all societies' cultural institutions can be compared. From this comparison, universal laws of human/social development could be derived, and used to assess the stage of civilization of each society. The theory of evolution provided this method of cultural analysis with an ultimate model for comparison: the European man.

Within this perspective, the description of particular societies and cultures was seen as instrumental to the end of generalization. Besides, the actual procedures for gathering and assembling 'facts' or data about societies were never questioned. As in any generalizing science, the stage of description was meant to 'give the facts', and the method of comparison was to account for them. This view was eventually responsible for a crucial, substantial split between on one side anthropology, as the actual generalizing science, and on the other ethnography, as the mere preparatory stage of data-gathering, subservient to the theoretical-scientific stage (where comparison and generalization took place). In some sense, ethnography was not really part of anthropology. The most prominent anthropologists between the end of the nineteenth and the beginning of the twentieth century[2] were 'armchair anthropologists', so-called because, rather than travelling to the field, they read about anthropological facts as reported in a wide range of sources: diaries, letters, travel reports from explorers, soldiers, missionaries, and natural scientists. None of these anthropologists would ever really question the way in which facts were collected or reported in the source material.

This style of 'armchair anthropology' was put under severe criticism by a new generation of anthropologists, under the influence of Malinowski. The anthropologist was now encouraged to adopt the attitude of a 'participant observer'. He was to leave the armchair, and go to the field, in order to collect his own data. However, it is interesting to note that this new style of anthropology was still under the influence of the positivistic idea that data were 'out there', in the field, waiting to be observed, recorded, catalogued, and eventually compared with other analogously recorded sets of data. Evidence of this is that the comparative method was still considered, by this generation of anthropologists, to be the method to follow. It was taken to be the equivalent of the experimental method in the natural sciences,[3] fieldwork functioning like a scientific laboratory workplace, where data were gathered and then tested.

> In its effort to be scientific, positivistic anthropology preoccupied itself with formulating and testing generalizations, which necessitated a focus on comparison. Problems of comparison were virtually the only problems that ever entered the methodological discussion. . . . The ultimate objective of any comparative research was to establish operationally defined variables which were then related together. . . . but the variables themselves were hardly ever seen as problematic. They were . . . all treated as objectified manifestations or forms of objectively existing social and cultural reality.[4]

It is important to have clearly in mind what the role of description and the function of ethnography were in positivistic anthropology, in order then to understand the radical change of paradigm, which occurred, in more recent times, within the discipline. In the new paradigm, the very concept of factual description was put under scrutiny. The activity of recording data during fieldwork, and that of organizing them in terms of anthropological reports – in one word, ethnography – became a crucial concern among anthropologists.[5] Ethnographical research was now seen as a theory-laden stage of anthropological inquiry, which not only affects, but enables and informs the way in which anthropological knowledge is eventually produced. However, as we will see, one of the main consequences of this paradigm shift was to deny that anthropology can be a science like natural science.

One typical illustration of how anthropological research can be carried out under this alternative paradigm is Clifford Geertz's 'interpretive' approach.[6] Right at the beginning of his famous book *The Interpretation of Cultures* Geertz writes:

> If you want to understand what a science is, you should look in the first instance not at its theories or its findings, and certainly not at what its apologists say about it; you should look at what the practitioners of it do.[7]

In anthropology (social anthropology), what practitioners do is ethnography. Understanding what *doing ethnography* implies is, for Geertz, understanding ethnography not as a method, but rather as an activity. To explain what kind of intellectual activity it is, Geertz makes use of a distinction first introduced by G. Ryle between 'thick' and 'thin' descriptions.[8] The difference between a twitch and a wink, Ryle once pointed out, cannot be perceived at the level of a plain observation. At this level, they can both be identified as a contraction of a facial muscle (a 'thin' description). In order 'to see' that the contraction of a facial muscle in the case of a winker is done on purpose (the winker tries to communicate something, he is sending out a message), we ought to put forward an interpretation ('thick' description) of what we observe, after exploring a whole variety of possible descriptions.

The same distinction, Geertz claims, applies to the object of anthropology. Human behaviour is complex, stratified, often obscure, and 'open to a variety of possible interpretations'. To understand human behaviour, the ethnographer must adopt a Rylean policy of 'thick' descriptions, or – in Geertz's own terminology – of *textual* interpretation.

> Doing ethnography is like trying to read (in the sense of 'construct a reading of') a manuscript – foreign, faded, full of ellipses, incoherencies, suspicious emendations, and tendentious commentaries, but written not in conventionalized graphs of sound but in transient examples of shaped behaviour.[9]

This view of ethnography is set against the more traditional, positivistic view, according to which the ethnographer 'observes, records, analyzes'.[10]

Ethnography is instead a constitutively interpretative activity: it requires a 'reading' of social events. Social events are indeed recorded in accounts, but ethnographic accounts are 'thick' descriptions of the symbolic significance of these events. In order to achieve the interpretative task, the anthropologist does not have to become a native, or to mimic natives. Only romantics or spies, says Geertz, would seem to find point in that. Instead, the anthropologist should try *to converse* with the natives. Anthropological 'texts' should then be seen not as the result of plain observation, but rather as the result of a dialogue between the anthropologist and the native.

In this dialogue, the anthropologist must use the meanings of his own culture to *translate* the way in which people belonging to a different culture make sense of themselves and what they do. This is why, ultimately, Geertz claims that anthropology is constitutively interpretative, or 'an understanding of understanding':

> What it means [that anthropology is interpretative] is that descriptions of Berber, Jewish, or French culture must be cast in terms of the constructions we imagine Berbers, Jews, or Frenchmen to place upon what they live through, the formulae they use to define what happens to them. What it does not mean is that such descriptions are themselves Berber, Jewish, or French – that is part of the reality they are ostensibly describing; they are anthropological – that is part of a developing system of scientific analysis.[11]

The procedure of describing another culture is more similar to the work a critic does to illuminate a poem, than to what an astronomer does to account for a star, as Geertz was to write in a later book.[12] To treat an anthropological event (practice, behaviour) 'as a text' is to present it in terms of a coherent construction. The construction is not there to start with, ready to be observed: it requires the invention of a form, an order, a framework of sense. Anthropological writings are then fictions, says Geertz – but not, as he specifies, in the sense of being false, or unfactual, but in the Latin sense of *fictio*, of 'something made', 'fashioned'.[13] So for example, Geertz uses the metaphor of a 'theatre' to analyse the State organization of nineteenth-century Bali: life in Bali is seen as a ritualized social drama, where people only have public identities. This shows how the 'logic' of an alien behaviour can be brought out by means of the anthropologist's idioms, and his systems of meanings. In other words, the discovery/construction of such a logic is 'an attempt to understand how it is that we understand understandings not our own'.[14]

We might now want to ask whether Geertz's variety of interpretive anthropology succeeded in opposing positivism, both in practice and in principle, and what model of knowledge it ultimately suggests for anthropology. Most importantly for us, we might want to ask whether there is a way to claim that an 'understanding of understanding' is an objective procedure of inquiry, as well as of classification of foreign behaviour. In order to discover this, let us consider one of Geertz's most famous case studies: his interpretive analysis of Balinese cockfighting as a social text.[15]

2. ANTHROPOLOGICAL OBJECTS I: COCKFIGHTING IN BALI

In April 1958 Geertz and his wife went to a Balinese village on a field trip. Ten days after their arrival, a large cockfight took place in the public square. Cock-fights are, except under special circumstances, illegal in Bali. Yet the villagers are prepared to take the risk of being caught by the police, and still have the fight. The Balinese show a lot of determination and seriousness in devoting them-selves to this kind of 'sport' – not to mention the large amounts of money they place on bets. This suggests that there is perhaps quite a bit 'to read' in cock-fights, and certainly more, Geertz suggests, than what a thin description of a chicken hacking another mindlessly to bits is able to reveal. Geertz's tentative, initial hypothesis is that in a Balinese cock ring it is not, despite appearances, the cocks that are fighting: actually, it is the cocks' owners.

To anyone who has been in Bali long enough, says Geertz, the social and psychological relation between men and cockerels is manifest. Everyday lan-guage is full of roosterish imagery: 'Sabung, the word for cock, ... is used, metaphorically, to mean "hero", "warrior", "champion", "political candidate", "bachelor", "dandy", "lady-killer", or "tough guy".'[16] Men actually spend a lot of time and care on these animals every day: they feed them, groom them, discuss them, and try them out against one another. In Balinese mythology, they are associated with the Powers of Darkness, with demons threatening to invade the village and devour its inhabitants. Perhaps, cockfighting can be looked on as a sort of sacrificial ritual? Geertz is not quite satisfied with this interpretation. As a next step, he goes into a fine-grained analysis of the scene of the fight, of the behaviour of the men participating in it, and most of all of the betting system. The 'centre bet', the one between the two owners of the cocks, is usually at even odds, and of enormous size relative to monthly income. Does this make the Balinese fools, or irrational people? Geertz argues that a utilitarian or rational choice explanation is inapplicable here. The fight is not held in order to maxi-mize money. Instead, it is precisely the apparent lack of 'rationality' in the bets that pushes us towards looking for a further explanation of the meaning of the fight. Geertz borrows from Bentham the concept of 'deep play' (a game where 'the stakes are so high that it is . . . irrational for men to engage in it'[17]), and he

makes us see, via this concept, that something more than, and something different from, monetary gain, is at stake in a cockfight. What is at stake are the self-
esteem, honour, dignity, and respect of the cocks' owners: symbolically, to win a
fight is to gain social status.

> [Social status] is at stake symbolically, for . . . no one's status is actually
> altered by the outcome of a cockfight; it is only, and that momentarily,
> affirmed or insulted. But for the Balinese, for whom nothing is more pleasur-
> able than an affront obliquely delivered or more painful than one obliquely
> received . . . such appraisive drama is deep indeed.[18]

So, Geertz's hypothesis is that a cockfight, or better a 'deep' cockfight, is a
'dramatization of status concern'.[19] In this sense, Geertz argues, cockfighting is
like an art form. It can be 'read' just like one of the great texts of our literary
tradition – *King Lear*, or *Crime and Punishment* – where ordinary, everyday
experiences are presented in order to suggest something else (a value, an ideal, a
goal). In order to grasp what ordinary experiences and human practices stand
for, the anthropologist has to go beyond the plainly observable, and into the
complex and hidden realm of underlying meanings.

Does textual inquiry then succeed in offering an alternative model of knowledge to positivistic anthropology? Are anthropological interpretations of the
kind offered 'objective'? We can now attempt to answer the first of these questions, by evaluating what Geertz's idea of an ethnographic 'text', as used in the
preceding case study, is able to point out as regards anthropological objects.
The second question will be addressed in the next section.

The idea of text as applied to anthropological objects allows Gertz to point
out at least three important features of the latter:

1) anthropological objects are *thick* objects, i.e. complex cultural forms
2) they are *symbolic* constructs, i.e. meaningful experiences
3) their meaningfulness is the result of an *interaction* between different symbolic
   systems, i.e. the result of a 'dialogue' and consequent reformulation.

Because of these features, to look at anthropological objects as texts seems to
convey rather successfully an anti-positivistic view according to which anthropological objects are not facts, they cannot be classified descriptively, and the
knowledge we acquire of them cannot be the consequence of a logical/
nomological/generalizing inference. However, by looking at the way in which
the idea of text succeeds in these goals, we have scope to wonder whether it goes
far enough in its anti-positivistic thrust. Starting from the third feature, in
describing how anthropological texts are produced, Geertz, rather surprisingly,

omits reference to the pragmatic dimension of such a production. The dialogue theorized by Geertz occurs, in fact, between *systems of meanings*. The natives (the actual people, uttering those meanings) never appear, in Geertz's model, as social actors, playing with and within their systems of meanings, during actual speech acts. The anthropologist himself is not properly a speaker, or an actor actively engaged in the practice he is to understand. By Geertz's own admission, 'We are not actors, we do not have direct access [to raw social discourse], but only [to] that small part of it which our informants can lead us to understand.'[20]

When Geertz talks about 'conversing' with the natives, what he has in mind is a sort of idealized scenario (a dialogue between meanings), not an actual exchange of information and of communicative strategies between the interpreter and the natives in the field.

[The] culture of a people is an ensemble of texts . . . which the anthropologist strains to read *over the shoulders* of those to whom they properly belong.[21] [my italics]

This is indeed a limitation, if Geertz aims at presenting his type of anthropological research as an alternative to the positivistic type. As Dwyer rightly points out,[22] textual inquiry reproduces a contemplative idea of anthropological knowledge, as being a relation between a subject, equipped with something like a method, and an object treated, paradoxically, as if it were silent, static and passive. We might end up somewhere reminiscent of a Malinowskian style of research, where the anthropologist is indeed reminded that he has to be a fieldworker, plant his tent in the natives' village, and mix with them. However, Malinowski also reminded his anthropologist that he had to get into the field already possessing a 'mental chart', which he was thereafter to materialize into 'a diagram, a plan, an exhaustive synoptic table of cases'. [23] 'Mixing with the natives' both for Malinowski and for Geertz seems to be nothing but a methodological prescription for practising good anthropology. What is not specifically asked in either case is how in practice such a 'mixing' works as an enabling condition for the construction of anthropological texts. This brings us to the second feature of interpretive objects listed above.

In describing anthropological objects as meaningful constructs, the role of language is overestimated (this is a limitation common to most hermeneutical approaches). Geertz often refers to the practice of ethnographic interpretation as being a 'translation', by which he seems to mean linguistic translation: to put an alien behaviour into a familiar form is to express one system of meanings into another. In the end, socio-cultural phenomena are not simply said to be meaningful, they are actually reduced to meanings. However, as has been noted, meanings might pervade culture, but they are not alone: 'they are interwoven with, for instance, ecological phenomena, or with psychological phenomena of a different type.'[24] Besides, there is a non-verbal, pragmatic dimension in the experience of fieldwork which, though crucial to the emergence of meanings, is neglected by textual analysis. Once again, Geertz might here appear not anti-positivistic enough. If he wants to draw a significant contrast between texts and factual reports, he should find a way to show that meanings are not 'found' in the field, but rather that they are the constrained result of both the verbal and non-verbal conditions of fieldwork. This leads us back to the first feature of anthropological objects as texts.

If the aim of using the idea of a text is to bring out the 'complexity' of cultural forms, then confining complexity to discourse, as well as ignoring the pragmatic dimension in the construction of meaning, also appears a rather limited operation both in scope and in depth. That the pragmatic dimension of theory construction in anthropology is an essential condition for successful anthropological work has been clearly illustrated, among others, by Jeanne Favret-Sadat. In her work on witchcraft and magic in the Bocage, she shows how, contrary to Geertz, the construction of objects of inquiry in anthropology is not achieved simply by translating meanings.

3. ANTHROPOLOGICAL OBJECTS II: WITCHCRAFT IN THE BOCAGE

Jeanne Favret-Sadat left on a field trip to a Bocage village in 1969. She lived there for two years, after which she visited the village, on and off, until 1975.[25] When she first arrived, she was prepared for the fact that nobody would talk to her about spells for quite some time.[26] Indeed, the Bocage people appeared from the very beginning to be reticent about the subject. Favret-Sadat soon realized that the only way to overcome this reticence was to let the villagers question the anthropologist's own position with respect to magic speech.

'Are you strong enough?' Favret-Sadat was asked whenever she tried to get people, who supposedly knew of stories of witches, to tell her about magic. It felt as if the people she interacted with were wondering what kind of an effect their stories would have on her. Would she be fascinated, or perhaps frightened (in both cases, a sign of her weakness)? Would she show indifference and detachment (a more ambiguous sign: it could mean that she is 'strong-blooded', that she has something to hide, or that she possesses 'forces' bigger than theirs)? 'As you can see,' Favret-Sadat comments, 'this is not exactly a standard situation, in which information is exchanged and where the ethnographer may hope to have neutral knowledge about the beliefs and practices of witchcraft conveyed to him.'[27]

By allowing this unusual situation to develop, she soon realized what the informants' initial reticence, silence and 'testing' actually conveyed: a power contest. Witchcraft in the Bocage does not consist of a series of pieces of information to be recounted, in a neutral, unproblematic manner. It is instead a series of speech acts endowed with a specific powerful nature. There are no *statements describing magic*, but only people who have the *power to use magic words*. Not just anyone can talk about magic, but only those who are caught up in it (either as a victim or as a practitioner). Therefore, it seems that the only way to learn about magic is for the ethnographer to abandon her professional role (external to the dialogue). The natives were allowed to approach the anthropologist as if she were a powerful subject (a witch, or a witch-doctor), or as if she were a supposedly powerless one (a victim, or a bewitched person), and sometimes as if she were both.

> For he who succeeds in acquiring such knowledge gains power and must accept the effects of this power; the more one knows, the more one is a threat and the more one is magically threatened. . . . I had to accept the logic of this totally combative situation and admit that it was absurd to continue to posit a neutral position which was neither admissible or even credible to anyone else. When total war is being waged with words, one must make up one's mind to engage in another kind of ethnography.[28]

In this different kind of ethnography, interpretation and understanding begin when the anthropological inquiry focuses not so much on the content of utterances, on what is said, but rather on 'speech acts': why this silence? what does this negation mean? who is speaking and to whom? why are words believed to kill? etc. etc.

> To talk, in witchcraft, is never to inform. . . . 'Informing' an ethnographer, that is, someone who claims to have no intention of using the information, but naïvely wants to know for the sake of knowing, is literally unthinkable. For a single word (and only one word) can tie or untie a fate, and whoever puts himself in a position to utter it is formidable. Knowing about spells brings money, brings more power and triggers terror: realities much more fascinating to an interlocutor than the innocent accumulation of scientific knowledge, writing a well-documented book, or getting an academic degree. . . . In short, there is no neutral position with spoken words: in witchcraft, words wage war. Anyone talking about it is a belligerent, the ethnographer like everyone else. There is no room for uninvolved observers.[29]

In other words, the construction of an anthropological text crucially depends on participation in communicative, regulated social games, or – to use Wittgenstein's famous expression – in a form of life. The ethnographer must perceive herself as just one speaker among others. In order to 'catch things' (to understand what goes on) she must let herself 'be caught' by things.

This also arguably shows how the conditions for the construction of anthropological texts depend on the resources available in the field (informants, social roles, discourses, meanings, social practices, non-verbal behaviour, etc.), and most of all on the dialogues negotiated in the field. The way(s) in which those resources enter these dialogues, and the way(s) in which dialogues embody the answers that the anthropologist is looking for cannot be predicted, nor piloted by her. Informants are often unco-operative, or they do not respond in a way that facilitates communication. Sometimes, they deliberately dissimulate, that is they answer in the terms they think their interlocutor expects of them. There are also times in which, as we have just seen, they require that the anthropologist changes her social (professional) role. Finally, and against Geertz's hermeneutic optimism, there might be times in which an anthropological text cannot be written at all. Or at least, what the anthropologist can write of it inevitably leaves out a whole series of features, which cannot be translated into, or expressed in a written form.

Does a focus on the pragmatic (fieldwork) dimension of ethnographic texts make anthropological inquiry more objective? I suppose Geertz could object that taking this dimension into account does not necessarily guarantee that we end up producing more reliable interpretations of a foreign culture. After all, pretending to be a witch, or to be bewitched, is a procedure of 'ontological simulation'. How can we say, then, that our descriptions *really* capture what our informants *really* believe, or *really* mean? It also raises the issue of how far the anthropologist is entitled to interact with the people he studies, to the point of practising deception, in order to gain knowledge from and about them. Geertz would ultimately be inclined to conclude that the problem of producing objective interpretations inevitably clashes with the discursive complexity which any anthropologist experiences in the study of his subject matter. Realistically, he concludes, the best we can do is to try to translate what some people say that they mean and do into what we think they mean and do.

> The moral asymmetries across which ethnography works, and the discursive complexity within which it works make any attempt to portray it as anything more than the representation of one sort of life in the categories of another impossible to defend.[30]

However, the question still stands: can we then ever claim that we have 'correctly interpreted' the Other? For critics like James Clifford, the answer to this question is not epistemological, but rather ethical/political.[31] In the context of an anthropological text, correctness is not a scientific or an epistemological standard. It should rather be treated as a moral imperative: we accept the responsibility of representing another form of life in the terms of ours. However, by claiming so, we implicitly subscribe to the idea that even a responsible anthropologist might eventually produce an incorrect interpretation. Consequently, interpreting the Other by constructing a text that presents it in terms which make sense to us, seems to be a far cry from explaining anthropological findings in objective terms. Yet, should we take this as the final word? Part of the problem with adopting a 'textual' view of anthropological inquiry – either *à la* Geertz or *à la* Favret-Sadat – is that we find it difficult (if not mysterious) to figure out how to reconstruct the link between what the anthropologist sees and what he represents. This is indeed an epistemological problem, and – *pace* Clifford – it should receive attention.

4. ANTHROPOLOGICAL OBJECTS III: NUER 'SACRIFICE' AND TXIKAO 'COUVADE'

What knowledge do anthropologists draw from their fieldwork experience? How do they succeed in conveying it? What general problems does this knowledge solve or raise?[32]

These are some of the questions which, says Dan Sperber, need to be addressed. No doubt, anthropology is an interpretative discipline of inquiry. Still, in acknowledging this feature, there are two related and yet distinct levels to consider. The first concerns the transition from fieldwork experience to the written report of that experience.

In his trunks, the anthropologist brings back a field diary, linguistic files, an herbarium, maps, sketches, photographs, tapes, genealogies, interview protocols, and notebooks filled with remarks scribbled on his knees, in the darkness of a smoky hut, or leaning against a tree in the forest, or in the evening, alone at last, under the light of a petrol lamp. These documents are about men, women, children, households, neighbourhoods, villages, fields, labors, crafts, food, plants, animals, markets, festivals, sacrifices, diviners' consultations, crises of spirit possession, conflicts, murders, vengeance, funerals, meetings, chiefs, ancestors, songs, dreams, and the reason why snakes have no legs.[33]

For the anthropologist all these 'documents' have indeed meaning (they are part of the experience he went through, and grew acquainted with). However, it is quite a challenge to try to condense them into a book and still be faithful (and truthful) to the reality experienced. Inevitably, 'between what the anthropologists have learned and what they manage to convey, great is the loss of knowledge'.[34]

The second level concerns the transition from written reports to the theoretical accounts of the experiences they report about. Ethnographic writings, at this level, are asked to provide the basic raw material for anthropological theorizing. Anthropology aims at reconceptualizing that experience in such a way that it can be presented in a synthetic, coherent, and possibly general form. To achieve this aim, the anthropologist has at his disposal a large collection of technical terms (taboo, kinship, myth, matrilinear lineage, etc.), which offer 'a kind of decontextualised condensation of very diverse local ideas'.[35] For example, 'myth' is a technical term which is used to cover a whole host of 'documents' (written and not), on the assumption that all these disparate documents have some features in common. 'Myth' is a family resemblance term, although of a particular kind: the resemblance it refers to is not of an ontological order. For Sperber, it is not a resemblance among 'things', it is a resemblance in meaning:

> Just as the appropriate use of 'goblin' by an anthropologist tells us nothing regarding the existence of goblins, the appropriate use of 'marriage', 'sacrifice', 'chiefship' does not tell us whether marriages, sacrifices or chiefships are part of the furniture of the world.[36]

Fieldwork experience at this level becomes even more remote when translated into this technical vocabulary, and the anthropologist, by trying to pursue the explanatory aim, is compelled to be less than faithful to the original experience in the field. Yet, this less than faithful terminology is used to express systematic relationships among supposedly existing properties of the cultural phenomena investigated. Structuralist and functionalist theories in traditional anthropology are good examples of how anthropologists go about explaining fieldwork data.[37]

Does this two-levelled role of interpretation condemn both ethnographic reports and anthropological theory to being non-objective, partial, and selective to the point of being biased, and finally unscientific? These are indeed some of the charges levelled against the interpretative nature of anthropological work. They are normally used to draw a contrast with what a 'descriptive' style of inquiry should be aiming at (that is, an inquiry which is meant to be objective, complete, consistent, adequate, unbiased, and verifiable). Still, can anthropology be really, or at all, descriptive? If it can, why at present is it not?

Interpretations and descriptions are in a sense alike, says Sperber, because they are both kinds of representations: they 'stand for' the object they represent, or even 'replace' the object in its absence. By standing in such a relation with the object, they are meant to reproduce it somehow adequately. There is, though, a crucial difference between them. A description is said to be adequate when it is true. By being open to a judgement of truth and falsity, a description can serve, directly, as either a premise or a conclusion of a logical argument, or else to confirm or disconfirm an explanatory statement, or to convey scientific evidence. Interpretations can also be adequate, but only indirectly, on condition that they are accompanied by a descriptive comment (something which tells us 'this is the interpretation of that'). A descriptive comment 'identifies the object represented and specifies the type of representation involved'.[38]

Returning to the question, 'Can anthropological work be descriptive?' we can first deal with the case of ethnographic reports (first level of interpretation). The problem here, Sperber claims, is that the descriptive comments we are often offered by ethnographers are, in one way or another, themselves interpretative. To demonstrate this, Sperber offers an analysis of a passage from *Nuer Religion* by Evans-Pritchard. This passage appears to be, at its most 'factual' level, a mixture of descriptions and quotation. However, if we look at it in more detail, 'not a single statement in it expresses a plain observation'.[39] Here is the passage in question:

I was present when a Nuer was defending himself against silent disapproval on the part of his family and kinsmen of his frequent sacrifices. He had been given to understand that it was felt that he was destroying the herd from inordinate love of meat. He said that it was not true . . . It was all very well for his family to say that he had destroyed the herd, but he had killed the cattle for their sake. It was '*kokene yiekien ke yang*', 'the ransom of their lives with cattle'. He repeated this phrase many times as one by one he recounted cases of serious sickness in his family and described the ox he had sacrificed on each occasion to placate the spirit *deng*.[40]

An expression like 'silent disapproval' is hardly an observation. It is more a conjecture. Or, saying that the man 'had been given to understand that it was felt that . . .', or saying that the Nuer was 'defending himself', are all extrapolations from a variety of complex behaviours. Ultimately, they are suggested as hypotheses of interpretation, which result from the interaction that the ethnographer had with his informants. The resulting description, says Sperber, is 'what the ethnographer selected from what he understood of what his informants told him of what they understood'.[41] Also, the natives' and informants' utterances are referred to in an indirect style ('he said it was not true'; 'he had killed the cattle for their sake', etc.). This form of presentation is a paraphrase of something as understood, but deprived of the context which made this understanding possible: namely, the actual *interaction* between the ethnographer, the native under scrutiny, and the ethnographer's informants.

Another example of the interpretative character of ethnographic descriptions is the use of the device of a direct quotation with its translation: '*kokene yiekien ke yang*', 'the ransom of their lives with cattle'. The translation offered by the ethnographer is the result of a series of steps. '*Kokene*' comes from the verbal form '*kok*' ('*kuk*' is the corresponding noun), for which there is no synonym in the ethnographer's own language. The closest we can get to grasping the meaning of '*kok*' is to try to locate the term itself in the wider context of Nuer culture (religious, economic, ceremonial).[42] '*Kok*' means both 'to sell' and 'to buy', that is it expresses an idea of reciprocal relationships and exchange. The closest words in English that Evans-Pritchard can come up with are 'ransom' and 'redemption' (as associated with the semantic field of the term 'sacrifice' both in its religious and economic contexts).

Having found the closest translation, Evans-Pritchard 'describes' how the Nuer conceive of sacrifice in the form of a 'gloss':

> A *kuk kwoth*, sacrifice to God, (or to some spirit), appears to be regarded as a ransom which redeems the person who pays it from a misfortune that would, or might, otherwise fall on him. By accepting the gift, God enters into a covenant to protect the giver of it or help him in some other way. Through the sacrifice man makes a kind of bargain with his God.[43]

Sperber does then wonder: can we claim that the ethnographer is actually describing assertions made by the Nuer? Is a gloss a plain translation? It seems that, at best, these assertions and the ethnographer's glosses are a sort of 'compromise between Nuer thought and the ethnographer's means of expression. In other words, they are typical interpretations.'[44]

So far, it seems that Sperber's analysis is similar to Geertz's: in the attempt to describe another culture, the ethnographer is offering a 'text', which helps the ethnographer to convey the natives' understanding of their own culture. Sperber, like Geertz, claims that the ethnographer achieves his results in the manner of a novelist. As in Geertz we read that Balinese cockfighting is like *King Lear*, in Sperber we read that Evans-Pritchard's *Nuer Religion* is just like Tolstoy's *War and Peace*: it contributes to our understanding of the world in which we live by giving us some insight into 'fragments' of human experience.[45] Also, interpretations achieve what cannot be achieved by other means, such as plain descriptions: if the ethnographer were just to describe plainly what he observes, what would be the point of that? We would just end up with the report of, say, someone slaughtering an animal (a 'thin' description).

However, the similarities end there. For Geertz, anthropology is just what ethnographers do, that is interpreting cultural meanings, and producing anthropological 'texts' which are not general, but rather 'deep'. This is what anthropology is all about. If we were to think of a possible explanatory format for this kind of anthropology, we might formulate it in terms of the following sequence of prescriptive moves:

a) look at an anthropological object as if it were a text (i.e. both as a symbolic construct, and as a complex cultural representation)
b) translate its meaning into our (the anthropologist's) own system of meanings
c) build up a new vocabulary of 'thick' descriptions.

Interpretations do not need any descriptive comments. For Geertz, they are themselves descriptions, though of a particular kind: indeed, the only kind which can be used to account for meanings (thick descriptions). By being descriptive in this particular way, anthropology is then a science, though itself of a particular kind. It is an interpretive science.

For Sperber, this view must be amended. If foreign meanings can only be reconstructed as texts which are familiar to the anthropologist but alien to the people and/or situations portrayed by them, in what relation do they stand to the state of affairs they reconstruct? How can we establish whether a chosen reconstruction matches better than any other possible thick description? In other words, we cannot avoid speculating about the validity of the interpretation under scrutiny. But asking questions about the validity of ethnographic interpretations does not imply that they are in principle devoid of any use or purpose. Speculation and doubt concerning these texts is not enough in itself to conclude that they are partial, unreliable, and misguided. What it does question, though, is whether the use or purpose they fulfil has any *theoretical* validity. Ethnography, Sperber claims, is in fact not anthropological theory at its best; it is just ethnography, that is a discipline in its own right, with an autonomous task to contribute to our understanding of cultural phenomena. If we fail to recognize this, then anthropology as a discipline, which purports to produce reliable knowledge about human experience (therefore a discipline with scientific ambitions), suffers.

However, if we turn to traditional anthropological theories (e.g. structuralist, or functionalist) to answer the question, 'Can anthropological work be descriptive?' we do not find better answers. As mentioned before, these theories are, despite appearances, heavily interpretative (their technical terminology is interpretative, and the empirical evidence they use, fieldwork data, is also interpretative). As a matter of fact, theoretical anthropology faces a dilemma. On the one hand, as with any empirical science, it needs data. The only data available are those collected by ethnographers, but these data, as illustrated above, are intrinsically interpretative. Sperber seems here to imply that if data are interpretative then they are not reliable; and if they are not reliable they cannot be used as a factual basis for producing theoretical generalizations. On the other hand, without ethnographic data theoretical anthropology as a 'science' of culture appears to be impossible. So, given that there is no alternative to interpreted data, the anthropologist ends up making use of them, pretending that his theoretical generalizations and systematizations reconceptualize them in a reliable and objective format. The dilemma, however, still stands. The anthropologist has only found a way to dissimulate it.

Is there a way out of this dilemma? The solution for Sperber rests not so much with an attempt to avoid interpretation (ethnographic data are what they are), but rather to find a different way to deal with it (different from either a Geertzian textual approach or structural/functionalist theorizing). To pursue this aim, we ought to start by rethinking what the object, or explanandum, of anthropological inquiry consists of. A general answer to the question, 'What is anthropology about?' is to say that it is about 'cultural things'. What 'things' can be cultural? There are two obvious candidates:

1) in ethnography, there are verbal representations (speech events, or utterances, as delivered to the anthropologist by his informants, as part of fieldwork experience)
2) in theoretical anthropology, behaviours and institutions (sacrifice, myth, marriage, religion, witchcraft, etc.) as reconstructed by anthropological theory.

However, there might be a third candidate. When we say that two Ebelo people contracted 'kwiss' (an expression heard by the anthropologist, which he translates as 'marriage'), what we are saying is that there is a people called Ebelo, and that they pronounce certain utterances, as a consequence of certain 'ideas' represented in their minds, which lead them to perform a certain ritual.[46] Where do these ideas come from? How can they take shape in the minds of individuals, and become so rooted and enduring as to convince a group of individuals to attribute to them social value, and behave accordingly? Theoretical anthropology should try to explain how classes of 'representations' cause individuals to act and to speak the way they do, and how some of these classes become both publicly acknowledged and socially enduring.

So, 'cultural things' in anthropology might be taken to refer to kinds of representations, and anthropological interpretations are ultimately about cultural representations. If cultural representations are the objects that anthropology is to investigate, how should anthropological inquiry be carried out in order to escape the dilemma of interpretation, as outlined above, and become a reliable, objective science? Here is Sperber's proposed alternative view.

All human beings share a capacity for producing, memorizing, and exchanging mental representations (beliefs, intentions, preferences). Through communication (and repeated communication), a number of these representations 'spread out' among a group of people (like an 'epidemic'), and may stay with single individuals for many generations. The anthropologist should try to establish through what processes of selection (individual and inter-individual) certain bits of mental representations become first public, and then, more specifically, 'cultural' (i.e. widespread and enduring representations among a population). Evolutionary biology and cognitive psychology can be useful to anthropology for identifying the object of anthropological knowledge (mental representations), and for providing reliable means to explain those micro- and macro-mechanisms that cause particular representations to be selected and shared among a social group (cultural representation).

> The causal explanation of cultural facts amounts, therefore, to a kind of epidemiology of representations. An epidemiology of representations will attempt to explain cultural macro-phenomena as the cumulative effect of two types of micro-mechanisms: individual mechanisms that bring about the formation and transformation of mental representations, and inter-individual mechanisms that, through alterations of the environment, bring about the transmission of representations.[47]

In this way, the object of anthropology becomes 'naturalized', and like any natural object it can be explained scientifically (i.e. causally). The task of anthropology (*explaining* culture) is then portrayed differently from that of ethnography.

> The main task of ethnography is to make intelligible the experience of particular human beings as shaped by the social group to which they belong. . . . Explaining cultural representations, interpreting them: two autonomous tasks that contribute to our understanding of cultural phenomena.'[48]

This does not mean that anthropology does not make use of ethnographic data. It means that anthropology can be given a better, more reliable method to deal with them, once they are adequately reconceptualized.[49] A cultural representation can be accounted for scientifically – and therefore objectively – as a special and more 'complex' case of a mental representation (which finds a scientific explanation in cognitive psychology).

For example, in studying a particular practice such as the Txikao couvade, an epidemiological approach is able to explain the belief in the efficacy of the practice from a cognitive and ecological point of view. In anthropological literature, the term supposedly refers to

> a set of precautions (e.g. resting, lying down, food restrictions) a man is expected to take during and just after the birth of a child of his – precautions which are similar to those imposed, more understandably, on the mother of the child.[50]

To explain why the practice, aimed at warding off some kind of misfortune, can persist among a group of individuals, the interaction between two variables must be taken into account:

1) a cognitive disposition (the spontaneous assignment of 'excessive weight to cases which have greater relevance in one's life')
2) an ecological factor ('the frequency of different kinds of cases' which allows us to predict either the persistence or the erosion of the practice itself).[51]

However, an explanation based on these two variables, and on the way they interact, refers to a general *type* of practice (a socially endorsed form of defence against various sorts of misfortune). How is it relevant to explaining the specific Txikao practice (the 'couvade')? According to Sperber, there are two issues involved here, which ought to be considered separately. Firstly, the anthropologist cannot avoid interacting with standard ethnographic work: 'To explain the Txikao couvade . . . one would have to study the particular context in which Txikao cognitive and communicative activities take place, trying to identify the factors which, through these activities, stabilize the institution.'[52] In other words, the anthropologist must rely on ethnographic data, as offered and described by fieldwork reconstructions. Secondly, in order to explain these data, the anthropologist should not try 'to devise some special hermeneutics': either a textual analysis, or the composition of some speculative table of similarities and differences. A cognitive explanation, in its specific epidemiological variant, affords a more reliable access to those data. It shows that the practice in question is the effect of the way in which inter-individual mechanisms of communication are constructed, reproduced and transformed out of individual mental mechanisms (mechanisms which find a good account in cognitive science).

This is certainly an attractive picture. Explaining cultural representations scientifically and interpreting them ethnographically are viewed as two independent activities, carried out in different, almost opposite, manners (for instance, the explanatory task tends to the general, the interpretative aims at the specific). In their own independent and different ways, both activities contribute to our understanding of cultural phenomena.[53] However, we might perhaps wonder, at this point, whether trying to advocate a scientific view of anthropology along these lines does not end up introducing some form of a 'scientistic' prejudice in the style of research, and ultimately a positivistic bias. We are in fact prompted to believe that in order to be scientific, anthropology should find an 'object' of inquiry which is naturalistic (= non-interpretative). It should also produce 'indifferent classifications' of such an object (classifications which take into account the causal mechanisms involved in the production and distribution of cultural representations, independently of what people make of those representations). Moreover, we are urged to look for a non-interpretive way to deal with ethnographic findings (i.e., they are treated as a set of initial conditions necessary for contextualizing, or giving access to, the general-case explanation). In this way, data can be used for the purpose of a 'science' of anthropology (i.e. the purpose of any empirical science). However, it seems to me that, by so doing, rather than putting ethnographic interpretations to good, reliable scientific use, we lose sight of the specific epistemological problem (or challenge) posed by those interpretations: what they say about some culture might be 'correct' even if it does not describe a given, or 'natural' state of affairs.

5. COMPLEX ANTHROPOLOGICAL OBJECTS

In this chapter I analysed three models of construction of an anthropological object of inquiry: a 'text' (Balinese cockfighting); a narrative reconstruction of socio-cultural interactions in the field (Bocage witchcraft); and a causally determined distribution of cultural representations (Txikao 'couvade'). All these models raise an issue of descriptive adequacy – namely, they make us reflect on the epistemological link between what is observed and what/how the anthropologist represents it. How objective is such a link? From fieldwork experience to ethnographic writings, and from ethnographic writings to anthropological generalizations, such a link appears to be interpretation-laden (what is observed is not independent of how it is observed). Since interpretation cannot be avoided (it is a part of knowledge claims in anthropology), is there a way to make use of it so that anthropological inquiry is not condemned to be descriptively unsound?

Geertz's and Sperber's suggestions stand at two ideally opposite poles. According to the former, what we observe is a meaningful experience, and the way we represent it is by means of another meaningful experience (meanings cannot really be factually assessed, they can only be interpreted). The interpreted nature of the object of inquiry requires here an interpreting procedure of inquiry. Such a procedure is 'descriptive' in the only sense of descriptive which makes sense in anthropology (an interpretative, or 'thick' sense). As we read above in Geertz, the 'discursive complexity' of anthropological objects is not amenable to a rigid model of objective representation (i.e. true description). However, we are left wondering whether his less rigid, interpretive model would ever be able to capture such 'complexity' (or indeed, be better in capturing it). Geertz's excessive optimism about the writing of anthropological texts opens the door to Clifford's scepticism when it comes to establishing standards for the correctness of the writing itself.

For Sperber too, what we observe is a meaningful experience, but the way in which this experience is represented need not itself necessarily be interpretative. By discovering the mechanisms responsible for the emergence and spreading of certain mental representations, which are in their turn responsible for the manifestation of meaning-dependent cultural experiences, we can account for the latter in the context of scientific explanation. In such a context, the complexity of meaningful cultural experience can indeed find an objective way to be described. Cultural representations are complex objects of inquiry not so much in that they are 'discursive', but rather in that they are cognitive and ecologically sensitive. Their complexity is 'naturalized', and once it is reconceptualized in this way, it can be explained objectively.

Favret-Sadat stands somehow in the middle. Against Geertz, she shows that there is more to anthropological objects than meaning; against Sperber, she demonstrates that the complexity of anthropological objects is qualitatively different from that of a natural object. Against both, she rescues the special and specific experience of fieldwork by acknowledging its own epistemic importance. As such experience clearly suggests, the procedures by which the anthropologist classifies alien human behaviour interact with the latter, and the complexity of human behaviour can be discovered and portrayed precisely because it cannot be reduced to that of a natural object. People are not indifferent to the way they are classified. This does not mean to deny that human behaviour includes a 'natural' aspect, which an anthropologist might find interesting to reveal and to include in his analyses. Nonetheless, it supports the claim that, if anthropological explanation loses sight of the interactive nature of its object-classifying procedures, its presumed objectivity is somewhat misleading.

Can we expect objective claims as a consequence of adopting interactive procedures of inquiry and classification? By classifying the inhabitant of some foreign community as an 'Other' (a *different* other), or a 'native', we implicitly subscribe to the view that the 'Other' (the 'object' of anthropological knowledge) is not just the inhabitant of a foreign community. As Fabian once pointed out, the Other is *made*.[54] What he meant was not that the individuals, peoples, and cultures the anthropologist talks about are invented. He rather meant that 'being an object' of anthropological knowledge is not a quality which belongs to individuals, peoples, etc., as if it were a natural quality. Being, say, a 'native' is an identity constructed out of the particular points of view and interests of the researcher, as well as of the larger background (social, cultural, etc.) the researcher belongs to.

If the object of anthropological understanding is 'made' in this sense, then the only way to ask questions about the objectivity of its construction is to inquire about the procedures which 'make' these objects possible, as well as about the 'looping effects' which take place in classifying them. To quote Fabian again, objectivity is a 'processual, historical notion'. Knowledge is an activity (knowledge production), rather than a state of mind. Objectivity, the result of such an activity, is to be reconstructed and analysed as a process of 'objectification'.[55]

CHAPTER 2

Sociological Objects

1. RECEIVED PARADIGMS

As mentioned at the beginning of the previous chapter, the discipline of sociology first developed in the nineteenth century, at the same time as anthropology emerged; and both developed at a time when positivism and evolutionism were the dominant ideologies of European culture. The two disciplines complemented each other: anthropology was viewed as offering crucial, almost laboratory-like tests for general sociological theories – in the sense, for example, that 'the functioning of more advanced societies can only be understood when we are informed about the organisation of less developed societies'.[1]

A good example of how the emergence of sociology is deeply embedded in evolutionism and positivism is the work of August Comte. As mentioned in the Introduction, Comte believed that each branch of knowledge passes successively through three different stages, which reflect the way the human mind has been evolving:

> In the theological state, the human mind, seeking the essential nature of beings, the first and final causes (the origin and purpose) of all effects, – in short, Absolute knowledge, – supposes all phenomena to be produced by the immediate action of supernatural beings. In the metaphysical state, . . . the mind supposes, instead of supernatural beings, abstract forces, veritable entities (that is, personified abstractions) inherent in all beings, and capable of producing all phenomena. What is called the explanation of phenomena is, in this stage, a mere reference of each to its proper entity. In the final, the positive state, the mind has given over the vain search after Absolute notions, the origin and destination of the universe, and the causes of phenomena, and applies itself to the study of their laws – that is, their invariable relations, duly combined, are the means of this knowledge. What is now understood when we speak of an explanation of facts is simply the establishment of a connection between single phenomena and some general facts. . . .[2]

In parallel with the three stages, and as a consequence of it, it is Comte's belief that the various sciences develop at different rates, depending on their degree of generality, simplicity and independence. Astronomy, the most general-simple-independent science, developed first, followed by physics, chemistry, and biology. The last in Comte's hierarchy is sociology. Sociology is the least developed; and yet, it has an advantage compared to the other sciences. It can rely, and build on, the results of the sciences which developed before it. Consequently, sociology does not have to invent its own method. Rather, it can adopt the same, or at least a similar, method as that already adopted by such 'mature' disciplines as mathematics, astronomy, and physics.[3]

This view endured well into the twentieth century, being promoted once again by the neopositivist philosophers who gravitated around the Vienna Circle, in the 1930s.

The goal ahead is unified science. The endeavour is to link and harmonize the achievements of individual investigators in their various fields of science.[4]

According to Neurath, the science which provided the model for unification was physics, and this for at least two reasons. Firstly, every science (every empirical science) rests on a materialist basis – so, at least in 'the widest sense', it is a kind of physics.[5] Secondly, physics has a fully developed system of concepts, which can be used, paradigmatically, for any science – including sociology. In the end, 'what is true of physics in the narrower sense also holds *mutatis mutandis* for sociology'.[6]

It is interesting to see that in manuals of sociology, the so-called 'naturalistic' perspective often refers to this tradition. This perspective is usually contrasted with another perspective, named 'anti-naturalistic', or 'humanistic', which denies the scientific credentials of sociology. The claim that there cannot be any science of human experience is part of a relatively long tradition, which goes at least as far back as to the nineteenth-century German historicists.[7] In the Anglo-Saxon world, the first systematic attempt to criticize a naturalistic view of sociology came at the end of the 1950s, with Peter Winch. Winch's view is normally referred to as the paradigm of the anti-naturalistic perspective. This is because, first of all, it denies that social inquiry deals with 'facts'. Social phenomena, Winch argued, are meaningful experiences. Secondly, and consequently, the methods of science (observation and causal/nomological explanation) are inappropriate to account for the essentially different subject matter of sociology. Winch's discussion of social action, as the typical object of sociological investigation, well illustrates this alternative view.[8]

Social action, Winch argues in a Weberian style, is intrinsically meaningful, in a way that the behaviour of natural objects is not. In order for an individual to act in a racially motivated manner, for example, he/she needs to have some idea, for example, of what 'racial' means, and/or to understand what (at least some of) the consequences of actions informed by his racial beliefs amount to. A molecule in a gas does not need to know, say, the formula of Gay-Lussac's law, in order to raise the temperature of a gas. However, unlike Weber, and in a Wittgensteinian style, Winch believes that the meanings which inform and motivate individuals' actions are born social. There is no relevant distinction to be made, *pace* Weber, between subjective or internal, and objective or external meaning of action (what an action means to me versus what it actually means, for everybody); nor any additional method to 'empathic' interpretation is required to understand social action.[9] In analogy with Wittgenstein's claim that to understand the meaning of an expression is to have the ability to follow the rules for the use of that expression in the different contexts set out by a community of speakers,[10] Winch argues that to understand social action is to understand its meaning by reference to, and on the basis of, the social rule(s) followed in performing that action.[11] Rules play the role of internalized norms of behaviour: they pre-exist action and they motivate individual behaviour. Ultimately, they make action identifiable, so to speak, 'from within' (though not subjectively), and understood 'as such' (objectively, that is intersubjectively).

Interestingly, both the naturalistic and the anti-naturalistic perspectives are, though each in its own way, normative. They both endorse the prescriptive assumption that there is to be some kind of unitary picture, or unified 'logic' of sociology: a logic of laws/causes/explanations on the naturalistic side; and a logic of rules/reasons/interpretations on the anti-naturalistic side. The picture each view advocates is unitary, in that each of the two 'logics' is prescriptively set out against the other. Against both perspectives, and more generally against all sorts of prescriptive attitudes in sociological inquiry, a number of approaches were developed during the late 1960s. Prescriptive sociology was accused of creating fictional objects of social inquiry, which had very little to do (if anything at all) with what effectively goes on in the social domain. One of the most radical, if not most provocative among them, was ethnomethodology.

2. AGAINST PRESCRIPTIVE ASSUMPTIONS: INDEXICAL SOCIAL OBJECTS[12]

There was a period, at the beginning of the 1970s, when the kind of work done by the ethnomethodologists, and their general approach to sociological practice, was seen as a threat to the integrity and the credibility of sociology as an established discipline of inquiry.[13] What was so dangerous about the ethnomethodological idea of sociology? In brief, and quite interestingly for our discussion, it was its widespread intolerance, sometimes pushed to radical ends, of any prescriptive attitude. The sociologist cannot describe, and still less explain society (either in scientific or in philosophical terms), since 'society' does not exist. It is a concept which has been invented by the sociologist (no matter of what inclination), and which he can manipulate according to the need of the theory of the day.[14] In actual fact, what we call society, or social order, is nothing more than what we 'conspire' together to produce, or concoct, in order to create an impression of order.

If we look at a classroom on a normal school day, for example, we assume that people involved in a series of routine activities are fulfilling predetermined roles, and are engaging in an institutionalized process of learning. Though not explicitly acknowledged, this assumption is nonetheless well in place. However, it survives only because people give each other the impression that everybody engaged in a certain activity is acting on the assumption that (i.e. they agree that) roles pre-exist people and determine people's activities. There is no such thing as 'being a student', if by that we mean filling a role (or following a rule) which pre-exists what happens in an actual context of interaction. Being a student is a 'doing' which makes sense only in a concrete teaching-learning situation. A teaching-learning situation, as a consequence, is an achievement, 'something done' (not something we step into, but something which real actors make happen).[15] Similarly, there are no rules 'causing' the practice in the first place. Rules are taken to be immanent in the practice, not transcendent, nor external to it.

If a sociologist sets himself the task of explaining such a 'doing', he should avoid making use of any prefashioned sociological terminology (causes, rules, roles, etc.). He must instead simply redescribe whatever 'is done' in terms of what appears to have been achieved, there and then. The ethnomethodologists often refer to this explanatory approach as 'indexical', and they set it out specifically against the prescriptive attitude of traditional sociological theory. The reason for calling it 'indexical' is that they conceive their approach as being analogous to the use we make, in our language, of such words as 'I', 'you', 'here', 'there'. These words acquire their meaning only in specific situations of use. In sociological explanation, roles, norms, rules, social relations (such as 'student', and 'teacher') do not have any meaning outside the concrete situations in which they are instantiated, or performed. The task of the sociologist is then, according to the ethnomethodologist, to acknowledge the *indexicality of social order*, and to *describe indifferently* the ways in which actors involved in specific interactions make an indexical order of action become concrete (accomplished).[16]

Consequently, to explain a social action is, for the ethnomethodologist, to adopt some kind of documentary technique.[17] The sociologist must first look at what actors do or say that they do (gather as many features and details as possible concerning the action done, and concerning the ways in which individuals engaged in this action describe what they are doing). He then must reproduce social doings (1) by accounting for them in terms of a non-interfering frame of description (a framework which only makes use of such words as 'context', 'situation', 'achievement', 'indexical', etc.); and (2) by adopting a policy of indifferent observation.

> [Methodological indifference means] abstaining from all judgements of adequacy, value, importance, necessity, practicality, success, or consequentiality of members' accounts.[18]

A documentary-type explanation then operates in two main ways. Firstly, it provides evidence for how people do things, by paying attention to details of action, of sense-making procedures, etc. Secondly, it suggests a framework for organizing this evidence, without adding, in the process, anything which is not already known (already part of the concrete action).

> [The] method consists of treating an actual appearance as 'the document of', as 'pointing to', as 'standing on behalf of' a presupposed underlying pattern. Not only is the underlying pattern derived from individual documentary evidences, but the individual documentary evidences, in their turn, are interpreted on the basis of 'what is known' about the underlying pattern. Each is used to elaborate the other.[19]

Does sociological practice in this ethnomethodological style succeed in its anti-prescriptive crusade? Does its non-prescriptively identified object of inquiry serve any useful role? There are two preliminary issues to consider. Firstly, does the rejection of any prescriptive sociology allow for a non-prescriptive kind of sociology to be put in its place? Secondly, does the rejection of prescriptive assumptions allow sociology to be an objective practice of inquiry? Starting with the first issue, the approach offered by ethnomethodology when rejecting the prescriptive attitude amounts, basically, to a refusal to play the role of being an alternative sociology – according to some, predefined characterization of sociology as a disciplinarian field. To think of sociology as a specific discipline based on a specific methodology, and aimed at producing a specific, unitary picture of the social world is, according to the ethnomethodologist, plainly a mistake. The ethnomethodologist wants to play a different game; in particular, he refuses to engage in a battle created by the prescriptive game, and which – precisely for this reason – is not necessarily the only game in town. As Garfinkel once pointed out, ethnomethodology is not an alternative sociology, but rather an *alternate* to sociology altogether.[20]

To escape prescriptive strictures, and yet still try to identify itself as a specific sociological practice, the ethomethodologist formulates a different question. Rather than asking whether social objects are like natural objects (as in naturalistic perspectives), or alternatively, whether they are philosophical concepts (as in humanistic/anti-naturalistic perspectives), he asks *directly* what individuals do when they interact socially, or publicly. By bypassing any model of sociological redescription, the object of sociology is taken to be a social 'doing', and it is investigated in its practical features as an 'achievement'. Can this non-prescriptively defined object be given an objective account? In order to be able to answer this question affirmatively, the ethnomethodologist has but one option open: since he rejects any methodology or any prescriptive appeal, he can only resort to a policy of 'indifferent observation'.

Does indifference qualify ethnomethodology as an objective practice? To deal with our second issue, there are at least two open questions with the idea of indifference. Is indifference actually possible, in the context of sociological practice? And is indifference a key to a non-prescriptive idea of objectivity in social inquiry? An answer to both questions can be framed in the context of a claim, sometimes made by ethnomethodologists, that they are 'ethnographers of everyday life'. As we found out in the previous chapter, ethnographers do not 'find' the meanings, by which the people they study express themselves, directly, by looking at the activities they observe, or by listening to how these people describe these activities. They rather produce these meanings, while engaging in real interactions during fieldwork. Such interaction does not amount to an indifferent recording of data: it is rather a dynamic, even creative activity of discovery. In other words, the ethnographer's work is far from being indifferent towards its object of inquiry: finding out what something *means* is not equivalent to listening to what an informant says (describes) of that something. Nothing said, or reported, can be taken *at face value* – as the ethnomethodologist recommends.[21]

Contrary to intention, the comparison with the ethnographer brings into focus the limitations of the ethnomethodological idea of indifference (with respect both to its possibility and its objectivity). To believe that sociological theories (in the widest sense of the term) can be removed from social scientific observation, and thereby achieve indifference (and therefore objectivity), is something of a myth. More fruitfully, rather than removing theory from observation, the relation between theory and observation should itself become an object of analysis. In other words, rather than answering a question such as, *What do social actors do?* by trying to bypass the purported 'interference' of theoretical assumptions, we should perhaps ask, *What do sociologists do when they observe social actors in their doings?* In what way (by means of what methods of sociological research) do they make 'actors' and 'actions' appear as, or become, objects of sociological investigation? By means of what procedures do they account for what they observe?[22]

To conclude, it seems that the ethnomethodologists are correct in one claim: that in order to challenge the belief in a unitary picture of sociology and its underlying logic, we must avoid formulating the basic question (that is, how to account for social phenomena) in the unilateral way recommended by normative models of sociology. How can this be achieved? The ethnomethodologists here only half see the answer. They suggest that the sociologist is to work at the level of practical theory, and by this they mean a theory which takes actors' doings as the object of its investigation. Social phenomena, they claim, are not what sociological models tell us they are. There is a 'reality in the making' in any social action or interaction, which needs to be brought to light, and not be taken for granted (the 'facts' of traditional sociology, for example, or the social rules of meaningful action of Winchian memory).[23] I would suggest that practical theory is also a theory which takes itself (i.e. a theory of *sociological* doings, concerned with the various sets of procedures adopted and employed by the sociologist, in order to observe and account for social objects) to be part of the investigation of that object. By adding this further level to the investigation, ethnomethodological indifference should give way to an analysis of the interactive relation between social doings and sociological procedures of identification, description, and classification of those doings. An objective analysis of the *complex object* of sociological inquiry can only be established after careful epistemological and practical analysis of that relation.

It must be said that a renewed ethnomethodological attention to the relationship between the sociologist's points of view and the concept of 'social reality' he appears to be working with seems a step in this direction.

> Ethnomethodology . . . is centrally concerned in examining sociological theories, in asking what they have to start with and how they make, from what they have to start with, the constructions that they have derived.[24]

This claim leads to a two-faceted reflection. On the one side, it seems to imply that the subject matters with which the sociologist deals, by being gradually identified through the procedures and investigations of sociological research, are the 'end product' of that research. This is said in the sense that they are only gradually recognized as being what they are as a consequence of the specific theoretical and empirical purposes of a piece of research. On the other side, it seems legitimate to acknowledge that the sociologist, as engaged in his theoretical, constructive activites, is himself a social actor, an individual member among others of the social order he investigates, though operating under a 'distinctive attitude' towards what he investigates. Arguably then, his activities and his attitude become an inextricable part of the understanding of the 'end products' of his research, as we are about to show.

3. SOCIOLOGICAL OBJECTS: STAGES OF RESEARCH AND LEVELS OF CONSTRUCTION

In manuals of sociological research, the description of how sociological research is carried out is normally given in terms of a sequence of stages. The idea one gets is that there is a 'method', or a generalized procedure that any sociologist should follow in order to get his results – and to get them in the best possible way.[25] The first stage consists of 'data-gathering' with a view to designing a specific kind of research, and to drawing up boundaries for the issues to be addressed. The second stage consists of the organization of data for analysis. Data are firstly 'prepared' for analysis: they are, for example, sorted into kinds or categories, or classified in such a way that they appear typical (a general instance) or atypical (a specific instance). Secondly, they are submitted to actual analysis: here a whole range of research strategies (quantitative as well as quali- tative) is employed to account for the data (that is, in order to explain them and to draw conclusions from them). A third stage consists of the writing down of the results of research, with a view to circulating them among the social scientific community, and offering them for debate and further discussion, or elaboration.

It cannot be denied that these levels are in fact 'stages' in the literal sense of the word (they happen in time, along a temporal sequence: e.g. we could not analyse data if we had not collected them first).[26] Still, this sequence of stages can also be thought of as a stratified complex of strategies, which variously and gradually configure the object of sociological research at different levels of description. At each level, an identified number of research strategies tell us different things about this object, depending on what each level is designed to do, and what it is intended to achieve. This is interesting from a philosophical point of view, as it allows us to conceive of these stages as different and related levels at which the objectivity of sociological research is to be assessed. Being objective about the subject matter of some sociological research can only be achieved by understanding how various research procedures 'shape up' that very subject matter during the various stages. Table 2.1 is a summary of the interrelated levels of research. In the rest of this section, I will analyse what each stage consists of, and how it operates.

Table 2.1 Stages of sociological research description

Stage 1	→	description of data as they appear from interviews, surveys, case studies, experiments
Stage 2	→	description of data as they appear from methodological analysis (axiomatization, symbolic analysis, narrative analysis, modelling)
Stage 3	→	description of data as they appear from written form (articles, books, reports, etc.)

3.1. STAGE 1: DATA-GATHERING

The description of this stage as 'data-gathering' is somewhat misleading. Strictly speaking, there are no 'data' to collect, at the beginning of a piece of research. Certain pieces of information only make sense as 'data' within the general design of a piece of research, and they are therefore chosen according to the type of research the sociologist intends to carry out. The 'choices' made at this initial stage of research are no doubt guided by certain protocols. These protocols tell the sociologist how in principle to conduct research (how to observe, measure, evaluate) and follow a generally acknowledged consensus. However, in practice, these protocols are not sufficient. The sociologist has constantly to make a whole series of contextual decisions, which go beyond the prescriptive content of the protocols themselves. These cannot be neglected, if we want to understand the process by which data are made available and become suitable for investigation.

Ad hoc decisions and contextual choices[27] are rarely made explicit in manuals of sociological research. This might misleadingly convey the idea that sociological research is objective, as data are collected *just* by following scientific protocols. However, by neglecting reference to these extra decisions and choices, the purported objectivity of the results is distorted, rather than preserved. Since these extra factors interact and 'interfere' with the protocols which guide the selection and assemblage of data, and since they are involved with the procedures by which the sociologist puts data together, micro-decisions and choices cannot be marginalized. Indeed, and at the very least, they should be considered when we come to assess the so-called reliability of data, and when we think about the kind of objectivity we can expect of the theories based on them. This is not to say that we should accept and encourage biased data. Rather, it means that an understanding of the origin and conditions under which data are assembled allows us to make adequately informed evaluations of the empirical basis of sociological research.

This applies to both quantitative and qualitative procedures. Measuring attitudes and opinions, or framing groups by means of statistical sampling, in principle encounters the same problems of design, selection, and research goals as, say, interpreting meanings or mapping common-sense beliefs. None of these procedures is a neutral technique of research, and all of them are amenable to questions of validity or reliability. Precisely for this reason, they constitute a specific area of philosophical interest. The case of experiments in traditional social psychology is a particularly instructive example.

'An experiment consists in an interaction between a number of people, in which instructions are issued, tasks are carried out, personas are presented, reputations are made or lost. An experiment is a social event.'[28] Asking questions about this sort of event, and about what sort of event it is, is therefore legitimate. In fact, it becomes all the more pressing when we consider, for example, that the function of traditional social psychological experiments was to categorize real-world social activities. How can we justify, or support the view that what happens in an experiment (constrained by the conditions under which the experiment is carried out) has any bearing on things that happen in real life? In fact, if we look at experimental set-ups, we find reasons to dispute that they achieve this task. For example,

Experiments take place in special places, often called social-psychological laboratories, with a simplified environment consisting of undecorated walls, plain furnishings, rarely more than two chairs, the mysterious blank face of the one-way mirror, and perhaps the intrusion of the unblinking eye of the television camera.

In real life, social events occur in highly differentiated environments, rich in sights and sounds, well furnished with symbolic objects, which direct or determine the interpretative procedures and the choice of rule-systems of the actors.[29]

The two settings are quite different: how can we map one onto the other, without being immediately confronted by the ambiguities of interpretations? In the simplified environment of the social-psychological experiment, actors do not know what rule-meaning system to follow (they are not familiar with the environment they are put into). The fact that they end up choosing one system does not mean that in a real-life, and supposedly analogous, situation they would choose the same one.

Also, 'who meets in a social-psychological experiment?'[30] Normally, and as we infer from the literature, the people involved in a sociological experiment are strangers. It is true that many social encounters are also between strangers. However, this becomes relevant from a sociological point of view: there are substantial differences in the modes of interaction between strangers and between people who know each other, and this affects the value and character-ization of the results of the experiments.

The picture becomes even more complicated when we question what position or role the sociologist does or should play in the experiments he conducts. The protocol would officially prescribe that the sociologist is to act like a detached 'scientist'. Can a sociologist experimenting with people act as a detached 'scientist', and if he cannot, are the results he obtains necessarily unreliable, or fruit-less? More generally, how does detachment guarantee that an experiment with people is carried out objectively? A famous experiment, run by Milgram in the 1970s, leads to reflection on questions of this sort.[31]

Stanley Milgram was a social psychologist, who set himself up to study how far people are prepared to go in obeying authority, even when their actions might end up violating, to an almost fatal degree, other people's rights. Milgram put together an experiment, the results of which he went on to describe and analyse in his book *Obedience to Authority*.[32] In Milgram's experiment, a group of individuals was asked to co-operate in assessing the relation between learning and pain. These individuals were told that they were allowed to administer electric shocks of various strengths to some other people connected to a machine, every time the latter group failed to accomplish a certain learning task. The experiment was, however, built on a sub-plot. The people connected to the machine were in fact 'friends' of the experimenter, and the machine was a fake one. But this was not revealed to the individuals put in charge of the machine, who were indeed under the impression that they were administering real pain to people. Milgram found out that the great majority of people were willing to carry on with the experiment, to the point of believing that they were adminis-tering shocks which were nearly lethal, provided that the experimenter con-sented. When the deceit was revealed, Milgram registered peculiar reactions: most of the individuals so deceived showed signs of more or less lasting psycho-logical problems afterwards. Those among them who had appeared the most nervous during the experiments, subsequently had a real breakdown.

Several issues can be raised. Firstly, the experiment can be analysed in terms of the knowledge it produced. Apparently, Milgram did not prove what he intended to prove: it was pointed out, for example, that what the experiment showed was not obedience to authority, but rather trust in the figure of a com-petent individual.[33] The relation between hypothesis and evidence does not seem to have worked. Secondly, the experiment raises ethical concern. Decep-tion is at the heart of Milgram's experiment (without deception, the experiment would have not been possible). Even supposing that some knowledge is gained, is it acceptable to deceive individuals in order to get those results? It seems that the experimental sociologist has a further and special problem, compared to the natural scientist. His 'object' of inquiry is an individual with the same moral rights as the experimental sociologist. Social research requires then some ethical code, which sets out what is permissible and what is not, morally speaking. Indeed, any social scientist, if or when asked, would claim that he follows a code, and that he practises research within the boundaries of this code. However, this is far from settling the matter.

For a start, we might accept (as any social scientist would) that sociological experiments are to be constrained by an ethical code, but then by following the code, we are prevented from pursuing knowledge as far as it would be possible to do so. So the results of the experiment might be incomplete, and the experimental sociologist might not be able to do his job properly, that is like a 'proper' scientist. Furthermore, while a sociologist might be aware of the moral constraints on experimental research, still his own moral, or ideological beliefs might also be at work, and ultimately be part of the very scientific results he has produced. It is one thing to claim that there are ethical questions involved in the practice of social science – while assuming that what is 'ethical' and what is 'scientific' are separable and distinguished. But it is quite another to suggest that the 'ethical' (evaluative) is embedded in the 'scientific'. This commits us to a claim that the 'ethical' is or becomes one of the means or even one of the conditions for pursuing empirical research.

> A science can be free of values in the form of an ethical code, but not free of values. Ethical values are manifest forms of partisanship. . . . manifest forms of partisanship have an advantage over latent or *de facto* forms, since they are usually the subject of discussion and debate. . . . When the values in the science are not in the form of a code but in the design of experiments, tests, or interviews or in the categories into which the data are sorted, neither the researchers nor their subjects are able to see, let alone debate, them. In short, the question isn't whether the data should or should not be partisan, but how and where the partisanship should be placed.[34]

3.2 STAGE 2: ORGANIZATION AND ANALYSIS OF DATA

Talk of a level of organization being distinguishable from a level of analysis of data might misleadingly make us think that classifications and then the methods for analysing data, once assembled in those classifications, are actually two separate stages. In fact, classifications are only ever made with particular methods of analysis in mind. For example, if a set of information is organized in a matrix, or according to some definitional operations or variables, this means that the ensuing account will allow for a statistical analysis, or for some other formalized procedure, such as the use of logical or computational models, or some methods of attitude scaling. On the other hand, if data are organized according to their symbolic functions, or their meaning, or their narrative content (stories in progress), then other procedures of analysis, qualitative rather than quantitative, would be employed.[35] Rom Harré, for instance, shows how the use of analytic models is of fundamental importance in the methodology of social psychology.[36] These models create simplified versions of social situations, which easily allow the researcher to single out the basic grammar of those situations.

Modelling a social situation is different from experimenting. The goal of an experiment is to reproduce a social action or behaviour. Models, instead, aim at illustration. An illustration has heuristic value: it is a perspicuous representation, in the sense that, depending on the grammar adopted to 'read' the situation, it emphasizes certain aspects while marginalizing others. A well-known example is the use of a dramaturgical model, first introduced by Goffman. Goffman's assumption was that in order to analyse real-life situations you can make use of an analogy with stage action. Scene, plot, actors' roles, styles of performance, all provide a sort of basic grammar by means of which roles, rules and actions in real life become interpretable.[37]

In saying that there is a direct and relevant relation between the way data are organized and the way in which they are analysed, it is not denied that sometimes data are analysed using mixed procedures, both qualitative and quantitative. For example, interviews can be treated both formally and textually; or else, in case study analysis, cases and stories might be divided up in subunits of analysis, which can then be treated according to probabilistic criteria.[38] These mixed analyses do not disprove the general claim that there is a relation between the organization of data and the methods of analysis of those data. Instead, it reinforces the claim that classifications are complex structures, significantly determined by which strategies of analysis are available.

3.3. STAGE 3: WRITING THE RESULTS

The final stage/level of sociological description, the writing down of results in the format of a scientific publication, is also a complex activity. There are various ways of thinking about sociological writing (or, as a matter of fact, about any 'scientific' writing).[39] The most naïve view is that such writing is a simple record of all the factual discoveries of a piece of research. A research report is a way of shaping knowledge in a written form – to paraphrase the title of an interesting book by Charles Bazerman; it is far from being a neutral operation of describing results:

Current writing practices (in conventional, interactional, and epistemological

dimensions) build on a history of practice and speak to a historically conditioned situation. A political scientist or a medical researcher writes as part
of an evolving discussion, with its own goals, issues, terms, arguments, and
dialect. . . . Psychology seem(s) also to have an important place. As a historically realized, social, epistemological activity, writing is carried on through
people. People write. People read. What a text is must take into account how
people create it and how people use it.[40]

Writing knowledge involves the choice of a genre, and a particular position
taken by the author (position of authority, reputation, right of making use of a
particular vocabulary, style of presentation, etc.). It also implies being able to
anticipate the possible comments and criticisms of the community in which the
scientific text is to circulate, and in such a way that the chances of the results'
acceptance are increased.[41] In some cases, the audience is not the academic
community, but a sponsor (an agency, a body of research, a policy-maker),
which has given financial assistance to carry out a specific type of research.
Writing knowledge for a 'client' is then conditioned, and often constrained,
by certain kinds of requirements and expectations. A 'technical' report is not
simply a 'tell it as it is' practice (which, of course, does not mean that it is by
necessity a biased practice).[42] Another, less naïve view of writing then appears,
according to which a rhetoric is involved in disciplinary writing, which leads any
other 'scientific' writer, including the sociologist, to consider (more or less consciously) his audience, and to select the most persuasive features of presentation
for his research among the standard formats.

Within the genre of scientific writing, the emergence of the experimental
article, for example, had a great importance not only in natural science, but also
in the social sciences. What does writing social scientific knowledge in the format of an experimental article involve? For example, by skimming through early
articles in experimental psychology, Bazerman points out how a specific format
was not only favoured, but also formally prescribed in compiling these articles.[43]
The latter had to be built on standard sections: 'title, abstract, introduction,
method, results, and discussion', and each section had to follow well-specified
guidelines.[44] In the articles, the authors appeared in the role of 'problem-solving
reasoners, figuring out how quantitative experiments might aid understanding
of philosophical issues', while the readers were either treated as being well
informed of latest work in the field – though not necessarily actively involved in
research – or as being generally concerned with understanding broad psychological questions.[45]

As a general conclusion, by looking at the description of how sociological
research is (to be) conducted through the magnifying glass of its fine-grained

practice, a more variegated and epistemologically challenging picture of sociology as a discipline of inquiry comes to the fore. The objects the sociologist studies are not totally independent of the theoretical strategies and procedures, which he employs when referring to, and analysing them. Social phenomena become objects of sociological interest in a continuum of complex moves (both practical and theoretical) which constitute the core of any sociological research.

4. A CLASSIC EXAMPLE: SUICIDE

The crucial difficulty with Durkheim's *Suicide* is not that he employs official statistics, but that he adopts for sociology the problem of practical theory. 'Suicide' is a category of the natural language. It leads to a variety of practical problems, such as, for example, explaining particular suicides or explaining the variety of suicide rates. To say that Durkheim's error was to use official records rather than for example studying the variation in the reporting of suicides is to suppose that it is obvious that events occur which sociologists should consider 'really suicides' . . . An investigation of how it is that a decision that a suicide occurred is assembled, and an investigation of how an object must be conceived in order to talk of it as 'committing suicide', these are the preliminary problems for sociology.[46]

This assessment of Durkheim's analysis of suicide as a type of social classification illustrates some of our concerns with the stages of data-gathering and organization, expressed in the previous section. In order to illustrate this, I will start from describing how Durkheim identifies suicide as an object of sociological investigation.

Durkheim's definition of suicide is as follows: 'every case of death resulting directly or indirectly from a positive or negative act of the victim himself which he knows will produce the result.'[47] Durkheim considers suicide as a conscious act (no plea for the agent's intentions is acknowledged, which, he claims, would be more suitable to a psychological, rather sociological, kind of explanation). Besides, and most importantly, he takes it to be a typical act (it can be analysed according to traits of similarity among individual suicides). A sociological analysis of suicide is indeed meant to express what is typical about a series of cases which display resemblances to one another. Individual or circumstantial features are then to be eliminated from sociological analysis, as they cannot be properly generalized (the object of sociology is to be identified as a collective phenomenon, identified by some collective properties). In order to study suicide as a typical social act Durkheim makes use of the methodological tool of suicide *rates*.[48]

Rates describe types. This means that they include all individual cases of suicides indiscriminately, *but only* in so far as their general (typical) traits are concerned.[49] It is precisely this elimination of special individual traits which gives the rate its stability (permanence).[50] By construing a rate in this way, Durkheim believed that what we are left with, in the end, is a 'filtrate' of pure social fact. Besides, by construing a rate according to the required procedure, social facts are classified in such a way that we are guaranteed that their classification does not depend on circumstantial features, but on 'the nature of things' alone.[51]

Once rates are collated, with the help of official statistics of occurrences of suicides, and general types of such occurrences are then established, social causes can be sought to match each type (i.e. the occurrence of each type can be inferred from a relevant social cause). By doing this, individual suicides can be explained by inferring the general type, of which they are an instance, from the relevant social cause. Finally, the inferential link can be expressed in terms of a sociological macro law.[52]

As the passage quoted above points out, however, the classification of suicides according to rates of occurrence takes for granted a whole series of issues which, once brought to the fore, makes us formulate a series of additional questions concerning the 'object' suicide. Concern is raised, as we read, not only about the use of official statistics as 'objective' providers of sociological data, but also about what the use of rates calculated on the basis of those statistics actually takes for granted regarding 'suicide' as a social category of analysis. Indeed, the first problem in analysing official statistics on suicide rates is one of *definition*.[53] A suicide is not simply a case of death. It is not even 'an objective quality of certain acts'. 'Suicide' is rather an 'interpretative category to which acts are assigned for certain practical purposes and as the upshot of a complex social event'.[54] Describing a death as a 'suicide' entails attributing a particular *meaning* to that death, and the attribution of meaning is itself a complex social practice.

There are also different possible ways for a death to be described as a suicide, that is there are several possible definitions of suicide. If this is so, a statistic of 'suicides' seems then to presuppose what in fact needs to be explained or established in the first place, i.e. what counts as a suicide.[55] Of course Durkheim would say that we put together actions or phenomena which have features 'in common'. But these features themselves are not 'brute' features, they cannot be simply and plainly observed as 'being similar'. Their resemblance implies a certain method of categorization. How do we know whether or not one compiler of statistical data has the same definition of suicide as another? And even if the sociologist and the statistician can agree on the appropriate definition, they may disagree on its application. One might restrict his application to overt cases of suicide, but another might feel it appropriate to include, for example, alcoholism, heroin addiction or smoking. Moreover, there might be agreement on the

view that suicidal behaviour must result in death, and therefore attempted suicides are ignored. However, by so limiting the study, relevant information that
could be derived from survivors is automatically excluded. It seems, then, that
in all these cases the choices made by the compiler(s) of the statistics affect the
work that the sociologist has to do on them.

The problem of definition is also strictly related to another pressing concern:
what *evidence* are these statistics based on? The statistician will clearly rely on
some sources of evidence in order to issue his numerical data: for example, he
will make use of death certificates, coroners' reports, or interviews with the
relatives and/or friends of the deceased. He needs to make a choice as to what
are the most appropriate sources, and in making these choices the charge of
being selective (and sometimes even too narrowly selective) might be raised.
Given that the Durkheimean sociologist will want to make generalizations at the
end of his study, it is questionable whether he has the authority to do so. Moreover, the evidence upon which the statistician bases his study is the product of
others' selections and interpretations. If families have been interviewed, they
may lie, for they may be reluctant to discuss the fact that their loved ones have
ended their own lives. Similarly, if asked to describe the social background or
profession of the deceased they may exaggerate, hoping to do justice to the
deceased's memory.[56] Alternatively, a coroner, in deciding upon a verdict of
suicide, will often have to rely on his common sense in order to give meaning to
very circumstantial evidence. Or instead, he might endorse the evidence offered
by a pathologist, whose training and experience has taught him that, given
certain medical information, suicide is the most probable cause of death in the
case under investigation.

By taking the problem of evidence into account, we can in the end hardly
agree with Durkheim when he claims:

> By proceeding in this way from the outset the sociologist is immediately
> grounded firmly in reality. Indeed, how the facts are classified does not
> depend on him, . . . but on the nature of things.[57]

The problems of definition and evidence associated with official statistics
should not simply discourage us from using such statistics (as well as rates,
questionnaires, scales, etc.) in social scientific inquiry. They should rather alert
us against the belief in a model of objective inquiry according to which certain
procedures are methodologically and normatively guaranteed to reproduce
social 'facts'. Classifying social facts is an interactive procedure, which works on
the two-fold assumption that the facts to be classified do not plainly pre-exist
their classification, and that classification is a social/sociological practice which
produces (rather than discovers) categories of description for social facts.

A further issue, raised by the problem of definition analysed so far, concerns the way in which a classification of suicides (events) relates to the kinds of people who commit them. As we know, the composition of a suicide rate is stated in such a manner that both the social and the individual aspects of the social fact of suicide are taken into account. However, the 'individual' aspects, which a rate can only include, are 'typical' traits. Durkheim justifies his choice of excluding 'non-typical' individual traits from sociological analysis by claiming that they are too specific and context-dependent to be included within the range of sociological factors which can explain suicide. However, by making such a choice, the 'typically' individual features profiled on the basis of rates of occurrence of suicides might in the end identify very abstract, and highly idealized traits of human beings – traits of 'average' individuals who do not really exist.[58] If the ultimate aim is, presumably, to explain why actual individuals commit themselves to certain courses of action, then it is indeed 'objectively' difficult to see how individual traits not necessarily comprised within types, simply can be disposed of, as if they were only contingently (accidentally) related to certain actions. '[To] put it baldly: explaining suicide – and explaining suicide rates – must involve why *people* commit it' [my italics][59]. It can here be repeated that the thrust of this objection is not to reject the use of rates, or other formalized methods of classification in social science.[60] The aim is instead to bring attention to the level and kind of description of the object under investigation that they produce. The objectivity of the results of the inquiry based on that description is then to be treated as a practical consequence of the inquiry, rather than as one of its normative assumptions.

Hacking has emphasized the interactive nature of social classifications.[61] In the case of human/social kinds, real individuals are often aware of being classified as being of certain types. Depending on the circumstances, they either comply with a classification (they experience themselves as being people of a certain kind), or reject it (they rearrange, or escape from the classification which presumes to say who they are). Both situations have effects not only on the people so classified, but also on how we construct types of individuals. Interactive human kinds are 'moving targets'.

In the case of suicides, this model does not seem to apply. How can a suicide interact with a classification if the person who has committed the act is dead? Yet, the idea of interaction is still useful and crucial to understanding how social kinds provide a reference for sociological inquiry. Classifying an individual who has committed suicide (and has been successful) as a particular type of suicide does not occur in a vacuum. As we saw earlier, to define a suicide, to identify cases or instances of suicide under one definition or others, to provide evidence both for definitions and real occurrences, etc., all require a whole range of institutional and social practices, as well as, most importantly, consideration of the people involved in those practices. These people are aware of social classifications, and socially interact with socially defined typologies. Types of suicides, despite obvious practical constraints, are still 'moving targets' for a sociologist of self-inflicted death.

CHAPTER 3

Historical Objects

1. THE NORMATIVE VIEW: EXPLAINING HISTORY BY HEMPELIAN LAWS

Is history objective? Can historical action be explained objectively? A number of philosophers of science in the analytic tradition have shown an interest in one form or another of these questions. History became a case study both in the theory of explanation and in the philosophy of action.[1] A prime example is Hempel. In answering the first question, he tried to show that history, although at present not in a satisfactory state, can be reformed in such a way that it becomes objective. The way to undertake such a task is to rethink, and remodel the types of explanation offered by historians, in accordance with the exemplary format of a scientific explanation. Such a format was for Hempel the deductive-nomological (D-N) model. Therefore, in order to answer the second question, he tried to prove that historical action can be typically accounted for in a deductive-nomological style.

Table 3.1 below illustrates the format of the Hempelian model of explanation, and the logical inference on which it is based.[2] According to the D-N model, a full explanation occurs when the description of the event to be explained (the explanandum) is inferred as the conclusion of a deductive argument. This description is derived from a set of premises (the explanans), which consist of a description of some initial conditions, and at least one general law under which the event may be subsumed. By following the inference, the explanandum appears to be nothing but an instance, or a logical consequence, of the explanans (if the explanans is true, then the explanandum cannot but be correctly explained).

Clearly, this type of explanation crucially relies on the explanans for its adequacy, particularly on the law (laws) included in it. In fact, a law must be part of the premise in the explanatory inference, if there is to be an explanation at all.[3] Laws, in this model, are defined as statements of universal generalizations of a conditional form (if X, then Y), which are capable of being empirically tested. They are intended to express regularities in observable behaviours. This means two things: firstly, that under certain conditions, there will always occur a certain behaviour, or certain properties of an object; secondly, that this behaviour or these properties are exhibited by each and every object of the same type. The basic idea appears then to be the following: 'same object/same behaviour'; i.e. given certain conditions we can reasonably expect a certain occurrence. In such a way, a law can be used to explain as well as to predict that occurrence. (If X then Y; Y because of X).

Table 3.1 The Hempelian model of explanation

D-N model		Explanatory inference
$C_1, C_2, \ldots C_k$	[initial conditions]	IF the explanans is true (all the statements in it are empirically confirmed),
$L_1, L_2, \ldots L_n$	[laws]	
E	[explanandum]	THEN the explanans must lead to a deduction of a description of the explanandum, i.e. to a correct explanation.

Hempel adds two further specifications to his model. Firstly, causal explanations are deductive-nomological in character (according to a Humean view of causation as temporal succession). Secondly, the laws which appear in the explanans are often of a probabilistic-statistical form, that is 'assertions to the effect that if certain specified conditions are realized, then an occurrence of such and such a kind will come about with such and such a statistical probability'.[4]

How does Hempel adapt this model to the case of historical explanation? His argument is built on two complementary steps. Firstly, he tells us that the D-N model, as he reconstructs it, is intended to show the logical structure and the rationale underlying explanation-seeking questions in empirical science. It does not describe the way in which scientists actually formulate their explanatory accounts.[5] We should not therefore expect to find it instantiated as such (in full-fledged form) in scientific activity. This allows him to say that what we will find in practice are, often, 'incomplete' formulations of this model.[6] Secondly, he compares the D-N model with other purported types of explanatory models in empirical science, leading us to conclude that the latter are not different in kind from the D-N model. The logical structure of the D-N model can be usefully employed to shed light on the logic and explanatory force of other explanatory accounts.[7] Indeed, an even stronger claim is eventually put forward, namely that where these other models appear to be irreducible to the D-N format, they should not be considered as genuine explanations at all.[8]

On the basis of these two steps, Hempel is then able to make a case for his picture of historical explanation, by arguing as follows:

1) the reason why explanations in history do not appear to be deductive-nomological is that they are often formulated in an incomplete manner. In this, they are not different from many explanations put forward in empirical science. Various forms of incompleteness are then analysed with a view to finding those most commonly instantiated in history;
2) incompleteness also explains why we are often under the impression that there are ways other than the D-N model to describe what a historical explanation amounts to. The logical structure of an explanation, as revealed by the D-N model, is then used to 'correct' other purported models of explanation in history, to remove apparent differences, and to distinguish between real explanations and pseudo-explanations.

1.1 EXPLANATORY SKETCHES

So in his first line of argument, Hempel accepts that most explanations in history do not appear as deductive-nomological in form. This is because, he argues, like many explanations in empirical science, they are formulated in an incomplete manner. Incompleteness takes many forms. It can be *elliptical* (certain laws or facts are left implicit), or *partial* (the explanans is insufficient to explain the explanandum), or *selective* (the explanation is complete only by reference to a particular description of a concrete event, regardless of the infinitely many different characteristics which make up the event itself). A further class of incomplete explanations which, says Hempel, are 'not explicit and specific enough to be reasonably qualified as an elliptically formulated explanation or as a partial one' consists of *explanation sketches*. A sketch

> may suggest, perhaps quite vividly and persuasively, the general outlines of what, it is hoped, can eventually be supplemented so as to yield a more closely reasoned argument, based on explanatory hypotheses which are indicated more fully, and which more readily permit of critical appraisal by reference to empirical evidence.[9]

An explanation sketch is, then, a 'short cut' to the complete explanation. The latter might not yet be available, but can still be arrived at, by pursuing further empirical inquiry along the logical lines suggested by the sketch itself. In other words, the sketch is not a pseudo-argument. It is rather an argument which, for whatever reason, has been left unfinished, and needs to be 'filled out'. The way to pursue the 'filling out' of an explanatory sketch (as well as to test whether a sketch is merely an incomplete argument) is to see whether it can be put in a D-N form.

Historical explanations often appear incomplete in this latter form. For Hempel, there are at least two reasons for this incompleteness, both of which depend on the formulation of the explanans:

> First, the universal hypotheses in question frequently relate to individual or social psychology, which somehow is supposed to be familiar to everybody. So they are taken for granted. . . . Second, it would often be very difficult to formulate the underlying assumptions explicitly, with sufficient precision, and at the same time in such a way that they are in agreement with all the relevant empirical evidence available.[10]

Both reasons raise concern. On one side, we might wonder what relevant explanatory use can be made of laws which state the obvious (other than making the explanation 'look like' a D-N explanation, i.e. a complete explanation in Hempel's vocabulary). On the other, we might question whether the lack of precision in the formulation of a law is only a *practical* impediment in explanatory sketches. Scriven, for instance, pointed out that if we want to explain a particular historical event (e.g. Cortes sending a third expedition out to Baja California, after the failure of the first two) by deducing the description of the event from a general law, we are confronted by the following alternatives.[11] Either the law we use to explain the historical event is general in form ('*All* confident wealth-seeking people undertake any venture which offers wealth') but most likely false. Or we use a closer-to-the-truth type of law – which would entail adding more and more specifications relating to the individual event in question – but such a law would not be general (e.g. 'All confident people with Cortes' background of experience, seeking very great wealth undertake any venture involving the hazards of this one, which offers very great wealth'). The extreme case, in this second alternative, would be that of a law which is most nearly correct, but which would admit of only one instance (e.g. Cortes' decision).[12]

There seems then to be a peculiar trade-off between truth and generality: if the law is general, it is not true; but if it is true, it cannot be general. This means that by adding more and more qualifications to our initial law, we are not 'filling out' an explanation sketch; we are simply violating the adequacy of the explanatory deduction. Or at best, we find ourselves in the position of explaining the event by means of the truistic claim that this is what happened because everybody like a certain X individual (e.g. Cortes) would have acted like him. This is not to deny, says Scriven, that historical explanations are often based on, or presented in terms of, statements or principles which appear to have the form of a law. However, they are not laws, and this can be proved by the fact that if we try to treat them as laws they appear either trivial, or truistic.

As a matter of fact, truisms are not completely empty statements, and this is why they are sometimes used by historians as part of their explanations. But we must be aware that they are truisms, so that we do not expect them to perform the covering role which general laws can (and are expected to) fulfil. In particular, truistic statements cannot be used for predictive purposes. For Hempel, explanation and prediction are structurally symmetrical. One of the most controversial consequences of this claim is that an explanation can only take place on, as it were, predictive ground. If we cannot use a law to predict an event, we are forced to say, if we stay with Hempel's picture, that we do not have an explanation either. Yet it seems difficult to claim that historical events can be predicted by laws, if we accept that – following Scriven – laws in history are at best truisms. If we then acknowledge this difficulty, and yet still want to argue that history is an explanatory discipline, we should perhaps find a way to argue that explanations in history occur without the need for prediction. However, by so arguing, we would be casting doubt on the very applicability of Hempel's model here.

1.2 VARIETIES OF HISTORICAL EXPLANATION

What about the second strand of Hempel's argument? How convincing is the view that all the apparently different explanatory models in history are in fact reducible to the deductive-nomological format (and that if they are not, then it is because some of these models, simply, are not explanatory)? Hempel considers three main candidates for historical explanation: explanation by reason; explanation by concept; and genetic explanation.

With regard to the first, Hempel takes issue with W. Dray's version of rational explanation. For Dray, to say why agent A did action X is 'to show that what was done was the thing to have done for the reason given, rather than merely the thing that is done on such occasions, perhaps in accordance with certain laws'.[13]

'The thing to have done' is the relevant clue in Dray's definition: to explain an action (e.g. Cortes') is to show in what way the action was *appropriate* (and not the one to be expected), and *reasonable* (there were 'good reasons' to act in the way that Cortes did). In other words, 'When in a situation of type $C_1, \ldots C_k$, the thing to do is X.'[14]

Hempel claims that the only way to attribute explanatory force to Dray's formula above is to translate it into the following format ('Schema R'):

A was in a situation of type C
A was a rational agent
In a situation of type C, any rational agent will do X

A did X

In other words, Hempel argues that Dray's formulation of rational explanation is not 'complete' if the assumption that A is a rational agent (he had reasons which led him to act the way he did) is not made explicit. By using again Scriven's example, we can indeed try to figure out Cortes' reasons for his decision to organize a third expedition. He was for example an ambitious man, and in the light of his ambition his decision becomes *reasonable*. However, in order to explain Cortes' decision we need to be able to say that ambition *caused* him to organize a third expedition. In fact, given Cortes' ambition, we could *expect that* Cortes would have organized a third expedition: that is, given Cortes' ambition, organizing a third expedition was indeed 'the rational thing to do'. For Hempel, Dray's sense of rationality (the one which makes an action appear reasonable) is not explanatory unless it is understood in the context of Hempel's sense of explanation: to explain why a certain action in the past was undertaken, is 'to put forward an empirical hypothesis . . ., to the effect that . . . the action can be explained as having been motivated by it'. The mere fact that such a hypothesis is not made explicit does not mean that it does not do its explanatory work. Therefore, Hempel concludes

> Dray's construal fails just at the point where it purports to exhibit a logical difference between explanations by reference to underlying reasons and explanation by subsumption under general laws, for to ensure the explanatory efficacy of a rational explanation, we found it necessary to replace Dray's normative principle of action by a statement that has the character of a general law. But this restores the covering-law form to the explanatory account.[15]

In order to decide whether Hempel's conclusion is sound, we need to analyse the underlying logic of Dray's model in more detail. Dray claims that his explanatory strategy is not deductive in form. Rather, to use his own words, it amounts to a 'calculation'. It refers to 'the agent's reasons for acting as he did', in the light of the circumstances in which he found himself, and the available means by which he could achieve his chosen end. The difference from Hempel's model (Cortes' action was caused by the motive he had for embarking on that action) is in fact remarkable. In Dray's model, the link between an action and its reasonableness is based on a kind of generalization which is neither necessary nor sufficient. What Dray offers is a 'principle of action', which expresses a

Table 3.2 Two alternative models of explanation

	HEMPEL		DRAY
1. Logical scheme:	**deduction**	vs.	**calculation**
2. Explanatory generalization:	**general law**	vs.	**principle of action**
3. Explanatory grounding:	**causes** (necessary)	vs.	**reasons** (appropriate)
4. Model of rationality:	**empirical hypothesis**	vs.	**critical appraisal**

judgement (i.e. an evaluation, or interpretation), rather than a causal link. Table 3.2 illustrates the points of difference between Hempel's and Dray's schemes.

Neither model of explanation can be translated into, or made compatible with, the other. 'Explaining why' a certain event occurred is answered differently (i.e. by means of a different logic) in each case.

The second purported model of historical explanation is explanation by concept. This takes the form of an answer to the question, 'What was it that happened in this case?'[16] Consider the following example. We explain a series of changes in late eighteenth-century France by saying, 'It was a revolution'. As it stands, we cannot say that the explanation offered is in any sense Hempelian (we are not answering a 'why-question' by quoting a law). Instead, we are providing a general idea by means of which we reconstruct 'what' actually happened.

Hempel's objection to this type of explanation is that we cannot claim that we have explained a certain event, if all we try to do is account for the phenomenon in question by means of some general ideas, not amenable to any empirical test. Trying to ascertain the meaning of an event by determining which other kinds of event are relevantly (i.e. significantly) connected with it cannot be considered an 'explanation'. We may in the end succeed in producing some 'emotive appeal', or some 'vivid pictorial associations'. However, Hempel argues, we cannot claim that we have 'furthered our theoretical understanding of the phenomena under consideration'.[17]

The only way to make room for an explanation within these procedures is, for Hempel, to try to reconcile them with his nomological model. Can a statement such as 'It was a revolution' be put in a law-like form? We could try to spell out a series of events – for example, elucidate on particular historical changes in agriculture, in industrial production, and in communications – and state that the conjunction of them *inevitably* (and not just coincidentally) led to a larger process of change which we call 'revolution'. This for Hempel is evidence enough that this explanatory strategy conforms to the covering-law model, that is 'if only vaguely and sketchily – the particular cases are assigned a place in a comprehensive pattern of connections'.[18] However, we might object, by pursuing the explanation in this way, we do not explain a certain historical change 'as a revolution'. Instead, we explain 'that a revolution' occurred because of the co-occurrence of a series of historical changes. The two explanatory strategies seem again to be rather different:

> To explain, say, what happened in France in 1789 'as a revolution' would surely not be equivalent to bringing it under any law of the form, 'Whenever $C_1, C_2, \ldots C_k$ then a revolution'. For to apply the concept does not necessarily represent the explicandum as the sort of thing which follows a certain type of antecedent event or condition, whether stated or merely understood.[19]

Indeed, both in the case of nomological explanation and in that of conceptual explanation we are trying to generalize what happened. However, the kind of generalization is different in each case. In 'saying-why explanations' it takes the form '*whenever X then Y*' (deductive inference). In 'saying-what explanations' it takes the form '*X, Y, Z amount to a Q*' ('summative' generalization), that is we are allowed to refer to X, Y and Z collectively as 'a so-and-so'. In other words, in the latter case we are generalizing a series of events by offering an interpretation of their occurring together in a particular time and place. We are not trying, as in the former case, to establish that the series of events referred to necessarily produced a certain outcome. To be sure, some regularity is suggested by the latter explanation. However, it is not the kind of regularity expressed by a law-like statement. 'Revolution', Dray argues, is a classificatory term drawn from the ordinary language of social description. It represents the joint occurrence of a series of events as a recurring social phenomenon not by implying the existence of a nomological link between a description of those events and a certain outcome (a revolution); the term rather allows us to say, of different historical occurrences, that they are 'revolutions' by suggesting a family resemblance between interpretations of specific events.[20] Subsuming a series of events under a concept follows a different 'logic' (intensional, rather than extensional) from subsuming them under a law.

The last model of historical explanation considered by Hempel is genetic explanation. This model presents the phenomenon to be explained 'as the final stage of a developmental sequence, and accordingly accounts for the phenomenon by describing the successive stages of that sequence'.[21] As an example, Hempel considers the practice of selling indulgences at the time of Luther. To answer the question, 'Where did the phenomenon come from?' the historian A. Gottlob, for example, asked himself why the popes and bishops started to offer

indulgences in the first place. By looking at its origin, and successive development, the phenomenon finally 'revealed itself as a true descendant of the time of
the great struggle between Christianity and Islam, and at the same time a highly
characteristic product of Germanic Christianity'.[22]

For Hempel, this type of explanation also qualifies for nomological representation, since each stage of development in a genetic sequence must relate to the
next not just by temporal contiguity, but by some necessary link.

> In a genetic explanation each stage must be shown to 'lead to' the next, and
> thus be linked to its successor by virtue of some general principles which
> make the occurrence of the latter at least reasonably probable, given the
> former.[23]

The general principles used in history consist of psychological uniformities
(often left implicit) which refer to the motivating reasons for action. The
explanation of why the popes started offering indulgences ultimately lies in giving the reasons why people like the popes 'will *generally* act, or will tend to act, in
certain characteristic ways'.[24]

However, by Hempel's own admission, genetic explanations in history are not
'purely nomological', as arguably they appear to be in physics (a stone in free fall
might be accounted for according to a genetic sequence where all different
stages forming the sequence are interconnected by universal law). In history,
nomological connections are combined with a certain amount of description.[25]
This is because, Hempel says, the final stage to be explained normally requires
far more data than those adduced by the initial stage of the sequence. Such a
difference in informative strength between the two stages can be remedied by
adding, along the way, a whole mass of historical details which, though not
directly explanatory, will become helpful for understanding the development
and direction of the explanation itself.

Hempel's reconstruction of genetic explanation in history appears far-fetched
for at least the following reason. Hempel seems not to be able to avoid running
two types of accounts – one nomological, and one descriptive – under a single
heading. In order to attribute prominence to the former, he must find a way to
relegate the latter to an auxiliary role. He admits that descriptive details might
themselves become crucial, in explanatory terms: for example, we might find
ourselves referring to specific bits of information in order to support the
cogency of certain connections between stages. However, Hempel denies that
the kind of support provided by the description of historical details is in any way
and by itself 'explanatory' (as it is not nomological in form). Nonetheless, this
seems at least to cast doubt on the fact that the nomological format can do all
the required explanatory work. We can even wonder what actually, in the end,

constitutes the 'explanation' of the phenomenon under study: is it the law-like connection between one stage and the next, or is it rather a detailed and consistent description of the phenomenon, which allows for a certain coherent story to be recounted?

Hempel rightly emphasizes that description is more important in history than it is in natural science, but he downplays the important fact that it is for this reason that in history, events cannot be explained purely nomologically, as particular instances of given kinds.[26] Descriptive details are not a reservoir of information to resort to, when the nomological explanation runs short of evidence. They might as well be what identify the very nature of historical explananda. As we will next analyse, acknowledgement of this fact has important consequences for the debate on historical explanation.

2. 'WHAT' DO HISTORIANS EXPLAIN?

The debate about historical explanation triggered by Hempel's view is ultimately a debate over what is the best explanatory methodology. As such, it is completely focused on the nature and function of the explanans (are laws required in a historical explanation? do they afford the right type of generality? do they guarantee the correctness of the explanation? do they make the explanation 'inevitable'? etc. etc.). There are two main perspectives from which these questions are answered by the various positions involved in this debate. One is descriptive: Dray and Scriven look at the practice of history, and they try to argue that history is 'in its own way' explanatory. The other is normative: Hempel looks first at the protocols of science, and then tries to make history conform to these protocols. However, what did not seem to be specifically questioned by either of these approaches is whether the adequacy of an explanation might depend not so much on the explanans, as on the way in which the historical facts to be explained (the explananda) are described.[27] As a further alternative, it can instead be argued that, depending on the description given, there are some explananda which might logically presuppose general laws, and be accounted for by them, and others which do not. In the end, it might be that the reason why the various positions in this debate look incompatible is not to be found in the logic of an explanation. This is the kind of insight put forward by Danto in his 1965 book, *Analytic Philosophy of History*.

> Phenomena as such are not explained. It is only phenomena as covered by a description which are capable of explanation, and then, when we speak of explaining them, it must always be with reference to that description. So an explanation of a phenomenon must, in the nature of the case, be relativized to

a description of that phenomenon. But then if we have explained a phenomenon E, as covered by a description D, it is always possible to find another description D' of E, under which E cannot be explained with the original explanation. If there are indefinitely many possible different descriptions of that phenomenon, there may be indefinitely many possible different explanations of that phenomenon, and there may, indeed, be descriptions of that phenomenon under which it cannot be explained at all.[28]

What are the consequences of Danto's general claim for the practice of history? In history, we might find many descriptions of the same set of events, and it might be impossible to cast some of these descriptions into the terms of the Hempelian model. However, this does not mean that the model is incorrect, nor that the events in question are unexplainable. For example, in order to explain why, during the celebration of the national holiday in Monaco back in the 1960s, the streets were decorated not only with the flags of Monaco, but also with American flags, we might say that there is no law which connects one event (Prince Rainier III married the American actress Grace Kelly) with the other event (the people of Monaco put out American flags during their national holiday). At this level of description, Dray is indeed right. However, each of the two events could be differently redescribed, and under a different description we might find it easy to produce a covering law, and make use of it in explaining the event so redescribed. Danto's strategy is different from Hempel's in that we are not told that the former explanation is 'incomplete' until it is supplemented by a covering law. Rather, the former explanation simply belongs to a different level of reconstruction of the object of inquiry. Danto offers the following three descriptions of the event E (different levels of description):

E' The Monegasques put out American flags side by side with national flags
         (description of the event before an explanation was available)
E'' The Monegasques were honouring a sovereign of American birth
         (description of the event after the event has been explained)
E''' The members of one nation were honouring a sovereign of a different
         national origin
         (description of the same event, but also of many other different events, still
         – arguably – of the same kind)[29]

Danto believes that this scheme ends up satisfying all the conflicting positions in the debate over historical explanation. Under description E''', the explanation can indeed rely upon use of a covering law (Hempel's position). However, such a law does not cover the event to start with, nor can the event be deduced from the law without first going through the redescription offered at the level of E'''. It is this redescription which somehow bears the burden of the explanation (Dray's position), in that it is responsible for almost a transformation in perception: E' is reconceptualized into a new set of relationships. Once we have E'', it appears relatively easy, almost 'trivial', to move to E'''' (Scriven's position). E'''' truistically describes at a higher degree of generality the habit mentioned in E''.

Danto's reconstruction of the debate about historical explanation is interesting for at least two reasons. Firstly, and more generally, it shows how limited it is to present the philosophical debate over historical explanation in terms of antithetical, and mutually exclusive, positions. Secondly, and more specifically, it is interesting because of the shift of focus (from the explanans to the explanandum) it recommends: it points out how the form and the very possibility of explaining an event is, to a large extent, dependent on the description given of that event. The implications of this shift are insightful. We are led to consider whether historical events, as dealt with by historians, can really exist independently of the way in which they are recounted. Further, we might wonder whether our explanations of them can ever be devised in such a way that they only refer to 'the way the events really happened'. The idea of *an objective past*, as well as that of a *perfect record* of the past, are, arguably, meaningless.

Danto asks us to imagine, for the sake of argument, a fictitious character. An Ideal Chronicler is somebody who is capable of witnessing a past event in the most complete way possible, and at the moment the event occurs. He is also able to record perfectly everything he has seen, that is to produce an ideal chronicle. Obviously, not all the possible true descriptions of this past event are known to be true at the time in which the Ideal Chronicler is compiling his record. For example, consider the report: 'The Thirty Years War begins in 1618.' Given that the war in question is so called because of its length, 'the sentence is true of some event (or series of events) in 1618, but could not appear in even an ideal chronicle of events for 1618'.[30] What Danto illustrates, by means of this example, is that a perfect witness to the past is not necessarily, in fact not at all, in the position of observing all which needs to be known about the past. And what is relevant about history is that the descriptions of historical facts might be true of the past without being known to be so in the past. These descriptions (or 'narrative sentences', as Danto defines them) refer to stories which 'historians alone can tell'.[31]

We could try to improve on the idea of the completeness of the perfect record. We could imagine, for example, that the ideal chronicle contains a transcription of everything which has come to happen – that is, all the possible true descriptions of past events (the whole set of narrative sentences). However, if all descriptions are allowed in, then inconsistencies are bound to arise. Is there just one French Revolution? According to François Furet,[32] there are at least three.

The 'French Revolution' is either the story of the origin of French national history and democracy; or the story (as 'narrated' by Tocqueville) of the natural and ultimate development of the work of the monarchy; or else, the story of a bourgeois revolution, which promoted new individualistic values (the story of the beginning of a new world). These stories of what purportedly happened in 1789 in France are, arguably, three equally true and yet mutually inconsistent narrative descriptions. It is as if we had three different narrators (the nationalist, the royalist, the Jacobin), and each time we see what happened via one narrator's eyes. If we imagine that an ideal chronicle should contain all three descriptions (it is a complete record), then we are bound to say that we are simultaneously seeing inconsistent accounts of the same thing; and an inconsistent chronicle is hardly an objective one. Conversely, if we want a consistent chronicle (as an ideal chronicle should indeed be), then we have to admit that the perfect record must be incomplete (it must exclude incompatible reports), and therefore it is not so 'perfect', after all.[33]

This has considerable consequences when we come to the problem of how to explain historical events.

> A phenomenon like the French Revolution cannot be reduced to a simple cause-and-effect schema. The mere fact that the Revolution had causes does not mean that they are all there is to its history.[34]

The Revolution as an event 'meant many things to many people', including the historians. As we said before, different descriptions of the same historical occurrence call for different explanations of 'what happened'. This claim not only casts doubt on singling out causal (or nomological) explanation as the ideal explanation in history. It also makes us wonder what the historian actually does when he claims that he reconstructs the 'causes' of certain past events. The causes of historical occurrences do not exist as facts which, at least in principle, can be (can be found as) perfectly recorded – say, in an archive, in a manuscript, or in a memory.

Archives, manuscripts, and memories, can all indeed be used as sources of 'factual evidence' for the reconstruction of the causes of past events. However, the interesting aspect of factual evidence in history is that it is itself a historical document, which needs to be subjected to the same critical examination as the events it is meant to bring to light or to explain. This is for at least two reasons. Firstly, in a manuscript, or in an archive, the historian finds events as *reported*:

> Reporting events is not a matter of neutrally transcribing what actually happened: . . . whether or not descriptions of Nazi crimes succeed in referring is

an issue loaded with ethical and political implications. Indeed, many – perhaps most – people's moral intuitions would probably tell them that even to express a willingness to consider whether the Holocaust took place, as if it could be an open question, is just repugnant, an unacceptable stand to take. But if there is anything to these intuitions (as there surely is), then the idea of a neutral domain of facts is seriously compromised by those who will have no truck with Holocaust revisionism.[35]

Secondly, the criteria for assembling, selecting and storing documented facts vary. Archives are a good example. It has been studied how there is a substantial difference, for example, between European archives as built in the nineteenth century and archives as rebuilt in our century, under the impact of computer technology. The way in which the historian refers to historical 'facts' since the advent of computerized data has been completely transformed.[36] In the nineteenth century, archives were put together according to criteria and procedures reflecting the ideological and methodological preoccupations of history at that particular time: national values tended to predominate, there was an almost exclusive emphasis on political and administrative sources; documents were classified only sequentially. In the twentieth century, for example with the development of the 'new history' in France, a new emphasis was put on producing serial classification of past events. The contexts for such classifications were models either for measuring change, or for building systems of change within patterns of stability, or also for discovering underlying equilibria in these systems. As a consequence, new sources of historical evidence were added, coming from the economic, fiscal, demographic, or geographic domains.

An important consequence of these studies is that they make us reflect on the fact that historical events are perhaps not the starting point of historical inquiry (even less so, an 'objective' starting point), but one of its results.

> History, in other words, is theory all the way down. The facts in which historians deal are themselves discursive constructs, and not items in the real world which are first collected and then assembled into stories.[37]

There are two ways to read the claim above. One (which I take to be the less enlightening) is to the effect that historical facts do not exist, they are fictions, fabricated by the historians, and as such they make history a highly subjective, and ultimately unreliable, kind of inquiry. Another reading, which I find more useful, draws our attention to the 'delicate and fascinating labour'[38] that goes into assembling facts, and into assessing, for the historian as well as for his audience, their significance and validity.

3. QUANTITATIVE AND QUALITATIVE HISTORY: SAMPLES OF RESEARCH

A feature of historical practice, which must be taken into account, is then how the selection and organization of historical facts in the reconstruction of some past event is pursued. As it has been put, 'it is not the sources which define the questions asked by a discipline, but the questions which determine the sources'.[39] Various and different procedures are followed and developed to categorize historical evidence. Depending on the procedure chosen, past events will be presented according to a particular description. This description will, in its turn, affect and constrain the kind of explanation which can be offered of those events (as we learnt from Danto). So, the conditions under which sources are selected and organized should be carefully monitored, as they affect the types of accounts offered at the end. This, nonetheless, does not mean that a particular kind of description/reconstruction of historical sources only allows for one type of explanatory procedure. We can illustrate all this by presenting some of the various ways in which historical research is carried out.

3.1 LITERACY IN SEVENTEENTH- TO NINETEENTH-CENTURY FRANCE

Quantitative research was very popular in the 1950s and 1960s among French historians, particularly the members of the *Annales* School (so called because of the name of their journal). Quantitative history covers at least two areas of historical practice: it is a particular way of reconstructing historical sources; and a particular type of explanatory procedure. The two areas cannot be set apart. In quantitative history, historical evidence from historical sources is assembled by means of statistical methods and computer technology. Historical data are formulated in such a way that they can be presented as a time-ordered series of documents. These series are made up of homogeneous and comparable units (e.g. wheat prices, dates of wine harvests, annual births, etc.), and then evaluated by comparing individual entries with those preceding or following them in that series, or in comparable series. In such a way, historical facts are not identified 'events'. They are rather presented as long-term developments, or 'trends', to be studied in terms of continuities and discontinuities within series of relatively homogeneous data.

The identification of historical facts depends on the coding of data, and this coding implies a number of choices as to how series are organized, what meaning they might have in relation to the questions asked, and the like. For this reason, Furet concludes:

The mask of some kind of historical objectivity hidden in the 'facts' and discovered at the same time as them, has been removed for ever; the historian can no longer avoid being aware that he has constructed his 'facts', and that the objectivity of his research depends not only on using correct procedures for the elaboration and processing of these 'facts', but also on their relevance to his research hypotheses.[40]

For example, one famous analysis using this historical style of research was the study of literacy in France, from the seventeenth to the nineteenth century, carried out at the École des Hautes Études in the early 1970s, and directed by Furet himself.[41] The project was to explain changing levels of literacy, by taking into account a rather dramatic contrast in literacy levels between two halves of France, defined by an imaginary line cutting the nation from St Malo to Geneva (north-east of this line, literacy was remarkably higher than south-west of it). The historians involved in this research drew on a wide range of sources (census, army statistics on conscripts, parish records of matrimonial acts, etc.). What they managed to establish, and to use as an effective inquiry tool, was a link between the ability to sign one's name and general reading and writing skills. In particular, by analysing marriage signatures on matrimonial acts, they were able to show that basic literacy was higher among women than among men in the eighteenth century.[42]

A major result of this research, as aimed at by the historians involved in the project, was the possibility of rewriting a piece of French history. The history of literacy had always been treated as part of the history of schooling, and the latter had been recounted in either highly political or ideological terms. On the one view, it has been seen 'either as the victory of the Enlightenment over obscurantism, or alternatively as that of the Church beset by republican persecution'. On the other view, it has often been confused with 'the history of ideas about the school and its ideological role'.[43]

However, as the statistics and percentages drawn from the sources analysed were taken to show, the two types of history do not proceed at the same pace. The great historical and political events of French history – including the French Revolution – did not appear to have had any decisive role in the evolution of rates of literacy. As Furet and Ozouf show in their own research, a series of *trends* in literacy skills could be identified by studying the history of French society 'from below', that is by taking into account ordinary people's behaviour and attitudes. These behaviours and attitudes could be retraced and followed up, to a large and significant extent, independently of the history of institutional and governmental policies (as a history 'from above' would prescribe).

Our inquiry becomes meaningful only if . . . it has succeeded in focusing attention on literacy itself, as a gateway to written culture; if it has restored to society itself the chief credit for this change. The Church, the State, the School are mere dramatis personae or agents.[44]

It is interesting that the participants in this research claimed that their description and analysis of literacy, as a social and cultural phenomenon, was as *precise* as possible. For them, precision can only be achieved by quantitative means:

Describing means measuring, precisely establishing the pace of the process, its spread according to sex and type of geographical and human environment. By analysing, we mean seeking to understand the chief variables that account for this phenomenon, and their possible consequences.[45]

Furet and other quantitative historians consider their methodology as a way to think of history as a science (one of the social sciences). This claim has stirred criticism on different fronts. On one side, it was claimed that quantitative historians had not always made the case for the reliability of the figures in their statistics. On the other, it was suggested that quantitative history was reductive in its approach.

[Quantitative] historians can count signatures to marriage registers, books in private libraries, Easter communicants, references to the court of heaven, and so on. The problem remains whether these statistics are reliable indicators of literacy, piety, or whatever the historian wants to investigate.[46]

Furet's advocacy of quantitative research is relevant to us, but not so much because it might lead us to believe that the use of formalized methods of inquiry guarantees the objectivity of the type of inquiry. Rather, it is because it makes us aware of the constructed nature of what the historian takes to be 'facts', and suggests that the objectivity of a piece of research cannot be assessed independently of the methods by which historical facts are identified and (re)constructed.

3.2 'MENTALITIES'

A rather different way to select historical sources and to pursue historical explanations (which, interestingly, originated in the same French school of historiographers) was the so-called history of 'mentalities'. Here is what J. Le Goff, for example, writes:

After 1095 something stirs in Western Christendom, and individuals and masses alike throw themselves into the great adventure of the Crusades. In attempting to analyse this momentous period, we may refer to demographic growth and nascent overpopulation, the commercial ambitions of Italian city-states, the Papacy's desire to reunite a fragmented Christendom by taking on the Infidel. But none of these factors is sufficient to explain everything, or indeed, perhaps, to explain what is most important. For this, we need to understand the pull of Jerusalem, the earthly equivalent of the celestial City, and its central collective imagery. What are the Crusades without a certain religious mentality?[47]

In order to explain historically the phenomenon of the Crusades, we ought to explain what kind of 'religious mentality' (habit of thought, mental structure)[48] prompted large groups of individuals to take part in them. Essentially, what is at issue in a study of mentalities are the values, beliefs, intellectual apparatus, or taken-for-granted assumptions, all shared by groups of individuals in different periods of time.[49] Of these groups of individuals, the historian of mentalities tries to establish whether common, underlying collective mental structures can be used to account for their socio-historical behaviour.[50] In particular, the categories of social groups taken into account by this style of research are those of common individuals. Once again, it is a history 'from below', though argued for on the basis of a different choice of sources from those of quantitative history.

In trying to show that a certain mentality played a role in the occurrence of the social events of a historical period, what kinds of historical sources should be used as evidence? As we saw earlier, in pursuing quantitative research, sources such as economic or demographic documents were selected and considered, with a view to the building up of series. In a qualitative type of research into the Crusade mentality, other sources of documentation will become relevant. The historian will analyse literary or artistic material, will make use of philology, hagiographic records, and even archaeological findings, such as weapons, or burial objects. This does not mean that this type of historical research excludes in principle the use of any quantitative sources in its explanations. In fact, a number of historians tried to pursue studies of mentalities using quantitative means. One of them was Michel Vovelle.[51]

Vovelle developed a study of the baroque mentality of 'piety' in eighteenth-century Provence based on a statistical analysis of about 30,000 wills. By means of this analysis, he provided evidence for the fading away of a series of consolidated trends (e.g. a declining interest in grandiose funerals, or the progressive disappearance of invocations of the Virgin Mary).[52] He interpreted this as the sign of a progressive 'dechristianization' of the people of Provence in the eighteenth century, and of their parallel adoption of more secular life-styles. Vovelle's attempt, as has been pointed out, is limited, in that its results seem to ignore anything not within the scope of statistical methods: 'we have gained in precision, but we are in danger of losing meaning.'[53] In general, it seems that trying to make use of quantitative sources to argue for, and achieve, qualitative results proves to be a challenging task (how can 'hard' statistical methods be applied to 'soft' data, such as feelings, beliefs, attitudes?).[54] This, however, is once again interesting for us. As pointed out earlier, it shows how a particular construction of an object of inquiry sets limits on the kinds of questions which can be formulated about it.

A final, general point can be made regarding the study of mentalities, which proves applicable also to quantitative research. If we think the object of historical inquiry to be a mentality, a series, or a trend, then it appears difficult to apply either the Hempelian model of explanation, or even the alternative model proposed by Dray. Both models seem to portray history as the result of intentional acts, or as the carrying out of individual aims. History, for both Hempel and Dray, seems to be a history of actors' events, of individual decisions, and individual calculations, with respect to which it is always possible to retrace causes and reasons. With mentalities, or with trends, this is hardly the case. History becomes a global model of trans-individual structures, and of long-term changes and transformations, the causes and reasons of which can only be retraced by appealing to the sources and resources used in identifying these structures, changes, and transformations.

All this has relevance for the philosopher interested in history. Alternative ways of 'doing history' do not necessarily amount to mutually exclusive models of research. Historical explanation can be viewed as a 'mixed narrative' (or a complementary model, as Danto already suggested in the 1960s). A mixed narrative is not a perfect chronicle. Different categorizations of historical facts create different opportunities for explanation, and an adequate philosophy of history should indeed take this aspect of historical practice into due account.

4. MAKING HISTORY IN MUSEUMS

So far I have discussed how historians of various inclinations identify their object of inquiry: how they select and look at historical sources by means of different procedures, and how they address sources with different questions. I also pointed out that sources are not the 'brute facts' of history. Historians find them, generally, in the form of written records, or reports. For this reason, they cannot neglect the conditions and the circumstances under which sources are both assembled and transmitted. Sources have their own history, and this crucially influences the way in which the historian will answer his specific research questions on the basis of his material evidence. As we read for example in *The Modern Researcher* (a classical manual on how to practise history), the distinction between 'gathering facts' and 'expressing ideas' cannot work as a protocol for historical research. 'Most of the facts we [historians] gather come dripping with ideas',[55] we are warned. Besides, '"bare facts" generally are of little *interest*, in themselves'[56] – let alone cases where their authenticity is under specific scrutiny (e.g. the exact date of a battle, or of a birth, etc.).

However, in the previous section, I noted how historical evidence is often not confined to written records. In the case of the historian of mentalities, for example, it might become helpful to rely on material findings (weapons, pottery, coins, etc.). It becomes then interesting to ask whether there might be a significant difference, in procedure, skills, or knowledge acquisition, in making a physical object the focus for the construction of historical evidence, rather than, say, reading a manuscript. Besides looking at how history makes the object of its inquiries, we can also find it instructive to reconstruct how objects, real objects, make history.

There is indeed a category of professional historians who specifically practise history in the latter way. Museum historians make history through things. Things constitute their primary sources: they are treated as 'bearers of information', though in a different way, as compared to documents.[57] Gaining information from a physical object entails a different set of skills from those used by the historian engaged in traditional, document-based, historical research. The conditions under which objects become significant in historical terms are crucial in gaining access to their possible meaning, and in understanding what these objects are intended to be evidence for.

There are at least three relevant areas of object categorization to be taken into account in museum-style history. The first is the identification of the position held by these objects in their social, political, cultural, and temporal contexts. The immediate challenge for the museum historian engaged in making history with things, consists of identifying the very things (their function, their use). Take a flat iron, for example.[58] It can be a doorstop, an ornament in a modern home, a weapon, a piece of scrap iron sacrificed in a wartime metal campaign, a bookend. A thing like a flat iron counts several, and often incompatible, meanings, some acquired at the time of its construction, others afterwards and in different contexts. In a collection (and in exhibitions as well), all these meanings can happily coexist, and be indicative of as many stories to tell. In this sense, museum curators are more experimental in their approach to history than traditional, or more narrowly academic historians: 'instead of looking for "truth" or a continuous uninterrupted narrative, they study the past through an open-ended exploration which is comfortable with plural, even contradictory, stories.'[59]

The second area of object categorization concerns the position which objects hold when displaced in a museum context (a collection, an exhibition, etc.). Often, it is the artificial space provided by a museum, which elicits further symbolic opportunities for the objects there displaced. It can even be claimed that it is the museum which, by displaying certain ranges of objects, defines what counts as historically and culturally meaningful.[60] The history of medical museums is quite instructive in this respect.[61] There is a remarkable difference, for example, between the early types of medical museums in Europe and the types we are used to nowadays. The former were usually located in the work-places, or the apartments of professional physicians, and their curators mostly belonged to the profession. The objects on display, which were often curiosities discovered during travels to unfamiliar places, or from excavation of ancient buildings, were not just collected for purposes of idle admiration. They were understood and catalogued 'in terms of medical "principles" held to correspond to a particular function or part of the body'.[62] They were also used to experience and experiment upon nature. It is fair to say that these early museums were 'privileged sites of knowledge'.[63] In contemporary times, we have instead become accustomed to the museum as a public, institutional service. Consequently, the attention has shifted towards covering a more general social ground. Medicine is now exhibited in the framework of health matters,[64] or as part of an attempt to 'humanize' medical science. This is achieved by focusing on the actual practice of medicine (both its research stage and its healing stage).[65]

A further point to consider is that there are cases in which the objects put on display belong to cultures which are different from that to which the museum where they are displayed belongs. A concern often expressed with international collections is that their curators may either misunderstand the history of these 'foreign' objects, or sometimes misrepresent them, in the attempt to make these objects understandable to their expected audience.[66] This brings to our attention a third area which is relevant to making objects historically meaningful: the museums' visitors, to whom the historical material is addressed, in collections and exhibitions. It cannot be forgotten that history as practised in museums has a public, educational function.[67] The level of engagement of an audience with the objects as collected and exhibited might not be a criterion by which to judge the truth, or reliability, of the story recounted via those objects. Objects themselves set limits to interpretation, besides enabling possibilities of understanding. However, the role of the audience adds a further dimension of inquiry to the historian's ability to question what can be known, and how to make it known, via the objects he displays.

> ... visitors to exhibitions cannot be treated as passive recipients of an ideological position, conveyed through all the physical aspects of the

museum. Rather, they have experiences as a result of *interacting with* the
museum environment. . . . By going, looking, participating, they in some
measure assent to the claims made by museums about the insights that
looking at objects provide.[68] [my italics].

Interaction with objects occurs then at two levels: the level of the historian/
curator, who chooses one (or sometimes more than one) narrative of display for
objects; and the level of the audience/visitors, who exercise their abilities to use
the objects so displayed (as well as the chains of ideas and memories they trig-
ger) to enter the story which these objects are made to recount. The two levels
are asymmetrical. Even when museum-historians try to anticipate visitors'
understanding, responses are typically open-ended. 'A museum can never be
read as a single text. Even if we consider the most basic question of who or what
museums are for, there is never a unitary answer.'[69]

This is particularly visible with collections of objects from different cultures,
as mentioned above. But it is also, for example, a recurrent problem with science
museums in our own culture.[70] With the latter, the problem of open-endedness
appears even more challenging, given the authoritative position that science
holds as the provider of objective knowledge in our society, and the unspoken
assumption which goes with it, namely that the objects of science should equally
be able to teach indisputable lessons of meaning.[71]

The point of this section, which might have appeared a digression from the
issues discussed in this chapter, is to reiterate, and to provide further evidence
for, how historical practice, in its various forms, makes use of a rich array of
procedures and techniques of discovery and analysis. In dealing with the ultimately unattainable goal of recovering an objective past, attention to the nature
and use of these procedures and techniques raises interesting questions about
the category of historical *facts*. At the very least, we are led to reflect on how any
purportedly objective reconstruction of the past is to start from the way in which
facts are 'objectified' via specific techniques of historical inquiry. Although historical classifications are not evidently interactive (in the way in which, arguably,
anthropological and sociological ones are), still attention to the complex and
heterogeneous practice of dealing with past social events adds insightful evidence as to how social scientific research pursues objective reconstructions of its
subject matter.

CHAPTER 4

Economic Objects

1. ECONOMIC THEORY AND METHODOLOGICAL CONCERN

There is rising speculation over the difficulties of the mainstream project in economic theory (mainly, its formalistic strand) to predict real-world events, as well as to inform policy decisions. The often-rehearsed joke, 'An economist is an expert who will know tomorrow why the things he predicted yesterday didn't happen today,' betrays real concern. What are the sources of the difficulties? One explanation offered draws attention to the lack of serious methodological discussion among economists. Especially among mainstream practitioners, there is a hostility to methodology. It is a widespread belief that methodology should be left to philosophers, and that the practice of economics does not require any acknowledgment of methodological issues. Moreover, often when economists do take methodology into account, they seem plainly to endorse positivistic precepts.

Critics of this attitude have pointed out firstly, that even if methodology is not openly and specifically discussed, this does not mean that methodological assumptions do not enter the practice of the discipline. In fact, were such implicit assumptions made explicit, the reasons for the apparent failure of economic practice to deliver the goods might become clear. Secondly, they claim that a positivistic methodology is ill-suited to the subject matter of economics. However, there is disagreement among critics about what ought to be done to correct the present situation. According to one approach, for example, we need to readdress the question of methodology (or perhaps, we should say, to address it anew) by first comparing theory and practice, and then seeing what of this practice is missing in the theory. By doing this, it will become clear that what is missing is an inclusion of ontological questions. Economics, mostly due to its more or less explicit positivistic inclination, fails to address questions concerning the nature of economic objects. Economic objects are specific to the economic field of inquiry, and yet they are part of the social field (or of social reality). Partly for this reason, they exist independently of their epistemological representations in economic theory. Economics then should put reality back in place. This is the critical-realist route taken, for example, by T. Lawson.

According to another approach, the question of methodology should be readdressed by ridding ourselves of the misleading idea of a methodology altogether. In its place, an analysis of the machinery of economic discourse, or as it has been defined, of the 'rhetoric' of economic discourse, will prove more appropriate. Positivistic methodology, with its stress on clarity, rigour, objectivity, formalization, etc., can itself be interpreted as being a rhetorical device, namely an attempt to concoct an image of economics as a 'hard' science. However, there is bad rhetoric, and there is good rhetoric. If we want to criticize successfully the damaging effects of positivistic methodology, we ought to find out what good rhetoric means as an alternative procedure of analysis. To achieve this task, we must look at economic discourse 'at work', namely at how economists work in practice, and how they write about what they work on. D. McCloskey is especially associated with this approach.

The first solution stays within a normative domain: it advocates the need for an alternative methodology to be put in place of positivistic methodology. The second solution is anti-normative and pragmatic: it denies the need for a methodology altogether, and it recommends a pragmatic approach (in a sense which will be qualified) in pursuing economic inquiry, as well as in analysing it. I find this way of viewing the normative/anti-normative divide rather artificial, and not particularly useful. In what follows, I will start from a discussion of the 'non-normative' perspective, and then proceed to showing how the 'normative' perspective allows us to formulate questions concerning the object of economic inquiry which, though barred by the latter, are not necessarily incompatible with it. A non-normative perspective should not exclude certain questions from being addressed (arguably itself a normative attitude); it should only avoid the prescriptive attitude according to which the only questions worth being addressed are those suggested by one particular methodology.

Trying to bypass the normative/anti-normative prescriptive distinction, I will then analyse examples of how certain types of economic issues are described, and show how practical as well as theoretical procedures are used in order to solicit questions and create conditions for the identification and description of these issues.

2. RHETORICAL OBJECTS OF ECONOMIC PRACTICE

In *The Rhetoric of Economics* McCloskey points out how 'most journals of economics nowadays look like journals of applied mathematics or theoretical statistics'.[1] This was hardly the case before the 1930s.

The *American Economics Review* of the early 1930s . . . contained hardly any equation; assumptions were not formalized; the graphs were plots of series, and not common; the fitting of a line to a scatter of points was rare. . . . Of the 159 full-length papers published in the *American Economics Review* during 1981, 1982, and 1983 . . . statistics, diagrams and explicit simulation had become routine. Fully two-thirds of the papers used mathematics explicitly, and most of the others were speaking in a mathematics-saturated environment in which the words 'production function' and 'demand curve' would call upon the mathematics anyway.[2]

Both attitudes come at a price. The mathematical 'innocence' of early economists resulted often in an inability to talk clearly. Without mathematical understanding, issues such as marginal productivity, or bargaining strength, were hard to grasp. However, McCloskey argues, after the 'mathematical turn', clarification made economics fall into scientism, that is, a particular ideology of what constitutes scientific achievement. One way of explaining the appeal that this ideology exercised among economists is to point at the fact that the more formalized/axiomatized that economic articles look, the more scientific they appear, and therefore the more seriously they are going to be taken.[3]

The ideology of scientism is called by McCloskey 'modernism'. Modernism is for her nothing but a crude form of positivism, that is a perspective where prediction, control, observability, formalization, nomological explanation and deductivism are the key ideas. Milton Friedman's 1953 essay,[4] though scattered with ideas which, compared with classic positivistic ones, appear rather iconoclastic, can indeed be taken as a central document of modernism in economics.[5] Right at the beginning of his essay, Friedman describes positive economics as 'in principle independent of any particular ethical position or normative judgements', as providing 'a system of generalizations that can be used to make correct predictions', and as being testable 'by the precision, scope and conformity with experience of the predictions it yields'. For this reason, Friedman argues, 'positive economics is, or can be, an "objective" science, in precisely the same sense as any of the physical sciences.'[6] Of course, objectivity is harder to achieve in economics, since it deals with human action. This 'raises special difficulties', but it does not produce any fundamental difference between the two types of science.[7]

McCloskey argues that modernism has generally proven to be a poor method for science, and that as a general ideology of science it is by now also obsolete in philosophy. In particular, criticisms of positivistic quantitative research methods have shown the limits of formalized analysis. Formalisms by themselves do not mean more rigorous results. There are indeed various ways of 'cooking' statistical results in order to accommodate some of the modernist precepts about what should count as evidence.[8] In order to see the role played by this ideology in the field of economics, she urges us to turn to the history of economics in the last 40 or 50 years; or even to ask any economists whether they actually follow the precepts of this ideology in what they do. In a Feyerabendian style, McCloskey claims that if economists, past and present, had confined themselves to working according to those precepts understood literally, they would have had little if anything to say, and they could hardly have produced any significant results. This then makes us realize how, notwithstanding the officially endorsed methodology in economics, things in practice work in a different manner.

Economic methodologists like Mark Blaug seem to believe that the practice should be made to resemble the theory more. In his book *The Methodology of Economics*, Blaug appears to reproach economists for not allowing this to happen. For instance, he writes:

> Economists have long been aware of the need to defend 'correct' principles of reasoning in their subject; although actual practice may bear little relationship to what is preached, the preaching is worth considering on its own ground.[9]

Yet, McCloskey observes, why should this be the case? Why should a preaching unrelated to actual practice be worth considering at all? Why not, instead, look at what economists do in practice, and infer methodological instructions from the way they practise their discipline? In other words, is there an 'unofficial' methodology in economic practice, and if there is, what is it? For McCloskey, what we find in practice is not so much a different methodology, but what she calls a 'rhetoric' of economic discourse.

Rhetoric is, in fact, for McCloskey, the opposite of a methodology in the modernist sense. It is not an independent procedure, made up of prescriptive rules of scientific conduct, which any discipline aiming at being objective and scientific ought to follow. It is rather a 'literary way' to examine the economists' language in action, and to understand the structure and persuasive force of the economists' arguments. The purpose of a rhetorical analysis of economic discourse is to make such discourse not only clearer, but also better: 'a rhetoric of economics can expose what most economists know anyway about the richness and complexity of economic argument but will not state openly and will not examine explicitly.'[10]

When we hear the word 'rhetoric', we tend to become defensive. We immediately associate the word with the image of a shifty technique used to obtain assent, and to cover the absence of truth. This association is not unfounded. Rhetoric, in its early days, was indeed charged with having an exclusive interest in prevailing in argument. To be a rhetorician (actually, a 'mere' rhetorician) often meant to be an ill-purposed technician who used the flatteries of oratory and eloquence to hide the lack of 'real' arguments. This is obviously not the image McCloskey wants us to subscribe to, when she talks of the 'rhetoric' of economic discourse. There is another, non-derogatory image of rhetoric, which includes at least two aspects that the negative image completely neglects. Firstly, rhetoric can be employed to pursue a good cause, or to secure assent to what we 'somehow' trust are convincing beliefs. Secondly, the study of rhetoric also includes the analysis of how plausible arguments are devised and constructed.[11] These are the aspects of rhetoric that I believe McCloskey has in mind, when she urges us to replace methodology with rhetoric in economics:

> The invitation to rhetoric is not, I emphasise, an invitation to 'replace careful analysis with rhetoric', or to abandon mathematics in favour of name-calling or flowery language. The good rhetorician loves care, precision, explicitness, and economy in argument. . . . A rhetorical approach to economic text is machine-building, not machine-breaking. It is not an invitation to irrationality in argument. Quite the contrary. It is an invitation to leave the irrationality of an artificially narrowed range of argument and to move to the rationality of arguing as human beings. It brings out into the open the arguing that economists do anyway – in the dark, for they must do it somewhere, and the various official rhetorics leave them benighted.[12]

2.1 'THE LAW OF DEMAND' AND 'MARKET INTEGRATION': SAMPLES OF RHETORICAL CONSTRUCTION

How does this rhetorical method of analysis work? In the second part of the first edition of her book, McCloskey carries out a detailed discussion of cases of economic theories, conceptions, models, mathematical proofs, etc. as instances of rhetorical argumentation.[13] One of them concerns proofs of the Law of Demand. By analysing this example, McCloskey shows how, in the description and assessment of an economic concept, a rhetorical construction of evidence for it is an ineliminable part of its very description and assessment.

The assertion that 'when the price of something goes up the demand for something goes down' does not only engage economists in the making of a sound scientific proposition. It must also count as a piece of 'persuasive discourse, aimed at some effect about which rhetoric speaks'.[14] In fact, if we look at samples of economic papers where we are told that 'the demand curve slopes down', the questions we can formulate concerning the statement go well beyond what formal logic or empirical testability are able to establish. In particular, if we

look at the reasons, the good reasons, which make economists believe in the Law
of Demand, we will be surprised.

Some of these reasons comply with modernist precepts (some elaborate statistical tests, market-by-market applied research, experimental tests), but the
results obtained by following these precepts are often not compelling enough to
endorse persuasion. Yet, this does not leave economists in doubt about the Law
of Demand. They 'believe it ardently'.[15] There must, then, be other reasons
(other than scientistic ones), which persuade them that the law is valid.
McCloskey suggests a possible list for these further reasons:[16]

1) *introspection*: the economist asks him/herself the question, 'What would I do
   if the price of gasoline doubled?' to which he/she would answer, 'I would
   consume less.';
2) *thought experiments*: the economist, for example, might speculate about
   people's behaviour, were the price of gasoline to double;
3) *the lore of the marketplace*: for example, the economist might look at business
   people who, acting on the implicit rule that any opportunity for profit should
   not be wasted, might decide to reduce prices in order to induce a rise in
   demand;
4) *mere definition*: on a certain definition of income, the economist might claim
   that a 'higher price of gasoline leaves less income to be spent on all things,
   including gasoline';
5) *the use of analogical reasoning*: if the law of demand works for, say, ice cream
   and clothes, why should it not work, the economist might speculate, for
   gasoline too?[17]

Some of these devices have their counterpart in literary and artistic work. We
could find them used by novelists or textual critics alike. The interesting, and
challenging morale which McCloskey draws from finding them used by economists is that merely scientific protocols do only part of the work, and arguably
not even the most relevant or successful part. Besides, the protocols are often at
odds with what economists actually do. So, in the end, the protocols do not help
either descriptively or prescriptively (what is the point of saying how things
ought to be done, knowing that they cannot be done in the way so prescribed?).
McCloskey then provocatively concludes that an economic article is above all a
performance, or a 'speech act': an exercise not in applied methodology, but in
literary thinking.[18]

Another example discussed by McCloskey concerns the use of economic
quantification. Often, economic concepts reduce to their operational definitions. To be able to reduce any concept, or question about concepts, to numbers is the right (often only) step towards defining the concept, or answering

questions – or so the official rhetoric of economics says. However, this is also where this rhetoric goes astray. Numbers by themselves do not set any standards. The question, 'How large is large?' cannot be settled by looking at figures in isolation. This is not a new claim. What McCloskey asks, on the basis of this claim, is why and how numbers are so convincing to people. In order to answer this question, she discusses the case of market integration. The way to define integration is to measure the correlation between two aspects of a market and then, on the basis of some statistics, judge as 'small' the differential between them. However, a 'small' differential is itself judged on the basis of standards which cannot be evinced simply from the number we put on the correlation. As an illustration of how standards are set out, McCloskey describes the case of the so-called Genberg–Zecher criterion.[19]

> We speak of America's money supply as though 'America' were a significant aggregate for some purpose, but we do not speak of California's money supply or Vermont's. Behind the speaking, then, must lie an implicit standard. The standard is that a market area in bricks, saws, and sweaters defined to contain without comment California and Vermont is apparently not disparate enough to require a separate money supply. The degree to which the prices of bricks, saws, and sweaters move parallel in California and Vermont, therefore, provides a criterion (the Genberg–Zecher one) for measuring the degree of integration between America as a whole and Britain. If the degree of parallelism is no larger between America and Britain than it is between California and Vermont, then – for purposes of argument – one might as well include Britain as California in America's money supply.[20]

In general terms, the appeal of plain numbers, as well as the appeal of plain facts, derives its force from their being invoked and uttered for a purpose, and from being part of a pragmatic context. McCloskey here follows Austin in the dictum: 'We must consider the total situation in which the utterance is issued – the total speech act.'[21] Providing standards, evaluating figures, or asserting facts are social and persuasive activities. The decisions, which stand behind any of these activities, are not written 'in the stars or in statistical tables'. They belong in 'the rhetoric of conversation, not the logic of inquiry'.[22]

However, what is the point of applying this method of analysis to economic discourse? We might well agree that we ought to construct sound concepts by means of sound arguments, and that we should be able to say why an argument is sound, or sounder than others. Yet, what about being able to say whether an argument is 'getting it right'? McCloskey does not appear to think that this is an interesting, nor even an important, question to ask. We should always remember, she warns us, that pursuing truth is in the end one methodological choice among possibly many others. Truth, she says, is like a fifth wheel: 'inoperative except that it occasionally comes loose and hits a bystander'. She then proceeds:

> If we decide that the quantity theory of money or the marginal productivity theory of distribution is persuasive, interesting, useful, reasonable, appealing, acceptable, we do not also need to know that it is true. Its persuasiveness, interest, etc. come from particular arguments. . . . good or bad. After making them, there is no point in asking a last, summarizing question: 'Well, is it true?' It is whatever it is – persuasive, interesting, useful, and so forth. . . . There is no reason to search for a general quality called Truth, which answers only the unanswerable question, 'What is it that is in the mind of God?'[23]

Nor should we worry about whether anything we say is 'objective'. Saying that scientific knowledge is social and audience-dependent is not equivalent to saying that it is not reliable, or collectively biased. It is to say that it is as objective as our (social) standards of comparison, quantitative assessment and calculation validate it as being so.

So McCloskey seems to brush away, in one shot, both epistemological and ontological talk. Still, we might indeed be interested to know whether we 'got it right'. Saying that a certain philosophical doctrine, or a certain ideology of science, did not 'get it right', and cannot possibly 'get it right', does not mean that we can never get it right, or can never know that we get it right. Moreover, saying that we are as objective as our standards entitle us to say that we are is not yet to say anything about our standards. Arguably, much of the substance of these queries might still be addressed depending on what the 'it' we ought to be right about (or be objective about) consists of. Here is where the second critical route, mentioned at the beginning of this chapter, pushes the argument in a rather different direction.

3. REALIST OBJECTS OF ECONOMIC PRACTICE

Lawson has a rather different story to recount, though he starts from an assessment of the present state of economic theory which is very similar to McCloskey's. Economists, he claims, are either silent on the topic of methodology because intolerant of it,[24] or positivistic at heart. Both attitudes are detrimental to the practice of the discipline. By the former, philosophical discussion is denied to have anything positive to contribute to the way economic theory is constructed and applied. By the latter, a set of controversial constraints is imposed on economic theory. This, in the least damaging case, leads the economist routinely to neglect these constraints (and practise economics 'as he sees fit'); and in the worst case, it gives the discipline a bad or poor image of itself.

Nonetheless, Lawson – unlike McCloskey – suggests that, rather than getting rid of methodology altogether, or refusing to engage with prescriptive issues, we ought to look for a different, better methodology. A better methodology should allow us, first of all, to reconsider the possibility of economics being a social science free from positivistic protocols. This means that the question of naturalism in the domain of economic theory must be reconsidered.[25] It is interesting to emphasize the direction of analysis which a naturalistic interpretation takes in Lawson's approach. Rather than assuming a certain picture of science and taking that as the standard by means of which the object of investigation is to be defined and judged (an epistemological direction), it sets out instead to investigate what such an object must be like in order for a science of economics to be possible, and to spell out the details of construction of such a science (an ontological direction). In this way, as I mentioned above, a naturalistic perspective can still be prescriptive, but not in a positivistic way.

Secondly, a better methodology should allow us to identify, in an explicit fashion, the nature of the objects of economic inquiry. This nature should be as much as possible independent of the taken-for-granted representations of the objects that we find in use in economic theory, and instead be thought of as part of social reality.[26] In other words, a better methodology should avoid the traps of both scientism (the ideology of modernism/positivism) and of the so-called epistemic fallacy, that is the positivistic view according to which matters of ontology can always be reduced to, or translated into, epistemological terms.[27]

> Once we break from positivist influence, and in doing so acknowledge explicitly an ontological domain, and specifically a realm of intransitive objects which exist independently (at least in part) of the scientific inquiry of which they are the objects, . . . methodological analysis can be seen to possess the potential for making a critical and fruitful contribution to the conduct of science, including economics.[28]

Lawson believes that critical realism is the philosophical perspective which is able to pursue methodological aims successfully, and in a non-positivistic fashion. The leading, underlying argument of this perspective runs as follows. All theories of knowledge, science-oriented philosophies, social practices, etc. presuppose an ontology, that is some conception of the nature of reality. So, we must proceed by investigating what the world must be like for these theories, practices, etc. to be possible. Experience, as accounted for by positivistic philosophy, is a poor contender for reality, because it reduces reality to what we actually perceive, or what is actually manifest. Especially in the case of social reality, where human agency is the core concept, we need a more stratified ontological picture. This should include not only the actually perceivable but also the causally possible. In the case of social objects, of which economic objects are an instance, attention should be paid to the 'transformatively human' and 'intentionally causal' features of social reality.[29] How relevant is this view to the description of the practice of economics and to the reconstruction of its objects of inquiry?

3.1 'PRODUCTIVITY PERFORMANCE': A SAMPLE OF REALIST ANALYSIS

In 1983 Stafford carried out a comprehensive study of the various theories which attempted to explain Britain's comparatively slow rate of productivity growth over the last 100 years.[30] Slow growth was inferred by contrasting empirical evidence referring to Britain's industrial performance with evidence coming from non-UK countries. Slow growth, in other words, is a relative concept, significantly dependent on a *relation of contrast* which defines the borderlines for its investigation. This is an important qualification, since – as we will see – the kind of explanation offered of the problem so identified crucially depends on the way the problem is described in the first place.[31] Britain's low rate of productivity performance becomes a 'fact' as a consequence of a 'contrastive' question being asked.

That explanation depends on the description of the object to be explained, can also be inferred from looking at what factors, Stafford thinks, explain Britain's productivity performance. He refers to the UK's 'far more highly decentralised system of collective bargaining . . ., along with the associated relatively localised nature of worker organisation in the UK'.[32] This suggests that Stafford is choosing to discuss productivity in terms of the contribution of labour to the total product. A different discussion might have focused on 'the capitalist drive to accumulate, the ceaseless attempt to increase the rate of surplus value'.[33] Besides, it has been pointed out that mechanisms, which possibly have a bearing on productivity growth (e.g. UK government and/or management actions or resistances), have neither been included nor suggested in the explanation. This means that the explanation in question (indeed, any explanation) is partial. This is said not just in the sense that only some factors of the object under investigation are selected and focused upon, but also in the sense that 'the sorts of factors singled out will reflect the interests and understandings of the investigator'.[34] However, this does not in any way entail that the explanation is incomplete, nor that it is empirically inadequate. Within the field identified by the description of its object of investigation, the explanation could prove to be perfectly 'objective'. Lawson, nonetheless, wants to go further: he wants to claim that, compared to the current explanations of Britain's productivity performance offered in the literature, Stafford emphasizes a set of determining factors (social structures and mechanisms) which, if appropriately accounted for, make his explanation 'the most empirically adequate'.[35]

What then is the structure of Stafford's explanation? How can the determining factors emphasized by it be accounted for, and in such a way that the explanation can be considered successful (the most successful)? Lawson presents the argument underlying Stafford's explanation of Britain's relative productivity performance in a series of steps, which can be summarized as follows:[36]

1) Since what we are trying to establish is a relative ratio of growth concerning Britain's productivity performance, what we should look for is a factor (set of structures, mechanisms) which is present in the UK situation, and absent from other countries, and which might be responsible for Britain's performance.
2) It can be shown that in Britain, unlike elsewhere, most aspects of work are negotiated locally rather than nationally, and that workers are organized on a craft rather than industry basis.
3) The combination of the two aspects of the British system mentioned in (2) leads to mechanisms which 'inhibit coordinated decision-making and work against quick or smooth responses to changes in production possibilities'.[37]
4) The crucial factor is twofold: on one side, any change, say for instance in technology, has direct negative effects on employment opportunities (more machinery means more job redundancies), and therefore it creates an incentive on the workers' side to resist changes; on the other side, resistance calls for negotiation which, given the local rather than national forms of workers' organization, will be pursued in a decentralized system of collective bargaining.

The explanation, Lawson then concludes,

focuses on a set of structures that empowers workers . . . to exercise a significant effect on all manners of outcomes. The exercise of this power . . . is essentially a defensive strength. Workers bargain to maintain living standards and working conditions, or at least to be partly compensated for detrimental changes to work conditions, skills, status, and so on. However, negotiations can take time, and the likely opposition of workers may even deter management from taking up the potential for change.[38]

5) Compared to countries where negotiation is carried out by means of a national statutory system, a country like Britain, based on local bargaining, will inevitably appear to be less flexible and slower when it comes to change and productivity growth.

All this, says Lawson, is well documented empirically. However, and despite the fact that probably most economists would find the explanation adequate as it stands, this is hardly sufficient to understand the phenomenon in question. Why, for example, given that the British situation appears to be so clearly and correctly assessed, has it persisted virtually unchanged and unchallenged? The answer arguably lies in an understanding of the emergence and persistence of Britain's unique industrial system.[39] This answer can be pursued on three related levels, according to Lawson: an understanding of why a decentralized bargaining system emerged in the first place; an understanding of the social process which has made it persist; and an understanding of why such a system did not emerge and persist in other countries.

Each level of understanding (historical, social, comparative) must be considered in the effort to discover the (some) conditions and causal factors which put the mechanism in place in a specific country, made it work the way it did/ does, and 'locked it in' subsequently. Historical analysis, social theory and comparative studies are among the research strategies which enable the investigator to formulate the appropriate questions, and to make the relevant discoveries. By combining these various strategies, and pursuing the different types of investigation they make possible, economic explanation, and more generally economics as a field of inquiry, appears more complex, and indeed more 'messy' than any positivistic reconstruction of law-like regularities would lead us to acknowledge:

> Unlike the simplistic positivistic conception of science as elaborating event regularities, the process of uncovering and explaining significant causal structures and mechanisms, including geo-historically rooted and dynamic totalities, will usually be a painstaking, laborious, and time consuming, transformative activity, one that gives rise to results that will always be partial and contingent (and usually contested).[40]

Leaving aside the details of how such research can be carried out in the specific case here discussed,[41] what can we conclude about that object of economic inquiry which goes under the description of Britain's 'slow productivity growth'? If we follow Lawson's realist reconstruction, we can say first of all, that ontologically speaking it is a *structured* object, in the sense that it does not simply consist of whatever pattern of correlation is included in an empirical law. It refers to the structures, processes and tendencies which, by existing to some extent independently of the law-like pattern, make the occurrence of the latter causally intelligible.

Secondly, at an epistemological level, we can emphasize that it is a *complex* object, which can be made intelligible by means of different empirical reconstructions, without having to assume that a phenomenon such as 'slow productivity growth' can be found in the outside world independently of its theoretical identification. The phenomenon as described becomes empirically relevant as an object of inquiry, only after some research-dependent formulations of it allow for some questions to be addressed and for some consequent answers to be explored.

Finally, and methodologically speaking, the need to interrogate the practice of economic inquiry in order to figure out the kinds of objects which that practice refers to, should not restrict itself to assessing the persuasive power of economic discourse. For McCloskey, the persuasiveness and truth of economic discourse do not go together. In fact, we can be satisfied just with the former. The latter does not add anything of importance or interest. Lawson has a more elaborate view of truth, which allows him to include truth-talk. Truth is to be taken in an 'expressive-referential' sense, as a reminder that

> neither our theoretical constructions nor their referents can be reduced to, or identified with, the other – that the two do not literally correspond. . . . the term expression [as in 'expressive-referential'] also indicates that there are different, including better and worse, ways of capturing something.[42]

A realist methodology will guide the economist towards 'expressing' the referents of his discourse (or of his arguments, pieces of reasoning, laws, etc.) on the assumption that those referents are not entirely created, nor reducible to, their discursive construction.

This last point can be made in such a way that it concerns not only economics, but social science more generally. Any methodology presupposes an ontology (Lawson is right). Ontological questioning requires a descriptive inquiry (being able to say what the world must be like). This does not mean that what there is simply amounts to what we can know about it (positivistic move), or say about it (hermeneutic move). What can be put in a descriptive form does cover the domain of what is meaningful or intelligible, but what is meaningful or intelligible (especially when relative to a particular stage of development in our knowledge and inquiry) does not cover the whole domain of what happens to exist. However, we also should not forget that 'what happens to exist' in the social domain is not *ipso facto* an 'object' of inquiry for social science. This is why the descriptive task of ontological questioning can only be achieved by a constructive epistemology. To paraphrase Lawson in a Kantian fashion, if a social scientific methodology without a social ontology is empty, a social ontology without a constructive epistemology is blind.

4. THE 'PARTIAL' OBJECTS OF ECONOMICS

The two approaches analysed in this chapter both take as their point of departure the practice of economic inquiry. By 'practice' they mean the economists' field of inquiry, which variously comprises the arguments, the theories, the research strategies, the measurement techniques, the explanatory hypotheses and the object-descriptions, which the economists employ in their investigations and analyses.

Two general questions can be asked from this starting point: what do economists talk about? how do economists talk? With respect to the first question, the rhetorical approach claims that economic discourse is about persuasion (it is a self-referential discourse), whereas the realist approach argues that economic discourse is about real structures and/or mechanisms (it is expressive of a referent that partly transcends this discourse). With respect to the second question, the rhetorical approach sets out to investigate how economic discourse works, on the assumption that there must be pragmatic reasons for why it is persuasive. The realist approach undertakes the same kind of investigation, on the assumption that the reasons which make such a discourse persuasive, or successful, are not only pragmatic, but also ontological.

The two approaches follow two different methodological strategies then, which nonetheless share a common feature: that what economists talk about and how they talk about it cannot be kept separate. Productivity growth, market integration, or demand curves, all become meaningful objects of economic inquiry only once a descriptive apparatus is introduced to allow for certain questions to be formulated, and for some definitions and classifications to be put in place. To use an old terminology, they are 'ideal-types' of objects.[43] This is said not in the sense that there is an ideal theory which 'fixes' their meaning and reference as a standard of use, but rather in the sense that part of the nature of their being objects of inquiry is produced by a theoretical context. Such context does not necessarily reduce economic phenomena to discursive constructs, nor does it downplay the role of empirical evidence.[44] It rather fruitfully interacts with the latter, by creating conditions of intelligibility for both the phenomena and the facts which we can make use of in order to understand those phenomena.

Is objectivity possible then in economics? There are at least two lessons which we can infer from the two positions analysed in this chapter. Firstly, as we learn from McCloskey, truth and objectivity cannot be set apart from the practical means and the theoretical constructions which make the economists' arguments work (they are not universal methodological precepts). Truth for McCloskey is 'made rather than found'.[45] This, however, does not imply, McCloskey prudently adds, that no economic theory can ever be objective, or equally, that any theory is as objective as any other.

> The social construction of economics or other sciences is not dread Relativism. . . . The world is still there. But we are still constructing it. It is like fishing. The fish are there by God's command, but humans make the nets. To catch fish we need both. It is pointless to argue that the socially defined and net-caught but sea-dwelling and corporeal fish are 'really' social or 'really' objective. They had better be both, or we are not going to eat fish on Friday.[46]

However, if we follow McCloskey, how can we tell, or can we ever tell, that we have caught some fish by means of our economic nets? A second lesson, which we learn from Lawson, is that the object of economic inquiry can only be partially expressed by that inquiry. This is due to two reasons: firstly, to the inherent *complexity* of that object, and secondly, to the *historical, contextual* and *transient* nature of our knowledge. However, a partially expressed object is not equivalent to a falsely or distortedly reported object. It is an object identified under one or some specific (and specified) components.

> If I focus on a person's eyes in an attempt to gauge his or her reaction to what I am saying, or if I describe them in reporting my impression to others, I do not . . . *necessarily* misrepresent the person's reaction in any way. . . . To take a partial approach is not *per se* to deform. It can involve a distortion; but the one is not equivalent to the other.[47]

Focusing on certain features of an object while neglecting others is for Lawson the typical process involved in abstraction. Of course, choosing a focus raises issues concerning the vantage point of analysis, the level of its generality, and the space-time extension relative to both.[48] Nonetheless, by admitting that a focus is ultimately a context-specific feature, it is not implied that what is out of focus can be assumed away, nor that contextual features exist in isolation.

> Such features cannot be considered as isolated momentary phenomena, like punctiform events. Each must be seen as expressing the remaining features, or whole, to which it is related, as well as (or including) its own history.[49]

This view of abstraction is set against both the positivistic idea of generalization implied by the elaboration of regularities between events, and against the form that abstraction takes in mainstream economic modelling. In the former case, Lawson argues that, for regularities to play their role, events and states of affairs must be 'emptied of their context-related, but often essential, content'. In the end, regularities obtain, but at a price: that of producing only broad generalizations. In the latter case, for models to work, they are built as closed systems, that is the features they focus upon are treated in isolation, under the controlled conditions created by the models themselves. However, Lawson objects, closed systems are ill-suited to dealing with social phenomena.[50] Social phenomena belong in social systems, and social systems, as 'structured process(es) of interaction',[51] are open in character. This partly explains why economic phenomena as dealt with by economic models often provide either poor explanations of what goes on in real social interactions, or limited guidelines as to what decisions to make (or what policies to enforce) in the social situations of which they are models. The artificial and controlled conditions created by the models are either often remote from the complex, plural, stratified variables encountered in real situations, or are too restrictive as to what they are able to process with the language they employ and the assumptions they make.

An instructive example is the model of measurement of the quality of life (qaly) invented by health economists at the end of the 1970s. In Rosser and Kind's formulation,[52] one year of good health is given value 1, and one year of bad health has value 0: between 1 and 0, various states of health are suggested, each of which is given a value. A 'state of health' is defined on the basis of two parameters: an objective invalidity, and a subjective pain. Objective invalidity is subdivided into eight levels, and subjective pain into four. Neither invalidity nor pain is defined by reference to specific diseases (see Table 4.1).

The values to be given to each state were established via interviews. A sample of about 70 subjects (patients, doctors, nurses and a number of healthy people) were asked, firstly, to 'mark' each state according to the severity of each state, and to express numerically comparative judgements between states – for example, by how many times is a person in the state X 'more ill' than a person in the state Y. Secondly, they were asked to determine (by being given appropriate statistical information concerning the prognosis of patients) the proportion of resources that should be allocated to the cure of the various states (see Table 4.2). Finally, they were asked to locate within the same model, and to submit to the same numerical treatment, the state of death. (In Table 4.2, death is assigned a score of zero.)

According to Rosser and Kind, the model could be successfully used to establish the quality of life of a patient after a cure, as well as to decide in what way available resources for treatment could be equally and efficiently distributed. At the very least, the model was intended to be a reliable tool for indicating how socially limited resources should be distributed among a community of ill

Table 4.1 Classification of states of sickness (Rosser and Kind; 1978, p. 349)

Disability

1. No disability.
2. Slight social disability.
3. Severe disability and/or slight impairment of performance at work. Able to do all housework except very heavy tasks.
4. Choice of work or performance at work very severely limited. Housewives and old people able to do light housework only but also to go out shopping.
5. Unable to undertake any paid employment. Unable to continue any education. Old people confined to home except for escorted outings and unable to do shopping. Housewives able only to perform a few simple tasks.
6. Confined to chair or to wheelchair or able to move around in the home only with support from an assistant.
7. Confined to bed.
8. Unconscious.

A. No distress.
B. Mild distress (slight pain which is relieved by aspirin).
C. Moderate distress (pain which is not relieved by aspirin).
D. Severe distress (pain for which heroin is prescribed).

Table 4.2 QALY (Kind, Rosser and Williams, 1982, p. 160)

	Distress			
Disability	A	B	C	D
1	1.000	0.995	0.990	0.967
2	0.990	0.986	0.973	0.932
3	0.980	0.972	0.956	0.912
4	0.964	0.956	0.942	0.870
5	0.946	0.935	0.900	0.700
6	0.875	0.845	0.680	0.000
7	0.677	0.564	0.000	−1.486
8	−1.028	–	–	–

people. The model, however, does raise a number of issues. Some have to do with the methods of calculations of quality adjustment factors, others with the assumptions and/or hidden premises which the model relies on in measuring quality by qalys. In what follows, I will review only some of the latter issues, and show what lies behind the idea that the quality of somebody's life is indeed a measurable concept.[53]

There seem to be 'facts' about human life which are objectively ascertainable, and these can arguably be used as criteria to decide whether one life is more worth living than another. Good health is one of them: it is a fact that good health is the highest ranked preference among people. What Rosser and Kind's model actually asks us to do, then, is to choose between *types* of life, on the assumption that there is an *ideal* life (that of a healthy person) which is the most preferable, in the absence of any intervening circumstances. This assumption is maintained to the point of claiming that a brief but healthy life is better, and therefore preferable, to a long but unhealthy one. What this comparison does not take into account is that everybody might have the same *desire to live*, as long and as well as possible, despite intervening circumstances. In other words, calculating qaly comparisons seems from the start to exclude the way individuals perceive and rate their own lives. A policy based on such comparisons would seem therefore to be ignoring some morally relevant factors. By focusing on general benefit, the model makes us neglect fairness towards individuals.

Moreover, the assessment of benefit entails an implicit endorsement of some hidden premises. What are these premises? Perhaps one way to find this out is by questioning whether Rosser and Kind's model is value-free. I said that the model seems to advocate, as a term of comparison, a picture of 'ideal life' construed on the basis of measurable 'facts'. However, in order for such a picture to work in the way the model requires, a series of assumptions have to be put in place. For example, it needs to be assumed that individuals are altruistic, to the point where they will not perform an action in their own interests (e.g. undertaking some medical treatment which is, though, not widely available), just because that action might prove detrimental to others (some people more than others might benefit from that very treatment, according to qaly criteria). Or we must assume that individuals are not biased towards certain kinds of diseases or handicaps. Or we must assume that they do not hold any belief (religious, moral, or other) concerning the absolute value of human life.

All these assumptions add up to the implicit adoption of a moral perspective, tacitly presupposed by the model: that the ideal life, in the end, is not only a healthy life (factually speaking), but also a life which is viewed as ideal by altruistic, unbiased, unprejudiced individuals (normatively speaking). Somewhat paradoxically, the model seems to assume that only idealized individuals can make the right decisions concerning the life and death of real people. This is an interesting result to take into consideration when we try to assess the objectivity of a qaly model. In fact, it seems, the model leaves its moral presuppositions unstated, hidden behind the purported objectivity of its measurable standards. Nonetheless, these presuppositions are essential for the model to work: it is because of the particular way we evaluate the ideal life in principle, that we can in practice trade one life against another.

Does then Rosser and Kind's model deliver? Can it be used, as intended by its creators, as an objective indicator of the limits of a bearable life? In the original matrix (Table 4.1), states such as 'being confined to bed, with moderate pain' or 'being in a wheelchair, with intense pain' are given the same value as death;

while 'the permanent loss of consciousness' or 'being confined to bed, with intense pain' receive a value even inferior to that given to death. In such cases, it would appear almost uncontroversial to justify euthanasia, as it would be in the objective interest of the very patient in question. The 'preference' of a suffering individual for terminating his or her own life is based on an objective assessment of that life's desirability. The subjective desire to live is assessed by how much pain can be objectively endured. However, social debates surrounding euthanasia teach us that decisions about the right to die, when the desire to live has ceased, can hardly be made only on the basis of a concept of quality as calculated in the way suggested by Rosser and Kind's model. A distinction might be useful to show what more is at stake.

The bearability of the 'biological life' of an individual, arguably, does not correspond to the desirability of his 'biographical life'. Interestingly, the distinction between the two types of life is crucial to the debate about where to draw the line for individuals to count as 'persons', and the related discussion concerning the moment or state in which a 'person' should be declared dead. If an individual is more than his biological life, can we decide that, when this 'something more' is not present any longer, the individual has ceased to exist? And of what does this 'something more' consist? Is it his biographical life? Or else, are there some biological facts about individual human beings which make them specifically human? If there are, and should these facts disappear from somebody's life (or else, should they never have been part of somebody's life), is the individual in question then no longer human (his humanity is dead, and what is still alive is not a human being any longer)?[54]

We also need to ask: desirability and bearability for whom? Let us imagine a spectrum of possible organic states. On one side, we find those states (say, the permanent cessation of the functioning of the organism as a whole, or the irreversible loss of the higher-brain functions) where the individual is incapable of attributing meaning to his existence, since the individual in question is not a competent individual. At the other end of the spectrum, we find states in which a competent, self-conscious individual is vexated by aspects of a biological life for several reasons intolerable and with no hope of recovery. The issue of the 'desirability' and 'bearability' of one's existence appears to be different in the two cases; at the very least, it involves different actors. In the case of the incompetent individual, desirability and bearability constitute an indirect judgement reached on behalf of the patient by some other individual (the doctor, the family of the patient, the hospital management). In the case of the competent individual, the desirability of his own life is a direct judgement reached by the patient on the basis of his own experience (what he can or cannot bear) and of the information acquired by other individuals involved (again, the doctor, the family, etc.). Such 'evidence' allows the patient to square his desire to stay alive with the individual costs from bearing the consequences of his choice (for example, in terms of pain, loss of dignity as a person, etc.). In both cases, the issue of the desirability/bearability of somebody's life certainly is relevant to the decision about whether or not to allow its prolongation, but there are other relevant factors too.

This is not to say that models, such as the one illustrated here, are worthless, vacuous, and trivial. Indeed, they can significantly contribute to devising hospital policies, or help the medical profession in making institutional decisions. However, their partiality should be acknowledged from the beginning. Partiality here means a number of things:

1) the choice of focus (in this case, comparative benefit)
2) the choice of measuring tools to apply to social aspects of human life (the quality of life)
3) the tacit choice of value-laden assumptions (what makes a life worth living, whose lives are more/most worthy, the comparability of lives in terms of their 'worth', the acceptance that 'quality' can be objectively assessed by empirical and/or mathematical tools, etc.).

Partiality *per se* is not an argument against use. It is rather (or at least it should be taken as) an empirical challenge for a model, when this model is confronted by the rich, articulated and complex social phenomena of the world in which we live.

CHAPTER 5

Geographical Objects

1. A NATURAL OR A SOCIAL SCIENCE?

Geography as a discipline can be defined as 'the study of the Earth's surface as the space within which the human population lives'.[1] A well-known formal definition of what geography attempts to do (geography as a practice of research) is the one put forward, at the end of the 1950s, by Richard Hartshorne:

> geography is concerned to provide accurate, orderly, and rational description and interpretation of the variable character of the Earth's surface.[2]

Taken at face value, these two definitions allow us to introduce some preliminary thoughts concerning the object of geographical inquiry. Firstly, the Earth's 'surface' contains not only trees and valleys, foxes and volcanoes, but also human populations interacting with all this, to a large extent with a view to survival. As a matter of fact, it is because of this interaction (though not only because of this) that we can think of the Earth's surface as *variable* in character. Secondly, and again because of this interaction, the list of items, as comprised and studied by geography, can be widened to include such things as borders, territories, landscapes, etc. – entities which are, rather puzzlingly, partly 'natural' and partly artificial (imposed, or constructed).

As a consequence, geography might be perceived as occupying a rather ambiguous position within the traditional partition of knowledge. What kind of discipline is it? Is it a natural, or a social science? In classical Greece, where geography finds its origins as a distinctive field of study,[3] this question would not have made any sense. In classical Greece, there was not such a distinction between nature and people. People were part of nature, not apart from it. As a consequence, the 'geography' of an area would have included a description of both (nature and people). The question of the status of the discipline is a much more recent one. It emerged when geography established itself as an academic discipline – that is, towards the end of the nineteenth century in Germany, and much later in Britain and America.[4] In the university context, geography had to comply with the already crystallized division, within academic disciplines, between the natural sciences and the humanities/social sciences. Because of the ambiguous status of its subject matter, geography found itself sometimes included in the natural science faculties, and sometimes in the arts or social science faculties. One of the results of this ambiguity was the tendency to split geography into two parts: a geography of the natural world, called 'physical geography', and a geography of the human/social world, named 'human geography'.

Haggett points out how many geographers found, and still find, this distinction artificial, or even worse, detrimental to the discipline. In fact, they claim, it ends up adding more confusion to the attempt to understand what the essential areas of study are within the discipline, and ultimately what the academic and intellectual profile of the discipline is.[5] However, and provided that it does not deny that the physical and the human strands of geography often have shared interests in methods, topics, and research procedures, it could also be argued that acknowledging some partition within the discipline might be useful. To an outsider (as I am), a 'separatist' perspective might suggest a way to recognize better where the emphases of geographical questions really lie. There is a difference between on the one hand, focusing primarily on the physical aspects of the earth (climatology, geomorphology, biogeography, etc.) and only derivatively on their effects on peoples; and on the other, studying specifically the human aspects (economic, social, political, historical) of the geography of a place, and the natural environment only in its interactions with those human aspects.

By following the 'separatist' suggestion, it seems then that the part of geography which is closer to being a social science is human geography. Yet, given that the subject matter of human geography falls, as we have seen, somehow in between the natural and the human world, the relation between the two worlds can itself be studied differently, depending on whether the focus of the analysis is more on the naturalistic side, or more on the humanistic one. So even by focusing on human geography, the question of the status of the discipline and the nature of its objects of inquiry is far from being settled.

2. 'SPACE AND PLACE': QUANTITATIVE RECONSTRUCTIONS

The geographers who tended to think of the relation between space and people in naturalistic/scientific terms were drawn, in the 1950s and 1960s, towards advocating a broadly conceived positivistic perspective. The major attraction of this perspective was quantification, that is the attempt to formulate the results of geographical inquiry in mathematical or statistical terms.[6] A related attraction was that this kind of formulation allowed the empirical testing and verification of those results.[7]

The focus of this positivistic/quantitative style of geography was 'space and place'.[8] The question, 'What is where?' was understood and analysed, according to Johnston, at the level of two related sub-questions:

1) What is the complex of phenomena which characterizes a particular place?
2) What is the pattern of distribution of these phenomena which characterizes a particular place?[9]

Because of this way of framing its object of inquiry, specific aspects of space were focused upon, to the detriment of others. One of these aspects was, according to Johnston, the role of space as an 'impedance factor':

> To cross space involves time, various costs, and other factors. These costs are to be avoided as far as possible, and so the organization of society is spatially structured to keep down, if not to minimize, the so called 'frictions of distance'. Thus to many, human geography became the study of 'spatial science' (or spatial social science), and attempts were made to develop theories reflecting this position.[10]

The concept of *spatial distribution* was at the core of this perspective. Space is conceived of as a 'system of distance relationships between objects'.[11] The study of the system can be pursued by means of spatial 'indicators', which identify spatial arrangements in the form of geometrical patterns.[12] Distribution appears then to be defined in terms of horizontal relations of distance which, in their turn, identify relative positions in space, or *locations*. In such a way, space can be studied in terms of models of distribution, and these models can be analysed by means of quantitative methods. Positivistic/quantitative human geography developed as a 'spatial science'.

In order to answer the requirements of such a science, the collection and organization of facts and material concerning places, as well as of the human activities within them, was guided by two underlying precepts: the adoption of systematic procedures of analysis, and a reconceptualized idea of regions as 'geographic generalizations'.[13] In the end, regions were used, within this perspective, as devices for mapping large data sets around specific area groupings on the Earth's surface. The tools for achieving this combination of material evidence and systematization were the typical positivistic ones: laws, generalizations, empirical hypotheses, and formal/mathematical models. Some examples will help illustrate this style of analysis.

A first, well-known case is Christaller's central place theory and its application to retailing.[14] The theory was intended to provide a predictive account of the relative spatial distributions of urban settlements and retail establishments. It assumed that shopkeepers and customers are all utility-maximizers. This, in terms of the geography of an urban settlement, means that the former would set up their businesses in locations which minimize the travelling expenses of the latter and which, at the same time, maximize the efficiency and worth of commercial transactions for both categories of individuals. On this assumption, the theory predicted that shops would be located at the centre of the areas where their keepers intended to carry out their business. This prediction can be given a formal (geometrical) model-representation. This amounted to a hexagonal distribution of the location of shops in central places,[15] according to the 'range' and 'threshold' of the goods on offer in those shops (that is, according to the distance that a buyer would be willing to travel in order to acquire specific goods, and according to the size of business necessary to survive as a shop selling certain goods). A model so conceived represents forms of shopping choice and of retail location, by predicting patterns for minimizing distances among consumers.

Two other examples, as reported by Johnston, might be usefully recalled here. One comes from an area of inquiry, 'industrial location theory', first developed within economic theory, as an application of neoclassical economic concepts to geographical space.[16] The initial assumption of this theory was that all owners of manufacturing industries tend to locate their factories in places which secure a substantial reduction in the costs of production and of distribution to the market. Among these costs, the most relevant are those of transport. The main premise of this theory became that 'the location of manufacturing industry is undertaken so as to minimise transport costs'.[17] On the basis of this premise, geographers developed models of the distribution of industrial plants, which in their turn elicited a whole series of hypotheses concerning the choice of particular locations. Once the hypotheses were formulated, they were then tested empirically.[18]

The other example is provided by the theory of 'urban social areas', developed within urban geography (although it originated from the sociological work of the Chicago School on land-use patterns).[19] According to this theory, society is divided into groups, along ethnic, economic or various common-interest lines. Members of each group wish to live in areas where inter-group contacts are minimal. Distance between groups is considered here as a social barrier, and the spatial organization of urban residential areas reflects this view of distance as a social mechanism. This view, within a positivistic kind of inquiry, can be represented in terms of formalized models, which account for spatial segregation/congregation in relation to the morphology of urban areas.[20]

So, generally speaking, a typical description of this kind of analysis (which can frequently be found, more or less explicitly, in geographical reports or articles) comes in a sequence of interrelated stages:[21]

1) A research area is singled out, and a model for the chosen area put forward. The model normally projects a simplified version of the corresponding situation in the 'real world'. To use our examples above, the model should depict a pattern of land-use in the distribution of manufacturing industries or retail establishments, or a pattern of urban segregation or congregation.
2) Once formulated, the model should guide empirical inquiry, in the sense that it should help address questions, which can be relevantly answered in an empirical or experimental (in the style of fieldwork) fashion. These questions, put forward on the basis of a chosen model, constitute the geographical hypotheses. To use, for example, the case of industrial location theory, the hypothesis is that the 'intensity of land-use for industries decreases with an increase of distance from market'.
3) Geographical hypotheses are tested during the inquiry itself. Empirical research is specifically devised with a view to testing them.

Positivistic human geography, which spread widely and prospered in the 1960s, faced various kinds of criticism at the end of the 1960s and beginning of the 1970s. Some of these criticisms focused on the fact that positivistic analyses exclude traits which arguably are crucial to the subject matter's very nature.[22] It was claimed that the positivistic approach showed a lack of concern for the social, structural, and material conditions of human existence in their analyses of space and spatial distribution: a Marxist critique of positivistic geography started taking shape at the beginning of the 1970s along historical-materialist lines. And as we will see shortly, the positivistic approach was also criticized for disregarding the role of the human agent (intentions, beliefs, perceptions, etc.) in its definition and treatment of geographical space.

3. 'SPACE AND PLACE': QUALITATIVE RECONSTRUCTIONS

Positivistic human geography has been criticized for excluding reference to the actual people who live in the worlds they themselves have created as thinking human individuals. The model of the 'economic man', for instance, often used in geographical modelling, appeared to be an inadequate idealization of what a social actor is and does. A 'decision-maker blessed with perfect predictive ability and knowledge of all cost factors' is a far cry from either 'objective reality' or from 'the world as seen by the researcher'.[23] Human geography, we are told, must try to understand how people live in their environments (a study from 'inside' the regions and their inhabitants, rather than the perspective of an 'outside' researcher), if this kind of geography is to deal adequately with its own subject matter.[24] Although this kind of perspective was present in the early 1900s, especially within the tradition of historical geographers,[25] a proper case for a humanistic approach to geography only started being consistently advocated for in the 1960s. It developed in two ways. On the one hand, some geographers were generally inclined towards a humanistic perspective, though they did not hold any specific philosophical views which go under that name. On the other hand, other geographers made use of well-identified lines of philosophical argument in order to turn geography into a 'humanistic' discipline.

An example of the former practice can be found in Kirk. He distinguished the 'geographical environment' in terms of the phenomenal and the behavioural.[26] A behavioural environment includes the same facts as the phenomenal, although only as they are perceived by human beings – that is, according to their interests, preferences, modes of thinking, cultural and social traditions, etc.[27] As in positivistic human geography, space and place remain the focus of inquiry, but we are now told that they have to be dealt with as concepts which pervade, and are pervaded by, 'human experience'. This is why, in the same spirit, a number of humanistically inclined geographers investigated possible links between geography and literature. Literature, they claimed, can often provide interesting clues as to how humans experience their environment. Writers and novelists not only describe the world, they also help shape it. They often succeed in producing powerful images of landscapes and regions, which, in their turn, affect the way people feel about the world they inhabit.[28]

As for the second way of practising humanistic geography mentioned above, geographers find themselves rejecting the positivistic framework, by adopting philosophical perspectives which were markedly anti-positivistic (phenomenology, existentialism, and various forms of idealism and pragmatism). These philosophies offered a way to stop thinking of people as 'little more than dots on a map, statistics on a graph or numbers in an equation . . . travelling from place X to place Y; shopping in centre X rather than centre Y; etc. . . . .'.[29] They rather allowed geographers to concentrate on aspects which are, arguably, and most distinctively, human: 'meaning, value, goals and purposes', as we read in Entrikin.[30]

How does such a change in perspective inform actual research? A first example is provided by the use of an idealist perspective on geographical inquiry. The views of Collingwood had a remarkable influence. In his *The Idea of History*, he argues that there is an unavoidable 'subjective element' in history (i.e. in the performance of human actions) as well as in the study of history (the views of historians, informed by what he calls the 'historical imagination'). To understand historical events entails 'seeing history in its individuality, seeing every incident in it as an irreplaceable and unique element in an irreplaceable and unique whole'. This style of analysis is set against a positivistic reconstruction which seeks for 'instances of laws', and which looks at historical events and actions as 'mere re-duplication(s) of a ready-made type'.[31] People make history happen, by following plans, purposes, and intentions. The historian's work starts with identifying the 'outside' of an event (its 'external' context), but the aim is to unravel the subjective motivations which either influenced or prompted individuals to act (the 'inside' of the event).

It has been argued that a similar approach should be adopted in geographical inquiry. Harris and Guelke advocate a view which explicitly makes use of Collingwood's arguments. Harris claims that, in parallel with the 'historical imagination', a 'geographical imagination' is to be developed, with the aim of allowing geographers to immerse themselves in the study of a 'region' in a way similar to the historian's immersion in a 'period'.[32] Guelke believes that geographers should concentrate on the meaning that certain actions have in geographical terms, and understand spatial arrangements (settlements, landscapes, etc.) as the outcome of 'the thinking of the people who created them'.[33]

Another example of humanistic geography informed by anti-positivistic philosophy is the phenomenological approach. In a phenomenological perspective, phenomena are said to be what they are because they are consciously experienced. As a consequence, the task of phenomenological inquiry is that of providing an analysis and an understanding of the basic features of our (subjective) knowledge of phenomena, that is an analysis and understanding of the modes of thought which make phenomena appear to us in the way they do (and make them what they are for us). Space is one of them: space is treated, phenomenologically, as a pure phenomenon of consciousness, or of our subjective knowledge.

A similar view informs some humanistic reconstructions of space in geography. Relph, for instance, claims that in a humanistic approach space and place should be analysed as 'sources of security and identity for individuals and groups of people'.[34] There is a 'sense of place' in all of us, which we express in landscaping, city planning, housing, etc. This sense reveals what the individual as well as the social or cultural perceptions of a particular environment are. Eyles identified four specific 'senses of place', based on an analysis of how groups of residents relate to the places where they live (small English towns).[35] He called 'apathetic' the sense of place which expresses residents' indifference to the place. A 'social' sense of place emerges from the residents' identification of place with social and family relations within a community. An 'instrumental' sense of place develops from treating a place as the provider of work and means of survival. Finally, a 'nostalgic' sense of place builds on conceptions of heritage. What is interesting about Eyles's classification is the suggestion that the meaning of 'sense of place' cannot be limited to the geographical notion of a spatial environment. The same place means different things to different people, and this is something a human geographer cannot ignore. Space, as has been suggested, is 'an essential framework to all modes of thought'.[36]

The positivistic and humanistic approaches to human geography seem to be very far apart. The former advocates a scientific methodology, informed by quantitative research and aimed at the discovery of empirical correlations. The latter developed as a series of critical arguments against positivistic claims, rather than as a well-developed, alternative methodology. So when it comes to carrying out research on human geographical topics, the problem of whether to follow a naturalistic approach, or whether and how to include some of the critical elements emphasized by the humanistic approach, becomes rather acute. Besides, the humanistic preoccupation with the role of human agency seems to leave aside the relation that individuals have with the broader structural and material contexts of their actions (as focused upon by Marxist analyses). In what way, if any, could an anti-positivist approach to human geography include reference to both agency and structure?

Many practising geographers would argue that these are philosophical preoccupations, relevant neither to the framing of empirical research, nor to the actual procedures of research. However, the fact that these philosophical preoccupations are not explicitly acknowledged or formulated in terms, say, of the conscious choice of a method of research, does not mean that philosophical assumptions are not entering the realm of geographical inquiry. The way they enter such a realm, though, should be qualified – especially so as to avoid confusion, or even worse, ambiguously mixed solutions. One non-*ad hoc* mixed solution comes, for instance, from the realist camp.

4. 'SPACE AND PLACE': REALIST RECONSTRUCTIONS

Talking of realism as a 'mixed' position might be misleading. Realism is both an anti-positivistic and an anti-idealistic philosophical perspective.[37] To be sure, the kind of combination it suggests for social science is of a scientific view mixed with a meaning-dependent identification of the objects of social scientific inquiry. However, by 'scientific view' the realist refers to a form of naturalism grounded on the belief in the existence of causal mechanisms, which are responsible for (and not reducible to) the occurrence of empirical regularities. By 'meaning-dependence', he refers to an epistemological condition of access to those mechanisms, not to their full ontological status.

The following list of features will serve as a quick reminder of what a realist-type perspective of science/social science consists of:[38]

1) the world exists independently of our knowledge of it;
2) our knowledge of that world is fallible and theory-laden;
3) the world is differentiated and stratified: it consists not only of events, but objects, including structures which have powers and liabilities capable of generating events;
4) social phenomena are concept-dependent. We therefore have not only to explain their production and material effects but to understand, read or interpret what they mean;
5) scientific knowledge is a social practice, so the conditions and social relations of the production of knowledge influence its content.

The interest that human geographers showed in realism in the 1980s and 1990s was twofold. Firstly, a realist perspective justified the importance of asking qualitative questions about the nature of the objects of geographical research (quantitative questions seemed not to be able to go any further than the level of empirical correlation). Secondly, realism appeared a viable way to give both the humanistic and materialist critiques an opportunity to be integrated into a scientific research programme with empirical applications.[39] In realism, human geographers found a way to address ontological questions concerning the subject matter of their discipline by means of an epistemological perspective which was theoretically more sophisticated and, at the same time, more promising in terms of practical results, than the positivistic one.

Space and its role in understanding social relations was indeed one of the domains studied by realist philosophers.[40] Sayer, for example, builds up his analysis of space using the following two distinctions, each central to his realist perspective.[41] One is the distinction between *necessary and contingent relations*. An example of the former would be the relation between master and slave, or between landlord and tenant. This type of relation is necessary 'in that what the object is is dependent on its relation to the other' (someone cannot be a master, or a tenant, without a slave, or a landlord).[42] An example of the latter is the relation between patriarchy and capitalist social relations: in this case the nature of the two objects in the relation is independent of the relation itself (capitalist social relations can, arguably, be defined in principle independently of gender-relations).[43] The former relations identify the 'structure' of the objects of research (i.e. the necessary, or internally related practices, which constitute the nature of these objects), whereas the latter concern the various forms which structural relations take on particular occasions, or under specific conditions. This distinction goes hand in hand with Sayer's view of causation. Borrowing from Harré and Bhaskar, he claims that 'objects are understood to possess causal powers and liabilities to do or suffer certain things by virtue of their structure and composition, but whether these powers or liabilities are activated depends on contingently related conditions'.[44]

How are these two sets of relations to be analysed? Would one and the same method of inquiry be able to encompass both? A second distinction, put forward by Sayer, is between *abstract and concrete research*. 'Abstraction involves concepts designed to refer to particular *one-sided* aspects of objects.'[45] This means that abstractions refer to real objects without reproducing them in their often chaotic and certainly complex appearances. By abstraction we are able to select those conditions which we believe are most significant for identifying the natures of objects. This is why, according to Sayer, abstraction is particularly suitable for the discovery of the structural properties of objects.[46] Concrete research, by contrast, deals with the non-necessary (contingent) relations which pertain to objects, that is all those relations and conditions which are not 'structurally' defined, and yet which are taken to have been brought about by structural relations.[47] In concrete research, factors such as complexity, context-dependence, and qualitative change cannot be neglected, and therefore methods and research techniques need to be devised that deal adequately with those factors. By making use of a further distinction, first suggested by Harré, Sayer claims that concrete research should make use not only of extensive, but also of intensive research methods.[48]

How does this framework help in the understanding of the concept of space and its supposed effects on social domains and processes? In particular, does it help in figuring out whether and how space 'makes a difference'? Usually, says Sayer, geographical discussions concerning space make use of one of the two following concepts of space: 'an absolute concept in which space is empty and a relative concept in which space only exists where it is constituted by matter.'[49] The former concept is incoherent: as Blaut simply puts it, 'what is empty is nothing, and what is nothing cannot be',[50] and how can something which cannot be have effects of any sort? The latter concept often leads to the inference that if space is constituted by objects, then it is reducible to them. This is also objectionable. If we change the disposition of some sequence of objects, for example,

$$\text{from:} \quad \textbf{A B C} \quad \text{to:} \quad \overset{\textbf{B}}{\textbf{A}}\ \textbf{C}$$

we can easily see that, although the constituents of the space are the same, the spatial form is not.

To say that space is independent of the (types of) objects which are present is not to say that the absolute conception of space is right. Setting space apart from

objects would put us in danger of 'attributing powers to space (whether in terms
of geometry, distance, location, or movement) regardless of the causal powers of
the objects constituting it'.[51] Objects activate their powers depending on context
and local conditions, that is depending on the other objects they are in contact
with, 'and this in turn depends upon spatial form'.[52] So, the properties of any
spatial form depend firstly, on what types of objects are present and their situation relative to each other, and secondly, on the assumption that those objects
possess causal powers whose effects depend on spatial contiguity, among other
things. For example, in the sequence 'A B C' above,

> if we knew that B was the Berlin Wall and A and C the two Germanys, then
> the spatial relation of 'betweenness' in which B stood would have some
> material significance. Of course, there are many other spatial forms or rela-
> tions besides that of betweenness, but whatever the form, and however
> complex it is, the same conclusion follows.'[53]

Space indeed makes a difference, and such a difference can be appreciated
by analysing its role within a realist ontology of the kind suggested, Sayer
concludes. However, it is important to ask at what level space makes a difference, and consequently must be analysed. If 'abstract theory analyses objects
in terms of their constitutive structures, as part of wider structures and in
terms of their causal powers', and 'concrete research looks at what happens
when these combine',[54] then space is best understood at the latter level of
inquiry.

> Space *is* certainly important, but to say what that importance consists in, we
> normally have to move to a more concrete kind of analysis where we identify
> particular kinds of objects, relations and processes constituting it in concrete
> spatial conjunctures.[55]

Space makes a difference, and produces material effects, at the level of contingent relations. This is not to say that theoretical abstractions are irrelevant
and of no use in the analysis of space. They are meant to provide the 'con-
ceptualisations of the contingent conditions as well as the central processes of
interest'. What they cannot do is to 'anticipate much about the forms of . . .
spatial settings'. Only empirical, concrete research can 'discover the concrete
forms that social objects contingently take. In all cases, the concrete forms will
make some difference to outcomes.'[56] There is only a limited range of things
which can be said about space at the level of abstract theory, besides acknowledging that social objects are spatially extensive. This, according to Sayer,
partly explains why, for example, social theory does not, by and large, engage in

any deep-level analysis of space, and when it does, offers only vague references to it.[57]

However, Sayer also specifies that claiming that concrete research is the appropriate type of analysis for the concept of space (the level of contingent relations) is not an admission that space is 'less important' than the concepts defined and analysed at the level of abstract theory. 'Contingent' does not mean undetermined, or uncaused, within a realist perspective; nor does it mean that everything about space is contingent. Empirical research into the contingent aspects of spatial forms reveals the large variety of forms that space can take in practice. Such a variety, as we said above, cannot be fully accounted for by theoretical abstraction, although abstraction does provide a conceptual framework, which 'feeds into' and guides empirical research.[58]

Attention to concrete research, together with the ways empirical analyses conceptualize particular spatial forms, should be (and indeed is) of great interest to the practising human geographer (as well as to the social theorist). This is because, among other things, it is an interesting attempt to bridge the gap between the theory and practice of research, and to show how a realist-informed kind of research provides an alternative to positivism. Still, how can such an attempt be pursued in practice, or – as Pratt puts it – how can critical-realist analyses of space be 'put to work'?[59]

In his study of the location and form of contemporary industrial estates and uneven development, Pratt analyses the relationship between industry, space and society from a critical-realist perspective.[60] His overall aim is to offer an explanation of 'the way that the industrial built environment both enables and constrains the potential actions of its occupants as well as those others – for example employees – dependent upon them'. In order for this explanation to be possible, we need to focus on 'how the built environment is actually created in particular places and at particular times'. Such an understanding is made possible by conducting empirical research (both extensive and intensive) about one particular form which the built environment may take, that is the industrial estate.[61]

The concept of 'uneven re-production' certainly refers to economic production and its components (distribution, exchange and consumption), but more importantly it entails a fundamental link between the socio-economic realm and the spatial realm. Geographers know that 'space matters', Pratt claims, but just how much, in what forms, and to what extent space matters in industrial location theory, is normally left unexplored. In order to make space a condition of analysis, however, a reconceptualization of it is needed. Industrial location offers a concrete context in which such a reconceptualization can be carried out in practice.

Similarly to Sayer, Pratt argues that space is not a container in which social relations occur and develop. According to such an absolute conception, space is taken for granted, and thought of as if it can be separated from social relations. Social relations are indeed spatially extended, but – as Urry emphasizes – one cannot exist without the other.[62] Social relations exist in space, but also space is created as an effect of social relations. This 'symbiotic' relation exists in the realm of the particular, of the contingent, or – to use a term of the art – of the *locality*. Locality defines any 'particular and unique combination of a whole set of social relations that intersect at any one place', and such combinations may interfere with the outcomes of social relations in ways which cannot be predicted. This is why 'the need for work on the concrete production of space in particular places and times would seem to be necessary'.[63]

In the specific case of industrial estates, this perspective on space and social relations leads Pratt to view locality as a 'spatially . . . specific form of development' which 'cannot be defined in the abstract'.

That they [industrial estates] emerged . . . in a particular place, is significant and must be related to the social, economic and cultural context. Likewise, their contemporary form, location, and mode of development can only be considered by recourse to particular painstaking empirical analysis. Nevertheless that analysis must necessarily be informed by abstract theory.[64]

The combination of abstract and concrete research is carried out, in Pratt's case study, in accordance with realist prescriptions: the object of inquiry (the industrial estate) is reconceptualized in such a way that causal mechanisms and structural relations are put forward, which in their turn are assessed for empirical adequacy. The research strategy is developed from an analysis of interviews with developers. Such an analysis does not treat data emerging from interviews as facts reported upon by an informant, as a positivistic style of research would prescribe, but rather as interactive sources of meaningful communication between interviewers and interviewees. The aim is not so much to present a statistical sample. The challenge, as Pratt puts it, is not to reduce information in such a way that it can fit some tabular form, but rather 'to create some order out of the mass of information collected'.[65]

5. THE POSSIBLE WORLDS OF HUMAN GEOGRAPHY

There is much talk within human geography – and other social sciences – about advocating a pluralist standpoint, or about pursuing research in a pluralistic style. But, we should ask, what are the assumptions behind a pluralistic framework in geography? Let us look, for example, at the following quotation:

Much of the confusion that lies at the heart of geography today results from an awareness that there are simply many geographies and many possible worlds. Uncertainty arises because we know neither which geography to choose, nor which possible world we should aim for. We run the risk of becoming dogmatic by trying to force all worlds into one very limited format, and in doing so we ignore, belittle or forget the others.[66]

In this passage an implicit distinction seems to be at work, which must be considered before reaching any decisions about pluralistic ideals of research. In claiming that there are different 'geographies' it is being assumed that there are alternative methods for studying geographical subject matters, whereas what constitutes a 'geographical object' of investigation is the same in all cases. But by saying that there are different 'possible worlds we should aim for', it seems that a different claim is being made. What appears to be a geographical object of investigation (a 'possible world', as we read in the passage above) is largely the result of the geographical approach which both enables and constrains the range of possible configurations for this object.

This distinction is crucial when it comes to deciding how to practise geography, and to choosing procedures of research. An illustration of what the distinction amounts to can be inferred from Scargill's description of the diversity of approaches used to refer to, and account for, the Fenland area of eastern England.[67]

The historical geographer looking at this region might be interested primarily in recreating its past landscapes, the periods chosen for study corresponding with those of major changes in the evolution of the drainage system. The spatial-analytical geographer, by contrast, seeks to fit Fenland phenomena – crops, farms, drains, etc. – into his statistical model of distribution, at the same time observing the diffusion of selected phenomena from centres of innovation. To the physical geographer the Fens are first and foremost an example of a controlled ecosystem and interest lies principally in the response of plants and animals to the hydrological situation. The literature and folklore of the region provide the starting point for the humanist who will probably have read Dorothy Sayers' novel *The Nine Tailors* and will be interested in this as a portrayal of the life and character of the region. Some, however, could prefer a landscape approach, noting how the region has been illustrated in art. Finally, the Marxists might seek to interpret the geography of the Fens in terms of the crisis of capitalist landownership, observing how present patterns of farming are a response to EEC prices . . . and how wealthy farmers benefit from a system that was not intended for them.[68]

As with the French Revolution, in our chapter on history, we can here ask: 'How many Fenland areas of Eastern England are there?' The answer is one and many. It can be objected that in fact there is a substantial difference between the 'French Revolution' and the 'Fenland area'. The former is an interpretative expression, which refers to a range of past human actions. The latter is at least a partially descriptive expression, in the sense that it describes an actual and present spatial location. Yet, when we ask: 'What does the expression "Fenland area" refer to?', pointing, say, to its location on a map is just one of the possible ways of offering an answer, and not necessarily the most 'descriptive' one. Besides, even maps do not plainly and 'objectively' describe, or represent, geographical reality.[69] They certainly cannot be taken at face value. Boundaries, for example, are chosen in the light of what it is intended to be emphasized about an area. Moreover,

> the cartographer has to interpret data and transform it for the purpose of the map. The map's scale and symbols may well be decided by someone else, depending on the purpose the map is intended to serve.[70]

Map-making relies on a mixed body of knowledge, partly theoretical and partly practical, as well as on an array of technical and technological procedures for surveying, measuring, symbolizing, and drafting. Besides, as for example Harley points out, cartography, though officially presented as a 'science', is (should be taken as) an art, which takes into account the historical, political, ethnic, social, and sometimes aesthetic rules for the production of maps.[71] Map-making, in the end, is not only a descriptive activity of visual representation, but a series of cognitive and cultural procedures for the reconfiguration of space and place.[72]

Back to our question, 'What does the expression "Fenland area" refer to?' a whole series of alternative answers could then be put forward: crops, farms, and drains linked together in a statistical model of distribution; a controlled eco-system; a landscape, past or present; a series of legends and stories; a model of capitalist ownership; etc. etc. If one is inclined to argue that the crops-farms-drains answer is more descriptive, geographically speaking, than, say, legends or landscapes, then it must be explained what is to count as a geographical description, and why some descriptions are to be taken as more 'descriptive' than others, and according to what criteria.[73]

This latter remark is rather interesting, because it can be turned into a general point about objects in the human/social sciences. Remember what was said about anthropological knowledge: anthropological objects cannot be plainly observed and classified. Their observation and classification takes place in fieldwork, by means of a whole range of procedures and actual interactions.

Similarly, in the case of sociological and economic knowledge: social facts cannot be described until, in the course of research, a context of inquiry (an interview, an experiment, a model) makes some conditions for their description available. This is also somewhat true of history, where the conditions for describing past events are not separate from the ways in which the historian selects and makes sense of documentary evidence.

In general, this means that the objects of social inquiry are essentially different from everyday 'things'. When we talk of social 'objects' of inquiry, we somehow presuppose a difference (an epistemological difference) between the phenomena we are surrounded by in the social world and the objects which we turn into the referents of our social scientific investigations.[74] More specifically, the appreciation of such a difference presupposes a critical perspective on analysis, in a Kantian sense. Such a perspective denies the possibility of asking questions about social objects directly (as if their configuration pre-existed our capacity for describing and classifying them). Rather it prescribes the necessity of asking questions about the procedures and practical resources by means of which they become objects for us to investigate.

How, then, does objectivity fit in here? It should by now be clear that objectivity should not be taken as an abstract ideal derived from a certain logic of science, and prescriptively applied to any disciplinary investigation which aims at being objective. This ideal, as suggested in the Introduction, and as shown in the various chapters of this book, rests on an epistemological picture according to which objects simply pre-exist our theoretical capacity for describing them. Objectivity is a derivative concept within this picture: the objectivity of our theories is 'derived' from the existence of an objective world. Kant, of course, made us question this picture. In the *Critique of Pure Reason* he offered an account of how it is instead our mind which, through the imposition of general categories of understanding, is an active producer of 'objects' of knowledge, and which – at least to this extent – confers objectivity on what would otherwise be an unsystematic manifold of subjective impressions or experiential events.[75]

If we adopt this Kantian picture, and use it as a framework for the understanding of the status and function of the disciplines of social inquiry, we discover the need to begin from assessing how social objects are identified by the descriptions, classifications, or explanations of those disciplines, before proceeding to assess the objectivity of those descriptions, classifications or explanations themselves. This entails finding out what procedures (theoretical, practical) are used to produce those descriptions, classifications, or explanations.[76] This should allow us to say that the objects so described, classified or explained are at least partly 'constructed', or produced by, those procedures themselves.

It might appear that, if the objectivity of a discipline of social inquiry amounts to the fact that any social scientific discipline is responsible for configuring the 'objects' of its own inquiries, there is very little to say, or to rethink about objectivity. This is not the conclusion to be drawn, however. There are at least five points that this book has tried to put up for discussion:

1) Before assessing whether a theory is objective, we need to know what object(s) the theory is dealing with.

2) The objectivity of our social scientific theories is not derived from some presumed 'way that things are', but rather from the practical ways we frame things in our inquiries.

3) Not all social scientific inquiries are objective in the same way: there are different ways of constructing objects. Different inquiries make use of different procedures for identifying the 'objects' they set out to investigate. Equally, one specific inquiry might sometimes make use of procedures from other types of inquiry.

4) Social inquiry can also make use of procedures used by the natural sciences (e.g. quantification, nomological or causal analysis, etc.). However, this is not compulsory; nor should such use be given any priority or any special role in principle, when assessing the objectivity of the results of some investigation.

5) Objectivity is not (cannot be) a prescriptive concept of empirical social inquiry: it is not a norm, or standard of correctness laid out in advance of practical research. Talking of objectivity only makes sense in the concrete context of an assessment of a described object of inquiry.

Notes

Introduction

1. In this book I will use the term 'normative', unless otherwise specified, to define the tendency of establishing a standard or paradigm of correctness by means of prescriptive rules. In particular, the normative/descriptive distinction, which I will make use of in my analysis, has nothing to do with the normative/positive distinction as used, for example, in economics; nor is normative equated with evaluative, as in normative ethics.

2. It might be worth recalling, at the outset of our discussion, that the word 'science' has different meanings in different languages, and this indeed affects the way in which the question 'is social science *science?*' is addressed and answered. 'Social science' does not translate into '*Geistwissenshaft*', nor into '*sciences humaines*'. See S. Morgenbesser, 'Is it a science?', in D. Emmet and A. MacIntyre (eds) *Sociological Theory and Philosophical Analysis*, London: Macmillan, 1966. On the meaning of 'science' adopted in the discussions referred to in this chapter, see sect. 2 below.

3. See B. Flyvbjerg, *Making Social Science Matter. Why Social Inquiry Fails and How it Can Succeed Again*, Cambridge: Cambridge University Press, 2001, p. 3. For a review of some of these reasons for failure see F. Cunningham, *Objectivity in Social Science*, Toronto: University of Toronto Press, 1973, ch. 1.

4. As pointed out, for example, by E. Nagel, *The Structure of Science: Problems in the Logic of Scientific Explanation*, London: Routledge and Kegan Paul, 1961, p. 485.

5. This example is in C. Hempel, 'Science and human values', in his *Aspects of Scientific Explanation*, New York: The Free Press, 1965, p. 91.

6. The debate on race and intelligence is a very instructive example. To get to grips with some of its controversial issues, see, for example, R. Jacoby and N. Glauberman, *The Bell Curve Debate*, New York: Times Books, 1995; and M. J. A. Howe, *I. Q. in Question*, London: Sage, 1997.

7. K. Mannheim, *Ideology and Utopia*, London: Routledge, 1936 (2nd edn, Routledge, 1991).

8. M. Hesse, 'The strong thesis of sociology of science', in M. Hesse, *Revolutions and Reconstructions in the Philosophy of Science*, Brighton: Harvester Press, 1976, pp. 29–60.

9. See W. B. Gallie, 'Essentially contested concepts', *Proceedings of the Aristotelian Society*, LVI (1956), New Series.

10. Hesse, 'The strong thesis of sociology of science', p. 31.

11. Lakatos's dislike for sociological analyses of science, and more generally for sociological inquiry are renowned. See for instance: 'But the sociology of knowledge frequently serves as a successful cover for illiteracy . . . most sociologists of knowledge do not understand – or even care for – ideas.' I. Lakatos, 'Falsification and the methodology of scientific research programmes', in I. Lakatos and A. Musgrave (eds.), *Criticism and the Growth of Knowledge*, Cambridge: Cambridge University Press, 1970, p. 174, footnote 1; and 'one wonders whether the function of statistical techniques in the social sciences is not primarily to provide a machinery for producing phoney corroborations and thereby a semblance of intellectual progress where, in fact, there is nothing but an increase in pseudo-intellectual garbage.' Ibid., p. 176, footnote 1.

12. For an interesting discussion and analysis of the arguments for and against social constructivism see A. Kukla, *Social Constructivism and the Philosophy of Science*, London/New York: Routledge, 2000, especially chs 5–7.

13. On the 'science wars', see A. Ross (ed.) *Science Wars*, Durham NC/London: Duke University Press, 1996; N. Koertge, *A House Built on Sand*, Oxford: Oxford University Press, 1998; and K. M. Ashman and P. S. Baringer (eds.) *After the Science Wars*, London: Routledge, 2001. See also I. Hacking, *The Social Construction of What?*, Cambridge MA: Harvard University Press, 1999, ch. 1.

14. The pioneers of this critique are well known. As a reminder, see among others, P. Feyerabend, *Against Method*, London: New Left Books, 1975; and R. Rorty, *Philosophy and the Mirror of Nature*, Oxford: Blackwell, 1980. Both developed and radicalized Kuhn's views as argued in T. Kuhn, *The Structure of Scientific Revolutions*, Chicago: Chicago University Press, 1962, and T. Kuhn, *The Essential Tension*, Chicago: Chicago University Press, 1977.

15. The reference here is to the originators of the so-called 'strong programmes in the sociology of knowledge'. See for instance, D. Bloor, *Knowledge and Social Imagery*, London: Routledge and Kegan Paul, 1976.

16. There are various versions of the circle, as pointed out, for example, by J. Bohman, *New Philosophy of Social Science*, Cambridge: Polity Press, 1991, pp. 104–7, 113.

17. An example of how the argument works for natural science is S. Woolgar, *Science: The Very Idea*, Chichester: Ellis Horwood and Tavistock, 1988, chs 2 and 6. An example of how it works for social science is provided by some postmodernist ethnography, as described, for instance, in J. Clifford and G. Marcus (eds) *Writing Culture: The Poetics and Politics of Ethnography*, Berkeley: University of California Press, 1986. For a discussion of both, see Bohman, *New Philosophy of Social Science*, pp. 126–32.

18. Woolgar, *Science*, p. 30; quoted in Bohman, *New Philosophy of Social Science*, p. 131.

19. As mentioned above, the fact that similar successes are hard to achieve in social science casts doubt on social science rather than questioning the applicability of those methods outside the realm of natural science.

20. Positivism emerged in France in the first half of the nineteenth century, and only in the second half did it spread into other European countries, including England. Here it found a suitable ground in thinkers of empiricist inclination, such as J. S. Mill, and in those of a Darwinian descent, such as H. Spencer. See on this, entries on 'positivism' in J. Gould and W. L. Kolb (eds.), *A Dictionary of the*

Social Sciences, London: Tavistock, 1964; W. Outhwaite and T. Bottomore, *The Blackwell Dictionary of Twentieth-Century Social Thought*, Oxford/Cambridge, MA: Blackwell, 1992; A. Bullock and S. Trombley, *The Fontana Dictionary of Modern Thought*, London: Fontana Press, 1988. See also, T. Lawson, *Economics and Reality*, London/New York: Routledge, 1997a, pp. 292–3.

21. For Comte's law of the three stages of human development see A. Comte, *The Positive Philosophy*, Engl. abridged edn. London: Paul Chapman, 1853, vol 1, pp. 1–3. On Comte's view, see also Chapter 2, sect. 1.

22. That Mill echoed Comte's ideas is well documented by a correspondence between the two men. See O. A. Haac, *The Correspondence of John Stuart Mill and Auguste Comte*, New Brunswick: Transaction Publications, 1995. It is also well documented how Comte's ideas were better received, and far more debated, in England than in his native France. A good introduction to Comte's philosophy of science and sociology is K. Thompson, K. *Auguste Comte. The Foundation of Sociology*, London: Nelson, 1976.

23. 'It is by generalizing the methods successfully followed in the former enquiries [i.e. those which proved scientifically successful], and adapting them to the latter [i.e. the human sciences], that we may hope to remove this blot on the face of science.' The 'blot' refers to the fact that the human sciences never succeeded in establishing any considerable body of truths. See J. S. Mill, 'On the logic of the moral sciences', in his *A System of Logic*, ed. J. M. Robson and R. F. McRae, Toronto: Toronto University Press, 1974, Bk VI, Ch. I, p. 834.

24. Lukes rightly points out how *The Rules of Sociological Method* marks, in fact, a transition point in Durkheim's intellectual development. This work bears testimony to a developing concern, which was to become more explicit later on in Durkheim, on the role of 'collective representations' (concepts, values, beliefs) as independent explanatory variables. See S. Lukes, *Emile Durkheim, His Life and Work*, London: Penguin Books, 1992, p. 227. For the purpose of my discussion here, only the positivist aspects of Durkheim's *Rules* are referred to.

25. See E. Durkheim, *Suicide: A Study in Sociology*, Engl. trans. J. A. Spaulding and G. Simpson, London: Routledge, 1952. For a detailed discussion of this, see Chapter 2 below, section 4.

26. M. Weber, *The Methodology of the Social Sciences*, Engl. trans., New York: The Free Press, 1949, p. 76.

27. 'The problems of the empirical disciplines are, of course, to be solved "non-evaluatively". They are not problems of evaluation. But the problems of the social sciences are selected by the value-relevance of the phenomena treated. . . . the expression "relevance to value" refers simply to the philosophical interpretation of that specifically scientific "interest" which determines the selection of a given subject-matter and the problems of an empirical analysis.' Ibid., pp. 21–2.

28. G. Myrdal, *Value in Social Theory*, London: Routledge and Kegan Paul, 1958, pp. 132, 155.

29. G. Myrdal, *Objectivity in Social Research*, London: Duckworth, 1970, p. 71. See also G. Myrdal, 'How scientific are the social sciences?', The Gordon Allport Memorial lecture, Harvard University, 1971, Folio, LSE Library.

30. In Weber's own words, for example, social objects are 'ideal-types', in the sense that they are 'formed by the one-sided *accentuation* of one or more points of view and by the synthesis of a great many diffuse, discrete, more or less present and

Notes

occasionally absent concrete individual phenomena, which are arranged according to those one-sidedly emphasized viewpoints into a unified analytic
construct.' Weber, *Methodology of the Social Sciences*, p. 90.
31. On value-relevance, and its difference from 'value-judgement', see ibid., pp.
21–4.
32. G. Myrdal, *Objectivity in Social Research*, London: Duckworth, p. 52.
33. 'Introducing the subjective element into the analysis in fact increases the objectivity of the research and decreases the 'objectivism' which hides this kind of
evidence from the public.' S. Harding, *Feminism and Methodology*, Bloomington
IN: Indiana University Press, 1987, p. 9. What is meant here by 'subjective side'
is not simply a generic human being (or even worse, the philosophical construction of a subject of knowledge: a 'mind'), but a particular individual with a social
history, a biography, and – the feminists add – a gender.
34. As Fox-Keller reminds us, objectivity conceived along these lines can only lead
to 'objectivism' (i.e. a bad ideology of objectivity). What we need instead is a
dynamic view of objectivity, that is 'a pursuit of knowledge that makes use of
subjective experience . . . in the interest of a more effective objectivity.' E. Fox-
Keller, *Reflections on Gender and Science*, New Haven: Yale University Press,
1985, pp. 116–17.
35. H. Longino, *Science as Social Knowledge: Values and Objectivity in Scientific
Inquiry*, Princeton: Princeton University Press, 1990, p. 13.
36. Ibid., p. 102.
37. Ibid., p. 216.
38. See Bohman, *New Philosophy of Social Science*, pp. 121–3. Bohman's alternative
meaning of the concept of limit is part of a wider argument (a 'transcendental
argument for weak holism') aimed at denying that the 'hermeneutic circle' is
epistemologically vicious. For details of such an argument see Bohman, ibid.,
pp. 115–26.
39. See Chapter 1 in this volume.
40. As Geertz puts it in C. Geertz, *Local Knowledge*, New York: Basic Books, 1983,
p. 5. More on this view in Chapter 1.
41. Among 'weak' contextualists we find, besides Bohman, Searle, Davidson,
Habermas, Geertz and MacIntyre. This list is in Bohman, *New Philosophy of
Social Science*, p. 251, footnote 31.
42. Ibid., p. 253, footnote 41.
43. Ibid., p. 131.
44. For a discussion of this distinction see Hacking, *The Social Construction of What?*,
pp. 103–8.
45. Ibid., p. 105.
46. E.g., quarks in accelerators, or plutonium in reactors. Ibid., p. 105.
47. Ibid., pp. 103–4.
48. Ibid., p. 108.
49. Ibid., p. 104.
50. Ibid., p. 105.
51. R. Bhaskar, *The Possibility of Naturalism*, Brighton: The Harvester Press, 1979
(2nd edn. with new Introduction, London: Harvester Wheatsheaf, 1989).
Details of Bhaskar's idea of realist science can be found in R. Bhaskar, *A
Realist Theory of Science*, York: Alma Book Company, 1975. For details of the
critical-realist view and its relations with other philosophical perspectives,

see W. Outhwaite, *New Philosophies of Social Science: Realism, Hermeneutics and Critical Theory*, Basingstoke: Macmillan, 1987.

52. Bhaskar, *The Possibility of Naturalism*, p. 65.

53. Of course, Bhaskar's argument holds on the assumption that the comparison he develops between natural and social science, and the types of differences he infers from such comparison, are legitimate and relevant. In fact, this has been specifically denied. See, for example, T. Benton, 'Realism and social science. Some comments on Roy Bhaskar's "The Possibility of Naturalism"', *Radical Philosophy*, 27.

54. The inaugural event is normally taken to be the methodological dispute known as *Methodenstreit*. The historian Gustav Droysen initiated the dispute by arguing, in his *Grundriss der Historik* (Leipzig, Veit, 1875), against the positivist supporters of a science of society similar to a science of nature. He claimed that the object of historical inquiry was ontologically different from, and irreducible to, that of scientific inquiry. Historical experience (and by and large human experience) is intrinsically meaningful, and as such it is particular, non-generalizable, ultimately unique. Along similar lines, the neo-Kantian Windelband later developed what were to become a widely used methodological distinction between *nomothetic* sciences (of the like of physics and mathematics) and *ideographic* sciences (the historical and social sciences). As he explains in his 1894 'Geschichte und Naturwissenschaft', the former were aimed at the discovery of the laws of nature (in *Präludien. Aufsätze und Reden zur Philosophie und ihrer Geschichte*, 5th edn, Mohr, Tübingen), and at explaining the regularities of natural facts by means of those laws. The goal of the latter, instead, could only be that of understanding human behaviour and of social action, by interpreting their meaning. The distinction between the two types of 'science', and between their underlying 'logics' continued to develop well into the twentieth century, by opposing logical positivism on one side, and hermeneutical approaches on the other. For useful and clear reviews of these disputes, see G. H. Von Wright, *Explanation and Understanding*, London: Routledge and Kegan Paul, 1971; and W. Outhwaite, 'The philosophy of social science', in B. S. Turner (ed.), *The Blackwell Companion to Social Theory*, 2nd edn, Oxford: Blackwell, 2000.

55. See P. Winch, *The Idea of Social Science and its Relation to Philosophy*, 2nd edn, London: Routledge, 1990, p. 68.

56. Mill, *On the Logic of the Moral Sciences*, Bk VI, ch. III, pp. 844–5.

57. For a thorough review of Winch's work see C. Lyas, *Peter Winch*, Teddington: Acumen, 1999. For an interesting discussion of Winch's 'incompatibility thesis' see Bohman, *New Philosophy of Social Science*, pp. 60–61. P. Lassman has recently edited a special issue of *The History of the Human Sciences*, which contains articles on various aspects of Winch's work and on its implications for the practice of social science. See *Hist. Hum. Sci.*, 13:1 (2000) (with two additional articles in *Hist. Hum. Sci.* 13:2 (2000)). We return to Winch in Chapter 2.

58. N. Goodman, *Ways of Worldmaking*, Indianapolis: Hackett, 1978, p. 10.

59. J. Searle, *The Construction of Social Reality*, London: Penguin, 1995, p. 28.

60. Searle's widely quoted example is money: a green piece of paper stands for a one-dollar bill, in the context of a financial transaction.

61. Searle's own description of social constructivism amounts to the view that '"we" make the world, that reality itself is a social construct, alterable at will and subject to future changes as "we" see fit.' Searle, *The Construction of Social Reality*,

p. 158–9. It has been noted that this is a rather limited view of what social constructivism amounts to. In fact, various types of constructivists would not disagree with Searle's own position. For a discussion of Searle's position, see I. Hacking, 'Searle, Reality and the Social', *Hist. Hum. Sci.*, 10:4 (1997), p. 91. For how social constructivism might be reconciled with a position *à la* Searle, see, for example, B. Barnes, D. Bloor and J. Henry, *Scientific Knowledge: A Sociological Analysis*, London: Athlone Press, 1996, p. 88. See also B. Barnes, 'Searle on social reality: process is prior to product', in G. Grewendorf and G. Meggle (eds), *Speech Acts, Mind and Social Reality*, Dordrecht: Kluwer, 2001.

62. For a discussion of some of the downsides of reductionistic analyses of social objects of inquiry see J. Dupré, *Human Nature and the Limits of Science*, Oxford: Oxford University Press, 2001.

63. Hacking, *The Social Construction of What?*, p. 129.

64. 'The matrix in which the idea of the woman refugee is formed is a complex of institutions, advocates, newspaper articles, lawyers, court decisions, immigration proceedings. Not to mention the material infrastructure, barriers, passports, uniforms, counters at airports, detention centers, courthouses, holiday camps for refugee children.' Ibid., p. 10.

65. Although there are often many 'fuzzy edges' among them, or 'a number of different continua'. Ibid., p. 107.

66. 'One gets a grip on how a kind works only by studying it in some depth. A study of one kind may illuminate many others. But no matter how well chosen the example, it will serve only as a guide for understanding a group of kinds. It should never aim at being a model for all kinds. The motto is "motley".' Ibid., p. 131. The story of kind-making here recounted by Hacking is that of child abuse. Ibid., pp. 133–62.

67. On the history of the idea see, for example, L. Daston, 'Objectivity and the escape from perspective', *Social Studies of Science*, 22 (1992); and L. Daston and P. Galison, 'The image of objectivity', *Representations*, 40 (1992). On different meanings of 'objectivity', see A. Megill (ed.), *Rethinking Objectivity*, Durham/London: Duke University Press, 1994, Introduction.

68. Daston and Galison, 'The image of objectivity', p. 82.

69. In ancient Greek there is no word which stands for the concept of an 'object' as external to the mind of a 'subject', and to be represented as such by the mind itself (for instance, as an 'idea'). The Presocratics never raised the problem of 'objects' as referents of knowledge, and even in Plato – to whom we owe, as we read in all introductory manuals of epistemology, the first formulation of the question of knowledge: 'is knowledge justified true belief?' – we cannot find any term which stands for the generic word 'object'. All we can find are terms with a built-in reference to whatever an 'object' is an object of: '*aiothepa*' (objects of perception), or '*noeta*' (objects of thought).

70. In the post-Kantian tradition, these forms gradually shift from being a priori rules of the intellect to being contextual forms of knowledge, practically produced within the various disciplinary fields of inquiry. The shift is not of small consequence, as it develops in an anti-idealistic direction the Kantian view of the 'internal' criteria of knowledge. One obvious, contemporary example is M. Foucault's view of the emergence and 'constitution' of objects of inquiry as 'discursive formations', as in M. Foucault, *The Archeology of Knowledge*, Engl.

trans. New York: Pantheon, 1982. For an interesting discussion of how to define an object of inquiry, see Longino, *Science as Social Knowledge*, pp. 98–102. For an insightful analysis of the Kantian and neo-Kantian notion of form and its relation to the object of knowledge, see S. Borutti, *Filosofia delle scienze umane. Le categorie dell'Antropologia e della Sociologia*, Milan: B. Mondadori, 1999, pp. 88–9, 95–9.

Chapter 1: Anthropological Objects

1. E. Tylor, *Primitive Cultures*, 5th edn, London: John Murray, 1929, vol. I. p. 1
2. For example, and besides Tylor himself (1832–1917), Lewis Morgan (1818–81), and James Frazer (1854–1941). For a useful and concise introduction to the history of anthropological thought see P. A. Erickson, *A History of Anthropological Theory*, Peterborough: Broadview Press, 1998.
3. This comparison is not inappropriate, given that the effort of nineteenth- and early twentieth-century anthropologists was in large part aimed at emulating scientific methodology.
4. L. Holy, *Comparative Anthropology*, Oxford: Blackwell, 1987, pp. 3–4.
5. As Holy effectively sums up, anthropologists in the new paradigm move 'from a theory of anthropological facts as things to a theory of them as constructions'. Ibid., p. 5.
6. This approach originates in a diverse set of ideas about the concept of culture and the practice of anthropology. The label 'interpretive' lumps together a variety of sociological concepts, which come from Parsons and Weber, with a series of philosophical ideas, which come from diverse intellectual sources (phenomenology, structuralism, hermeneutics, semiotics and transformational linguistics, and the Frankfurt School of critical theory). See on this G. E. Marcus and M. M. J. Fisher, *Anthropology as Cultural Critique*, Chicago: Chicago University Press, 1986, pp. 25–6.
7. C. Geertz, *The Interpretation of Cultures*, New York: Basic Books, 1973, p. 5.
8. See G. Ryle, 'Thinking and Reflecting', and 'The Thinking of Thoughts', in his *Collected Papers*, London: Hutchinson, 1971.
9. Geertz, *The Interpretation of Cultures*, p. 10.
10. Ibid., p. 20.
11. Ibid., p. 15.
12. C. Geertz, *Local Knowledge*, New York: Basic Books, 1983, p. 10.
13. Geertz, *The Interpretation of Cultures*, p. 15.
14. Ibid., p. 5.
15. This case study is presented in ch. 15 of Geertz's *The Interpretation of Cultures*.
16. Ibid., p. 418.
17. Ibid., p. 432.
18. Ibid., p. 433.
19. Ibid., p. 437.
20. Ibid., p. 20.
21. Ibid., p. 452.
22. K. Dwyer, *Moroccan Dialogues. Anthropology in Question*, Baltimore: The Johns Hopkins University Press, 1982, p. 263.

23. B. Malinowski, *Argonauts of the Western Pacific: an Account of Native Enterprise and Adventure in the Archipelagoes of Melanesian New Guinea*, London: Routledge and Kegan Paul, 1922, p. 14.
24. D. Sperber, *On Anthropological Knowledge: Three Essays*, Engl. trans., Cambridge: Cambridge University Press, 1985, p. 10.
25. The Bocage is an area of Normandy (northern France). The people in that area speak a French regional dialect.
26. J. Favret-Sadat, *Deadly Words: Witchcraft in the Bocage*, Engl. trans., Cambridge: Cambridge University Press, 1980, p. 31.
27. Ibid., p. 11.
28. Ibid., pp. 11–12.
29. Ibid., pp. 9–10.
30. C. Geertz, *Works and Lives: The Anthropologist as Author*, Cambridge: Polity Press, 1988, p. 144.
31. See J. Clifford, *The Predicament of Culture: Twentieth-century Ethnography, Literature and Art*, Cambridge MA/London: Harvard University Press, 1988, Part 1, especially Ch. 2.
32 Sperber, *On Anthropological Knowledge*, p. 5.
33. Ibid., p. 6.
34. Ibid.
35. D. Sperber, *Explaining Culture: a Naturalistic Approach*, Oxford: Blackwell, 1996, p. 43.
36. Ibid., p. 18.
37. For a critical discussion of both structuralist and functionalist explanations in anthropology, see Sperber, *Explaining Culture*, pp. 43–9.
38. Sperber, *On Anthropological Knowledge*, p. 12.
39. Ibid., p. 14.
40. E. E. Evans-Pritchard, *Nuer Religion*, Oxford: Oxford University Press, 1956, quoted in Sperber, *On Anthropological Knowledge*, p. 14 [my underlining].
41. Sperber, *On Anthropological Knowledge*, p. 15.
42. Evans-Pritchard dedicates several chapters to discussing Nuer uses of the term in question.
43. Evans-Pritchard, *Nuer Religion*, p. 221; quoted in Sperber, *On Anthropological Knowledge*, p. 15.
44. Sperber, *On Anthropological Knowledge*, p. 16.
45. Ibid., p. 34.
46. Sperber, *Explaining Culture*, p. 20.
47. Ibid., p. 49–50.
48. Sperber, *On Anthropological Knowledge*, p. 34.
49. Sperber seems to subscribe to the traditional opposition between explanation and interpretation, and to the related view that the former is scientific because it is causal. However, he also appears to accept the more Weberian view that a full understanding of cultural phenomena should be both explanatory and interpretative. He acknowledges that our access to the object of anthropological inquiry is to some extent interpretive, but also claims that this does not prevent our account of it from being non-interpretive. If suitably identified, our object of inquiry can be investigated scientifically (i.e. empirically and causally).
50. Sperber, *Explaining Culture*, p. 36. On the practice of 'couvade' see, for example,

P. Menget, 'Time of birth, time of being: the couvade', in M. Izard and P. Smith (eds.), *Between Belief and Transgression: Structuralist Essays in Religion, History and Myth*, Chicago: University of Chicago Press, 1982, pp. 193–209; and P. Riviere, 'The Couvade: a problem reborn', *Man*, n.s. 9: 3 (1974) both quoted in Sperber, *Explaining Culture*, ibid. p. 36.

51. Sperber, *Explaining Culture*, pp. 51–2.
52. Ibid., p. 53.
53. Interesting work is done in the growing field of cognitive anthropology. See, for example, M. E. F. Bloch, *How we Think they Think*, Oxford: Westview Press, 1998; and R. Astuti, 'Are we all Natural Dualists? A Cognitive Developmental Approach', The Malinowski Memorial Lecture, London School of Economics, London: Mimeo, 2000. For a good historical account of the developments in the field of cognitive anthropology over the past thirty years, see R. D'Andrade, *The Development of Cognitive Anthropology*, Cambridge: Cambridge University Press, 1995.
54. See J. Fabian, *Time and the Work of Anthropology: Critical Essays 1971–1991*, Amsterdam: Harwood Academic Publishers, 1992, p. 208.
55. On Fabian's idea of objectivity, see ibid., pp. 9–21. Fabian's idea of 'objectification' has nothing to do with the pejorative sense often used (for example by some feminist writers) to draw attention to the fact that certain groups are perceived as mere things.

Chapter 2: Sociological Objects

1. See E. Durkheim, 'Debate on the relationship between ethnology and sociology', in S. Lukes (ed.), *Durkheim, The Rules of Sociological Method and Selected Texts on Sociology and its Method*, London: Macmillan, 1982a, pp. 209–10.
2. Comte named this 'the law of human development', or of 'human progress'. See A. Comte, *The Positive Philosophy*, Engl. abridged edn, London: Paul Chapman, vol 1, p. 2.
3. In the nineteenth century, it was widely believed that a science of society was indeed possible, as well as much needed. The most distinguished intellectuals of the time – Comte and Mill, but then also H. Spencer and E. Durkheim – were all drawn into a dream vision of creating the conditions for a 'social engineering', a science which would be able to control social conflict and predict social problems.
4. H. Hahn, O. Neurath and R. Carnap (1929), 'The scientific conception of the world: The Vienna Circle', in O. Neurath and R. S. Cohen (eds), *Empiricism and Sociology* Dordrecht: D. Reidel, 1973, p. 306.
5. O. Neurath, 'Empirical Sociology', in Neurath and Cohen, *Empiricism and Sociology*, p. 390.
6. Ibid., p. 415.
7. For details of this see the Introduction to this volume, note 53.
8. P. Winch, *The Idea of a Social Science and its Relation to Philosophy*, 2nd edn, London: Routledge, 1990, ch. 2. On Winch's interpretation of Weber's concept of meaningful action see ibid., pp. 116–20.
9. For Weber, the only way to deal with the 'objective' reason behind an action is

to treat it as its cause. This means that, in addition to the internal, or subjective description of an action (achieved by *Verstehen*, or interpretive, empathic understanding), an empirical method for verifying the initial interpretive hypothesis concerning that action, and for transforming it into an objective external motive, must also be put in place. As has been clearly summarized, in Weber 'sociological explanation begins when the observer attributes a motive to the agent, and ends when an empirical demonstration affords both that this was the motive and how it came to be so'. W. G. Runciman, *A Critique of Max Weber's Philosophy of Social Science*, London: Cambridge University Press, 1972, p. 43. It should perhaps also be noted here that Winch puts particular emphasis on the empiricist aspects of Weber's method, to the neglect of the Kantian aspects.

10. Rule-following is essentially a public practice, dependent on the essentially public character of language (meanings). It is on the basis of this view that Wittgenstein puts forward his well-known Private Language Argument, which is meant to prove the impossibility (logical impossibility) of the existence of a language invented by a single individual, and intelligible only to him. See, for example, Wittgenstein's discussion of the word 'pain', in L. Wittgenstein, *Philosophical Investigations*, ed. G E M. Anscombe, 3rd edn, Oxford: Blackwell, 1967, §§ 243–363.

11. So, for example, by appealing to commonly shared rules, we can establish that different actions have the same meaning. Besides, by the same appeal, we can establish whether actions are performed correctly (that is, in accordance with the rules). See Winch, *The Idea of Social Science*, pp. 31–3, 58.

12. In this and the following section I make use of material which first appeared in my 'Sociologie', in S. Borutti, *Filosofia delle scienze umane. Le categorie dell'Antropologia e della Sociologia*, Milan: B. Mondadori, 1999, Part III.

13. As Craib reminds us, there are stories of people being fired from academic jobs for being and acting like ethnomethodologists. See I. Craib, *Modern Social Theory*, 2nd edn, New York/London: Harvester Wheatsheaf, 1992.

14. The same applies to the idea of a social actor. The ethnomethodologists endorsed A. Schutz's assessment of what social actors amount to in sociological models: 'These models of actors [in traditional sociology] are not human beings living within their biographical situation in the social world of everyday life. Strictly speaking, they do not have any biography or any history, and the situation into which they are placed is not a situation defined by them but defined by their creator, the social scientist. He has created these puppets or homunculi to manipulate them for his purpose. Etc.' A. Schutz, *Collected Papers I: The Problem of Social Reality*, 6th edn, Dordrecht/Boston/London: Kluwer, 1990, p. 41.

15. See, for this example, Craib, *Modern Social Theory*, pp. 102–3.

16. Giddens rightly reminds us that Pierce was the first to use the expression 'indexical sign' to draw attention to the fact that the same word might acquire different meanings in different contexts. Most of the expressions used in ordinary discourse are indexical, and the ethnomethodologists take this to mean that 'such expressions are the very stuff out of which social activity is organised by its members as a practical accomplishment'. See A. Giddens, *New Rules of Sociological Method: A Positive Critique of Interpretativist Sociologies*, London: Hutchinson, 1976, pp. 36–7.

17. As adopted in much conversational analysis. For a description and discussion

of this model of explanation, see J. Bohman, *New Philosophy of Social Science*, Cambridge: Polity Press, 1991, pp. 79–80.

18. H. Garfinkel and H. Sacks, 'On Formal Structures of Practical Actions', in J. C. McKinney, and E. A. Tiryakian (eds), *Theoretical Sociology*, New York: Appleton-Century-Crofts, 1970, pp. 345–6.

19. H. Garfinkel, *Studies in Ethnomethodology*, Englewood Cliffs, NJ: Prentice Hall, 1967, p. 78.

20. The reference to Garfinkel is in G. Button (ed.), *Ethnomethodology and the Human Sciences*, Cambridge: Cambridge University Press, 1991, p. 7. On the heterogeneous nature of ethnomethodology as a way of sociological inquiry see ibid., pp. 139–40.

21. For a comparison between ethnomethodological 'documents' and anthropological 'texts' see E. Montuschi, 'Metaphor in social science', *Theoria*, 25 (1996).

22. The natives' village for the anthropologist is 'the field': that is, it is not just what it is, but rather what it becomes when put under anthropological scrutiny. Similarly, a classroom is not as such a sociological object of inquiry. It becomes so when it is observed 'in sociological terms', whatever this might mean.

23. This, as we will see in the final section, becomes particularly important in the analysis of how certain social phenomena, e.g. suicides and suicide rates, are identified and classified.

24. See for example, W. Sharrock, and G. Button, 'The social actor: social action in real time', in Button, *Ethnomethodology*, p. 146.

25. See for instance C. Robson, *Real World Research*, Oxford: Blackwell, 1993.

26. As, for example, in D. P. Forcese and S. Richer (eds), *Stages of Social Research*, Englewood Cliffs: Prentice Hall, 1970.

27. See for example, J. Roth, 'Hired hand research', *American Sociologist*, I (1965); R. Harré, *Social Being*, Oxford: Blackwell, 1979, pp. 113–16.

28. Harré, *Social Being*, p. 106.

29. Ibid.

30. Ibid., p. 107.

31. For a description and comment on this experiment see Harré, *Social Being*, ch. 6; and A. Rosenberg, *Philosophy of Social Science*, Oxford: Clarendon Press, 1988, ch. 7.

32. S. Milgram, *Obedience to Authority: An Experimental View*, London: Tavistock, 1974.

33. See Harré, *Social Being*, p. 105.

34. M. Root, *Philosophy of Social Science*, Oxford: Blackwell, 1993, p. 132.

35. For interesting and informative discussions of social scientific methods of analysis see the following: D. Silverman, *Interpreting Qualitative Data*, London: Sage, 1993; U. Flick, *An Introduction to Qualitative Research*, London: Sage, 1998; C. Raging, *The Comparative Method: Moving Beyond Qualitative and Quantitative Strategies*, Berkeley: University of California Press, 1987; T. R. Black, *Doing Quantitative Research in the Social Sciences: An Integrated Approach to Research Design, Measurement and Statistics*, London: Sage, 1998; M. S. Lewis-Beck, *Experimental Design and Methods* (International Handbooks of Quantitative Applications in the Social Sciences, vol. 3), London: Sage, 1993.

36. In the second edition of his *Social Being* Harré offers a more extensive and detailed analysis of the role and use of these models as methodological tools of

social investigation. See R. Harré, *Social Being*, 2nd edn, Oxford: Blackwell, 1993, chs 5 and 6.

37. Harré, *Social Being*, 2nd edn, pp. 148–61. For Goffman's own analysis, see E. Goffman, *The Presentation of Self in Everyday Life*, London: Penguin, 1969; and E. Goffman, *Frame Analysis*, Cambridge MA: Harvard University Press, 1974.

38. On the case study method, see, for example, R. K. Yin, *Case Study Research. Design and Method*, 2nd edn, Beverly Hills: Sage, 1994. See also B. Flyvbjerg, *Making Social Science Matter. Why Social Inquiry Fails and How it Can Succeed Again*, Cambridge: Cambridge University Press, 2001, ch. 6.

39. N. Gilbert (ed.), *Researching Social Life*, London: Sage, 1993, p. 329.

40. C. Bazerman, *Shaping Written Knowledge*, Madison: University of Wisconsin Press, 1988, p. 5.

41. This is what also happens in ordinary conversations, and this is why sometimes the two kinds of activities have been studied in parallel. See on this L. Van Langenhove and R. Harré, 'Positioning in scientific discourse', in R. Harré (ed.), *Science and Rhetoric, Anglo-Ukrainian Studies in the Analysis of Scientific Discourse*, Lampeter: The Edwin Mellen Press, 1993.

42. Robson, *Real World Research*, pp. 418–19.

43. With the publication of the 'Instructions in Regard to Preparation of Manuscript', which appeared in the *Psychological Bulletin*, in February 1929, the 'official style' for writing experimental science was first codified. See Bazerman, *Shaping Written Knowledge*, pp. 259–61.

44. Ibid., p. 260.

45. Ibid., p. 265.

46. H. Sacks, 'Sociological description', *Berkeley Journal of Sociology*, 8 (1963), p. 8.

47. E. Durkheim, *Suicide: A Study in Sociology*, Engl. trans. J. A. S. Spaulding and G. Simpson, London: Routledge, 1952, p. 44.

48. Previously dealt with as a moral problem (eighteenth century), suicide had become in the nineteenth century a specifically social problem, and it was treated as one in need of sociological explanation. A series of statistical studies, the formulation of suicide rates, and several inquiries into the possible social determinants of types of suicides were then pursued in different European countries. Durkheim's own study was then, among other things, an attempt to provide a systematic framework and a theoretical synthesis for the very many ideas, explanatory hypotheses and comparative studies produced by his predecessors and his contemporaries. See J. D. Douglas, *The Social Meanings of Suicide*, Princeton: Princeton University Press, 1967, pp. 3–12; and S. Lukes, *Emile Durkheim, His Life and Work*, London: Penguin, 1992, pp. 191–2.

49. '[The] suicide-rate is . . . a factual order, unified and definite, as is shown by both its permanence and its variability. For this permanence would be inexplicable if it were not the result of a group of distinct characteristics, solidary one with another, and simultaneously effective in spite of different attendant circumstances: and this variability proves the concrete and individual quality of these same characteristics, since they vary with the individual character of society itself. In short, what these statistical data express is the suicidal tendency with which each society is collectively afflicted.' See Durkheim, *Suicide*, p. 51.

50. S. Turner, *The Search for a Methodology of Social Science*, Dordrecht/Boston MA: D. Reidel, 1986, pp.152–6.
51. E. Durkheim, *The Rules of Sociological Method*, in Lukes, *Durkheim, Rules of Sociological Method*, p. 76.
52. '[Suicide] varies inversely with the degree of integration (regulation) of the social groups of which the individual forms a part.' Durkheim, *Suicide*, p. 209. For an analysis of how specifically social causes of suicide can be discovered, and for a description of the model of explanation of suicide rates, see Lukes, *Emile Durkheim*, pp. 213–17.
53. See for example, besides Douglas, *Social Meanings of Suicide*, J. Atkinson, *Discovering Suicide: Studies in the Social Organization of Sudden Death*, London: Macmillan, 1978; A. Cicourel, *Method and Measurement in Sociology*, New York: The Free Press, 1964; B. Hindess, *The Use of Official Statistics in Sociology*, London: Macmillan, 1973.
54. Harré, *Social Being*, p. 114, 1st edn.
55. Douglas goes as far as claiming that 'suicides cannot correctly be said to exist (i.e. to be 'things') until a categorization has been made'. See Douglas, *Social Meanings of Suicide*, p. 196, footnote 40.
56. '[A] reconstruction of the victim's biography ... is itself a process of social negotiation, not the construction of an objective record of the past.' Harré, *Social Being*, p. 114, 1st edn.
57. Durkheim, *The Rules of Sociological Method*, S. Luke (ed.) (1982), p. 76.
58. As Alfred Schutz famously expressed, social actors in traditional sociology appear to be nothing but 'puppets', fictitious characters deprived of their biographies and of their social and historical identity. See note 14 in this chapter.
59. Lukes, *Emile Durkheim*, p. 221. By his own admission, Durkheim often finds it difficult to keep the definition of social facts separate from the individual level. 'It is often hard', he writes, 'to say where the individual ends and the social commences'. He also recognizes that no amount of social pressure would make individuals who are not 'suicide-prone', commit the act. See Durkheim (1952), p. 313, footnote 11.
60. Against the excessive distrust of officially produced numerical data, see, for example M. Blumer, 'Why don't sociologists make more use of official statistics?', in M. Blumer (ed.), *Sociological Research Methods*, 2nd edn, London: Macmillan.
61. See Hacking's view, as discussed in the Introduction to this volume, sect. 3.

Chapter 3: Historical Objects

1. For a historical reconstruction of these two developments within analytic philosophy see G. H. Von Wright, *Explanation and Understanding*, London: Routledge and Kegan Paul, 1971, Part 1.
2. For a description of this model, see C. Hempel, *Aspects of Scientific Explanation*, New York: The Free Press, 1965a, pp. 335–47.
3. Both types of statement are necessary and sufficient conditions for the occurrence of an explanandum event – although, the necessity of the statement containing the initial conditions is, so to speak, subservient to the general law, in that

it is meant to make the law applicable to the specific event that it is asked to cover.

4. C. Hempel, 'Explanation in science and history', in R. G. Colodny (ed.), *Frontiers of Science and Philosophy*, Pittsburgh: University of Pittsburgh Press, 1962, p. 13. Both claims are highly contentious, but we do not need to enter any critical discussion on this issue here.
5. Hempel, *Aspects*, p. 412.
6. Ibid., pp. 415–25.
7. Ibid., p. 447.
8. Hempel's two-step argument is then built on a strong normative assumption, in the sense described in the Introduction: once the paradigmatic model for a correct explanation is fixed, any explanation which aims at being correct should follow this model.
9. Hempel, 'Explanations in science and history', p. 18. Hempel suggests referring to laws as 'universal hypotheses' to point out that the issue of satisfactory empirical confirmation can be stated separately. See Hempel, *Aspects*, p. 231.
10. Hempel, *Aspects*, p. 236.
11. See Scriven, 'Truisms and the grounds for historical explanation', in P. L. Gardiner (ed.), *Theories of History*, New York: The Free Press, 1959, pp. 454–55.
12. Ibid.
13. W. Dray, *Laws and Explanation in History*, Oxford: Clarendon Press, p. 124
14. Ibid., p. 132.
15. Hempel, *Aspects*, p. 471. For 'Schema R' see ibid.
16. Ibid., p. 453.
17. Ibid., p. 241.
18. Ibid., p. 455.
19. W. Dray, 'Explaining "what" in history', in P. L. Gardiner (ed.), *Theories of History*, pp. 404–5.
20. Ibid., p. 406.
21. Hempel, *Aspects*, p. 447.
22. Quoted by Hempel from H. Bohemer, *Luther and the Reformation in the Light of Modern Research*, Engl. trans., New York: The Dial Press, 1930. See Hempel, *Aspects*, p. 447, footnote 1.
23. Hempel, *Aspects*, pp. 448–9.
24. Ibid., p. 451.
25. Ibid., p. 449.
26. Ibid., p. 423.
27. Hempel gets close to this view when he admits that an explanation can only be said to be complete with respect to the specific description of the concrete event it purports to explain (a view that he claims to share with Weber). See Hempel, *Aspects*, p. 422.
28. A. C. Danto, *Analytic Philosophy of History*, Cambridge: Cambridge University Press, 1965, p. 218.
29. See ibid., p. 221.
30. See on this P. A. Roth, 'Narrative Explanations: the case of history', in M. Martin and L. C. McIntyre (eds), *Readings in the Philosophy of Social Science*, Cambridge MA/London: The MIT Press, 1994, p. 706.

31. Danto, *Analytic Philosophy*, p. 151.
32. F. Furet, *Interpreting the French Revolution*, Engl. trans., Cambridge: Cambridge University Press, 1981.
33. Roth, 'Narrative Explanations', p. 708.
34. Furet, *Interpreting the French Revolution*, p. 22.
35. A. Callinicos, *Theories as Narratives: Reflections on the Philosophy of History*, Cambridge: Polity Press, 1995, p. 76.
36. See F. Furet, 'Quantitative methods in history', in J. Le Goff and P. Nora (eds), *Constructing the Past: Essays in Historical Methodology*, Engl. trans., Cambridge: Cambridge University Press, 1985, pp. 15–18.
37. Callinicos, *Theories as Narratives*, p. 76.
38. Quoted by Callinicos from Lucien Febvre's inaugural lecture at the Collège de France in 1933. See Callinicos, *Theories as Narratives*, p. 75 and footnote 94.
39. Furet, 'Quantitative methods in history', p. 18.
40. Ibid., p. 20.
41. F. Furet and J. Ozouf, *Reading and Writing: Literacy in France from Calvin to Jules Ferry*, Engl. trans., Cambridge: Cambridge University Press, 1982.
42. Evidence for this discovery is presented in ibid. by means of a series of cross-related graphs and tables. On this form of presentation, and on this way of conducting research, see also P. Burke, *The French Historical Revolution: The Annales School 1929–1989*, Cambridge: Polity Press, 1990, p. 77.
43. Furet and Ozouf, *Reading and Writing*, pp. 302–3.
44. Ibid., p. 303.
45. Ibid., p. 4.
46. For criticisms of quantitative history see Burke, *The French Historical Revolution*, pp. 79ff.
47. Le Goff, *Constructing the Past*, p. 166.
48. These are some of the expressions used as synonyms of 'mentality' in Le Goff's major contribution to the history of mentalities, that is his study of the medieval imagination. See J. Le Goff, *The Birth of Purgatory*, Engl. trans., London: Scolar Press, 1984.
49. The precursors of this type of historical research are M. Bloch and L. Febvre. See M. Bloch, *Feudal Society*, Engl. trans., London: Routledge and Kegan Paul, 1961, especially Part I, Bk II; and L. Febvre, *The Problem of Unbelief in the Sixteenth century, The Religion of Rabelais*, Engl. trans., Cambridge MA: Harvard University Press, 1985. In a similar style, though in the English tradition, see, for example, W.J. Brandt, *The Shape of Medieval History: Studies in Modes of Perception*, New Haven: Yale University Press, 1966; W.E. Houghton, *The Victorian Frame of Mind*, New Haven: Yale University Press, 1957.
50. This, as Peter Burke points out, is what makes this style of history so difficult to accept for British historians, brought up in the tradition of empiricism and methodological individualism. A collective mentality, i.e. a collective mind, appears to them as a fictitious entity, which is too ambiguous to be used confidently as an explanatory tool (there are only really individuals who think!). See on this P. Burke, 'Reflections on the historical revolution in France: The Annales School and British Social History', in S. Clark (ed.), *The Annales School. Critical Assessments*, vol. II, London: Routledge, 1999.

51. See M. Vovelle, *Piété baroque et déchristianisation en Provence au XVIIIe siecle*, Paris: Plon, 1973.
52. Burke, *The French Historical Revolution*, p. 291.
53. Ibid.
54. Ibid.
55. J. Barzun and H. F. Graff, *The Modern Researcher*, 5th edn, Fort Worth: Harcourt Brace Jovanovich College Publishers, 1992, p. 134.
56. Ibid., p. 137.
57. G. Kavanagh, 'Making histories, making memories', in G. Kavanagh (ed.), *Making Histories in Museums*, London: Leicester University Press, 1996. There is indeed a sense in which physical objects can be treated as condensed 'texts', and are indeed treated as such by historians. Coins are a most suitable example. Gareth Williams (British Museum, London) tells me that, compared to manuscripts, or other forms of written evidence, coins have a potential advantage: the information they reveal goes back to the time when they were produced. A manuscript might be written years after the events it describes. This, nonetheless, does not make the historian's work of 'reading' a coin any easier, as it does not detract from the fact that coins are physical objects open to many interpretations.
58. For Kavanagh, this is the most standard kind of historical object, which can be found in most museum collections. See Kavanagh, 'Making histories, making memories', p. 6.
59. Ibid., p. 7.
60. See S. Schaffer, 'Object lessons', in S. Lindqvist (ed.), *Museums of Modern Science*, New York: Science History Publications, 2000, pp. 61–2.
61. See K. Arnold, 'Time heals: making history in medical museums', in Kavanagh (ed.), *Making Histories in Museums*, 1996.
62. Arnold, 'Time heals', p. 17. See on this also, P. Findlen, *Possessing Nature: Museums, Collecting and Scientific Culture in Early Modern Italy*, Berkeley: University of California Press, 1994.
63. Arnold, 'Time heals'. In these museums, anatomical dissections took place, theories on fossils were tested, or the magic of loadstone was explored. Museums became actual 'theatres of experiments', which 'allowed early curators to marshal their objects into facts that served a particular purpose'. See ibid, pp. 17–18.
64. As in the case of the 'Health Matters' Gallery in the Science Museum in London, where the emphasis is put on the social, political and technological aspects of the modern growth of medicine in Britain. Ibid., p. 22.
65. As in the 'Science for life' exhibition at the Wellcome Centre for Medical Science, London. As part of this exhibition, Arnold draws our attention to an interactive machine which prompts the viewer to discover the causes of a mysterious disease. This serves the purpose to make people acknowledge the role of luck in medical research, as well as to simulate the sense of frustration consequent to failure. Ibid., p. 23.
66. This was pointed out to me by Gareth Williams.
67. For the history of this function, see, for example, A. S. Wittlin, *The Museum: Its History and its Tasks in Education*, London: Routledge and Kegan Paul, 1949. For an analysis of the educational aspects of museums (visual communication and

learning) see E. Hooper-Greenhill, *Museums and the Interpretation of Visual Culture*, London: Routledge, 2000.
68. L. Jordanova, 'Objects of knowledge: A historical perspective on museums', in P. Vergo (ed.), *The New Museology*, London: Reaktion Books, 1989, p. 33.
69. Ibid., pp. 32–3.
70. Jordanova takes the practical difficulties concerning what to include and how to exhibit across the vast majority of anthropological and scientific museums as evidence of a 'deeper uncertainty as to what it is possible to learn from museum objects'. Ibid., pp. 39–40. On the educational relation between museums and types of audience and the social function of this relation, see also T. Bennett, 'Speaking to the eyes. Museums, legibility and the social order', in S. Macdonald (ed.), *The Politics of Display*, London/New York: Routledge, 1998.
71. Schaffer, 'Object lessons', pp. 61–2.

Chapter 4: Economic Objects

1. D. McCloskey, *The Rhetoric of Economics*, Brighton: Harvester Press, 1986, p. 3. Further developments of McCloskey's rhetorical view of economic discourse can be found, for example, in D. McCloskey, *If You're so Smart. The Narrative of Economic Expertise*, Chicago/London: The University of Chicago Press, 1990; D. McCloskey, *Knowledge and Persuasion in Economics*, Cambridge: Cambridge University Press, 1994.
2. McCloskey, *The Rhetoric of Economics*, p. 3.
3. Quite radically, McCloskey argues that the conversion to, and consequent faith in, the mathematical way of talking has produced a generation of economists (at least at the time when McCloskey first published her book) who are, by and large, 'bored by history, ignorant of their civilization, disdainful of other social scientists, thoughtless in ethics, and unreflective in method'. Ibid., p. 7.
4. M. Friedman, 'The methodology of positive economics', in his *Essays in Positive Economics*, Chicago/London: Chicago University Press, 1953.
5. Iconoclastic ideas in Friedman's essays could be seen as corrections and improvements on the modernist view underlying the image of positive economics, rather than tools for radical criticism. In this, he appears to be a 'transitional' figure – a bit like Popper, McCloskey suggests. See McCloskey, *The Rhetoric of Economics*, pp. 9–10.
6. Friedman, 'The methodology of positive economics', p. 4.
7. In a footnote, Friedman for example claims: 'The interaction between the observer and the process observed ... has a ... subtle counterpart in the indeterminacy principle arising out of the interaction between the process of measurement and the phenomena being measured. And both have a counterpart in pure logic in Godel's theorem, asserting the impossibility of a comprehensive self-contained logic.' Ibid., p. 5, footnote 3.
8. McCloskey discusses the role and significance of statistics in econometrics in ch. 8 of her *The Rhetoric of Economics*.
9. M. Blaug, *The Methodology of Economics or How Economists Explain*, Cambridge: Cambridge University Press, 1980, p. xii; also quoted in McCloskey, *The Rhetoric of Economics*, p. 21.

10. McCloskey, *The Rhetoric of Economics*, p. 36.
11. McCloskey discusses the meaning of the term 'rhetoric' in ibid., pp. 29–30. For the good and the bad image of rhetoric, see also E. Montuschi, 'Persuading science: the art of scientific rhetoric', *The British Journal for the Philosophy of Science*, 45 (1994); and E. Montuschi, 'Rhetorical aspects of scientific arguments', in R. Harré (ed.), *Reason and Rhetoric*, Lewiston: The Mellen Press, 1993.
12. McCloskey, *The Rhetoric of Economics*, p. 36.
13. *The Rhetoric of Economics* can be ideally divided in two parts. One part explains what a 'rhetorical analysis' of economic discourse amounts to. The other shows in practice how this type of analysis works in concrete instances of economic discourse. For 'rhetorical' reasons, McCloskey decided to invert the order of the chapters in the second edition of the book (as she explains in the Preface to the second edition, 1998), so that the applied part comes before the more philosophical (and less appealing, at least to traditional economists) one. All the quotations from *The Rhetoric of Economics* in this chapter are from the first edition.
14. Ibid., p. 58.
15. Ibid., p. 59.
16. For the complete list, see ibid., pp. 59–60.
17. It might be objected that each of these 'reasons' could be interpreted in terms of economic behaviour, and be processed by mathematical language. What McCloskey wants to point out here, however, is not so much their translatability into ordinary economic language, as their persuasive edge and function.
18. Mark Blaug disagrees with McCloskey's interpretation. In the Preface to the second edition of his *The Methodology of Economics* he writes: 'No doubt, there are many reasons for believing that demand curves are negatively inclined but there is little doubt that if statistical evidence repeatedly ran the other way, none of these reasons would suffice to make economists believe in the "law of demand".' See Blaug, *The Methodology of Economics*, Cambridge: Cambridge University Press, 1992, p. xx. This might indeed say something about what language economists find most 'persuasive', according to McCloskey's perspective.
19. See A. H. Genberg, 'Aspects of the monetary approach to the balance-of-payments theory: an empirical study', and D. McCloskey and J. R. Zecher, 'How the gold standard worked, 1880–1913', both in J. A. Frenkel and H. G. Johnson (eds), *The Monetary Approach to the Balance of Payments*, London: Allen and Unwin, 1976.
20. McCloskey, *The Rhetoric of Economics*, p. 145.
21. J. L. Austin, *How to Do Things with Words*, 2nd edn, Cambridge MA: Harvard University Press, 1975, p. 52, quoted in McCloskey, *The Rhetoric of Economics*, p. 151.
22. McCloskey, *The Rhetoric of Economics*, p. 153. For another example of how to dress economic arguments concerning human behaviour with numbers, and the rhetorical dangers related to mathematical exposition, see Dupré's discussion of Becker's *Treatise on the Family*, in J. Dupré, *Human Nature and the Limits of Science*, Oxford: Oxford University Press, 2001, pp. 133–5.
23. McCloskey, *The Rhetoric of Economics*, p. 47.
24. As an example of such clear intolerance Lawson quotes Hahn: 'Methodology like original sin won't go away, and Backhouse is right in saying that I myself

have sinned. Perhaps it would have been better if I had not . . . What I really wanted to advise the young to do was to avoid spending much time and thought on it. As for them learning philosophy, whatever next?' See F. Hahn, 'Answer to Backhouse: Yes', *Royal Economics Society Newsletter*, 78 (1992), quoted in T. Lawson, *Economics and Reality*, London/New York: Routledge, 1997a, p. 12.

25. Lawson, *Economics and Reality*, p. 45.
26. Ibid., p. 41.
27. This view, the realists claim, is based on the mistaken belief that statements about beings are reducible to statements about the knowledge we have (or acquire) of them. See ibid., p. 33 for a description of the fallacy. For the original formulation of the fallacy, see R. Bhaskar, *A Realist Theory of Science*, York: Alma Book Company, 1975, p. 36.
28. Lawson, *Economics and Reality*, p. 40.
29. Ibid., p. 63. For a concise version of Lawson's critical realist view of economics, see T. Lawson, 'Economics as a distinct social science: on the nature, scope and method of economics', *Economie Appliquée*, L:2 (1997b). Lawson's view is explicitly reminiscent of Bhaskar's version of critical realism. For a description of Bhaskar's realist model of social objects of inquiry see the Introduction to this volume, sect. 3.
30. B. Stafford, 'The Class Struggle, the Multiplier and the Alternative Economic Strategy', in M. Sawyer and K. Schott (eds), *Socialist Economic Review*, London: Merlin Press, 1983. For a discussion of this case study, see Lawson, *Economics and Reality*, pp. 255–8.
31. Sebastiano Bavetta tells me that a similar situation occurs in the literature concerning the measurement of freedom. Despite the impression, often created by the contributions to the debate, that the various models of measurement are all measuring 'the same thing', it can be shown that each model in fact creates its own definition of freedom by focusing on certain questions; as explained, for example, in his 'Measuring Freedom: a review of the axiomatic and the statistical approaches', London: Mimeo, 2001.
32. Lawson, *Economics and Reality*, p. 256. A similar explanation can be found, more recently than Stafford's, in M.W. Kirby, 'Institutional rigidities and economic decline: reflections on the British experience', *Economic History Review*, XLV:4 (1992), quoted in Lawson, *Economics and Reality*, p. 330, n14.
33. Lawson, *Economics and Reality*, p. 268. He refers here to the view of P. Kennedy, 'British Economic Decline: Bourgeois Methodology versus Marxism', Glasgow: Mimeo, 1993.
34. Lawson, *Economics and Reality*, p. 263.
35. Of course, this is itself an assessment which depends on 'context and availability of relevant evidence': 'there is always the possibility of further hypotheses being proposed whose comparable empirical adequacy will then require examination.' Ibid, p. 270.
36. For a more detailed description of the nature and substance of this explanation see T. Lawson and A. Kilpatrick, 'On the nature of industrial decline in the UK', *Cambridge Journal of Economics*, 4 (1980), reprinted in D. Coates and J. Hillard (eds), *The Economic Decline of Modern Britain*, London: Harvester Press, 1986.
37. Lawson, *Economics and Reality*, p. 257.

38. Ibid.
39. Ibid., p. 259.
40. Ibid., p. 270.
41. For these details, see ibid., pp. 259–67.
42. Ibid., p. 244.
43. 'An ideal-type is formed by the one-sided *accentuation* of one or more points of view and by the synthesis of a great many diffuse, discrete, more or less present and occasionally absent concrete individual phenomena, which are arranged according to those one-sidedly emphasized viewpoints into a unified analytic construct. . . . [It] cannot be found empirically anywhere in reality.' See M. Weber, *The Methodology of the Social Sciences*, Engl. trans., New York: The Free Press, 1949, p. 90.
44. This arguably holds also in the case of McCloskey. To study the rhetorical construction of economic discourse seems only to deny that what economics talks about could be assessed *independently of* the purposes and interests of those engaged in some discourse. As for the issue of realism, McCloskey simply brackets it, or sets it aside – though, by quoting W. Barrett, she specifies that 'bracketing . . . is not identical with the epistemological doubt whether the object really exists'. See McCloskey, *Knowledge and Persuasion*, p. 205. The quotation is from W. Barrett, *The Illusion of Technique: A Search for Meaning in a Technological Civilization*, Garden City, NY: Anchor, 1979, p. 129.
45. McCloskey, *Knowledge and Persuasion*, p. 211.
46. Ibid., p. 212.
47. Lawson, *Economics and Reality*, p. 240.
48. Ibid., p. 228.
49. Ibid., p. 232.
50. However, the idea of models as closed systems can also be used to criticize a positivistic regularity view. In fact, it can show how regularities are not fundamental, but they can only be 'a consequence of the repeated successful running of a socio-economic machine' (meaning a model). In other words, regularities do not precede, but are generated under, the *ceteris paribus* conditions set out by a model. Against the positivistic view that regularities are fundamental, and that they can run on their own, regularities are instead taken to be derivative of a stable and well-functioning configuration of components as assembled in a machine-model. See N. Cartwright, *The Dappled World*, Cambridge: Cambridge University Press, 1999, ch. 6.
51. Lawson, *Economics and Reality*, p. 165.
52. R. Rosser and P. Kind, 'A scale of valuations of states of illness: is there a social consensus?', *International Journal of Epidemiology*, 7:4 (1978); and P. Kind, R. Rosser and A. Williams, 'Valuation of quality of life: some psychometric evidence', in M. W. Jones-Lee (ed.), *The Value of Life and Safety*, Leiden: North Holland Publishing, 1982. Tables 4.1 and 4.2 reproduced below are both taken from A. Edgar, 'Measuring the quality of life', in P. Badham and P. Ballard (eds), *Facing Death: An Interdisciplinary Approach*, Cardiff: University of Wales Press, 1996. For a discussion of Rosser and Kind's model see E. Montuschi, 'Measuring life and choosing death: moral, empirical and social aspects of euthanasia', London: Mimeo, 2000.

53. For a discussion of some of the questions raised by qalys, see, besides Edgar, 'Measuring the quality of life', also J. Broome, 'Qalys', in his *Ethics out of Economics*, Cambridge: Cambridge University Press, 1999.

54. Consider, for example, the 'irreversible loss of the higher-brain functions' often suggested, in legal debates, to be a criterion for deciding whether an individual is effectively dead. On this debate, see J. Lizza, 'Persons and death: what's metaphysically wrong with our current statutory definition of death?', *Journal of Medicine and Philosophy*, 18:4 (1993).

Chapter 5: Geographical Objects

1. P. Haggett, *The Geographer's Art*, Oxford: Blackwell, 1990, p. 8.

2. R. Hartshorne, *Perspectives on the Nature of Geography*, Chicago: Rand McNally, 1959, p. 21. It must be noted that Hartshorne's definition is far from being generally representative of what geography should concern itself with, as we will soon realize. It rather reflects the preoccupations of the 1950s geographers with adopting quantitative methods and attempting to discover universal spatial laws. This was in part a reaction to geographers' earlier concern with the uniqueness of places on the Earth's surface, and with the identification of particular *regions*. See on this P. Cloke, C. Philo and D. Sadler, *Approaching Human Geography*, London: Paul Chapman, 1991, pp. 6–7.

3. The first to use the word was Erathostenes (3rd century BC), although geographic questions started being investigated long before him, for example by Homer. The first known map is due to the Sumerians (2700 BC), even before Homer's time.

4. P. Haggett, 'Geography', in R. J. Johnston, D. Gregory and D. M. Smith (eds), *The Dictionary of Human Geography*, Oxford: Blackwell, 1994, p. 221. See also R.J. Johnston, *Philosophy and Human Geography*, London: Arnold, 1986, ch. 1. On the identification of its own subject matter, and for its position among the academic disciplines, see A. Holt-Jensen, *Geography. History and Concepts*, London: Sage, 1999, ch. 1; and ch. 2, especially pp. 30–34.

5. Haggett, 'Geography and Human Geography', p. 221.

6. Johnston concedes that not only positivist geographers make use of quantitative methods; nevertheless, 'much research using quantitative methods in human geography has been closer to the positivist than to any other approach'. See Johnston, *Philosophy and Human Geography*, p. 52.

7. For a review of this approach, see Johnston, *Philosophy and Human Geography*, pp. 33–54; and Holt-Jensen, *Geography* ch. 4. Harvey, for example, writes: 'The whole practice and philosophy of geography depends upon the development of a conceptual framework for handling the distribution of objects and events in space.' D. Harvey, *Explanation in Geography*, London: Arnold, 1969, p. 191. It is interesting to notice that Harvey's book is considered to be a paradigm of positivist human geography, even though its author never refers to or says a word about positivist philosophy or methodology. This is why positivism has often been labelled 'the hidden philosophy' of geographers in the spatial-science tradition. See on this, for example M. R. Hill, 'Positivism: a "hidden" philosophy in geography', in M. E. Harvey and B. P. Holly (eds), *Themes in Geographic*

Thought, London: Croom Helm, 1981. See on this also Cloke *et al.*, *Approaching Human Geography*, pp. 12–13.

8. For an 'authoritarian definition' of space and place, see Holt-Jensen, *Geography*, p. 141, quoting from the 'National Curriculum Geography Working Group, 1989': 'The study of *place* seeks to *describe and understand* not only the location of the physical and human features of the earth, but also the processes, systems, and interrelationships that create and influence those features; the study of *space* seeks to explore the relationships between places and patterns of activity arising from the use people make of the physical settings where they live and work.'

9. Johnston, *Philosophy and Human Geography*, p. 34.

10. Ibid.

11. G. Hard, *Die Geographie, Eine Wissenschafttheoretische Einfurung*, Berlin: De Greuyter, 1973, p. 184; quoted in Holt-Jensen, *Geography*, p. 85.

12. See as an example Haggett's model for representing spatial distributions, built on five geometrical elements (movements, channels, nodes, hierarchies, and surfaces). See P. Haggett, *Locational Analysis in Human Geography*, London: Arnold, 1965; and P. Haggett, A. D. Cliff and A. Frey, *Locational Analysis in Human Geography*, London: Arnold, 1997. For a description of model building in spatial human geography, see Holt-Jensen, *Geography*, pp. 83–5.

13. See for this definition P. E. James, 'Towards a fuller understanding of the regional concept', *Annals of the Association of American Geographers*, 42 (1952), p. 199; quoted in Cloke *et al.*, *Approaching Human Geography*, p. 11. The old concept of region focused on the essential unity of some territory, acquired as a consequence of a long-term interaction (sometimes defined in terms of vertical relations) between nature and humanity. See, for example, P. Vidal de la Blanche, *Principles of Human Geography*, Engl. trans., London: Constable, 1926.

14. W. Christaller, *Central Places in Southern Germany*, Engl. trans., Englewood Cliffs: Prentice Hall, 1966. See also B. J. L. Berry, and J. B. Parr, *Geography of Market Centres and Retail Distribution*, 2nd edn, Englewood Cliffs: Prentice Hall, 1988. Christaller's theory was actually used in planning the establishment of new settlements in northern and eastern Europe. See Holt-Jensen, *Geography*, pp. 79–81.

15. Hexagonal representation was chosen because 'hexagons are the most efficient geometrical figures for the exhaustion of a territory without overlap'. See R. J. Johnston, 'Central place theory', in R. J. Johnston, D. Gregory and D. M. Smith (eds), *The Dictionary of Human Geography*, p. 57.

16. It should be noted that when geography pulled together positivism and system analysis in the 1960s and early 1970s, the dominant paradigm of research was economics. The paradigm changed, during the 1970s, to historical materialism, and further on, in the 1980s, to structuration theory.

17. Johnston, *Philosophy and Human Geography*, p. 36.

18. As shown, for example, in P. Dicken, *Location in Space*, London: Harper & Row, 1978; and D. M. Smith, *Industrial Location: An Economic Geographical Analysis*, New York: John Wiley, 1981.

19. On urban geography, and its relation to location theory, spatial science and positivistic methodology, see R. J. Johnston, *Geographers and Geography: Anglo-American Human Geography since 1945*, 5th edn, London: Arnold, 1997. See also

H. Carter, *The Study of Urban Geography*, London: Arnold, 1988; and the pioneering T. G. Taylor, *Urban Geography*, New York: E. P. Dutton, 1946.

20. See D. W. G. Timms, *The Urban Mosaic*, Cambridge: Cambridge University Press, 1971. On this, see also R. J. Johnston, *City and Society: An Outline for Urban Geography*, London: Hutchinson, 1984.

21. For the description which follows, see R. J. Johnston, 'Writing geographically', in J. Eyles (ed.), *Research in Human Geography*, Oxford: Blackwell, 1988, p. 176.

22. Quite interestingly, even the Harvey of *Explanation in Geography* (a book which was considered a typical product of positivistically inspired human geography), changed his mind concerning the explanatory power of quantitative analysis in positivistic style. Reflecting a general climate of increasing dissatisfaction with positivism, Harvey embraced, only a few years later, a rather different kind of analysis. See D. Harvey, *Social Justice and the City*, London: Arnold, 1973.

23. See Holt-Jensen, *Geography*, pp. 93–4; and Johnston, *Geographers and Geography*, p. 150.

24. It should be noted here that there have been attempts to deal with the specific behavioural traits of individuals within an essentially positivistic framework. This is the so-called 'behavioural geography', which flourished in the 1980s. See, for example, H. Couclelis and R. Golledge, 'Analytic research, positivism and behavioural geography', *Annals of the Association of American Geographers*, 73 (1983).

25. See, for example, S. W. Wooldridge, 'The Anglo-Saxon settlement', in H. D. Darby (ed.), *An Historical Geography in England before 1500*, Cambridge: Cambridge University Press, 1936, where the countryside is viewed through the eyes of the farmers living in it; or the French school of regional geography and landscape, e.g. Vidal de la Blanche, *Principles of Human Geography*. Interestingly, Vidal de la Blanche's regional geography was much liked by the Annales School of historical research. On the 'pre-history of humanistic geography', see Cloke *et al.*, *Approaching Human Geography*, pp. 63–7.

26. See W. Kirk, 'Historical geography and the concept of behavioural environment', *Indian Geographical Journal*, 25 (1951).

27. It is interesting to notice that when later, in the 1970s, the views and goals of practising geography in a humanistic style became clearer and more developed, the framework of argument was still very similar. For example, Tuan claimed that a humanistic geography should aim at 'an understanding of the human world by studying people's relations with nature, their geographical behaviour as well as their feeling and ideas in regard to space and place'. See Y-F. Tuan, 'Space and place: humanistic perspectives', *Progress in Geography* 6 (1974), p. 213. See also Y-F. Tuan, 'Humanistic geography', *Annals of the Association of American Geographers*, 66 (1976); and Y-F. Tuan, *Space and Place: The Perspectives of Experience*, London: Arnold, 1977.

28. See D. C. D. Pocock, 'Place and the novelist', in *Transactions, Institute of British Geographers*, NS6, 1981; and Y-F. Tuan, 'Literature and geography: implications for geographical research', in D. Ley and M. S. Samuels (eds), *Humanistic Geography: Prospects and Problems*, London: Croom Helm, 1978.

29. Cloke *et al.*, *Approaching Human Geography*, p. 69.

30. J. N. Entrikin, 'Contemporary humanism in geography', *Annals of the Association of American Geographers*, 66 (1976), p. 616.

31. R. G. Collingwood, *The Idea of History*, Oxford: Oxford University Press, 1946, p. 210.
32. C. Harris, 'The historical mind and the practice of geography', in Ley and Samuels, *Humanistic Geography*, pp. 125–6.
33. L. Guelke, 'Idealism', in M. E. Harvey and B. P. Hollis (eds), *Themes in Geographic Thought*, London: Croom Helm, 1981, p. 132. See also L. Guelke, *Historical Understanding in Geography: An Idealistic Approach*, Cambridge: Cambridge University Press, 1982.
34. E. Relph, *Place and Placelessness*, London: Pion, 1976, p. 6.
35. J. Eyles, *Senses of Place*, Warrington: Silverbrook Press, 1985.
36. R. D. Sack, *Conceptions of Space in Social Thought*, London: Macmillan, 1980a; see also R. D. Sack, 'Conceptions of geographic space', *Progress in Human Geography*, 4 (1980b). For a review of positions, and a description of the concept of 'sense of place', see Holt-Jensen, *Geography*, pp. 158–66.
37. See on this the Introduction to this volume, sect. 3.
38. This is an abridged version of the list offered by Sayer in A. Sayer, *Method in Social Science. A Realist Approach*, 2nd edn, London: Routledge, 1992, pp. 5–6.
39. A forerunner to the attempt at combining agency and structure can be found in Giddens's structuration theory, introduced into geographical literature, for example, by A. Pred, 'Place as historically-contingent process: structuration and the time-geography of becoming places', *Annals of the Association of American Geographers*, 74 (1984). However, as has been pointed out, Giddens's ideas proved difficult to use as practical guidelines for geographical research. See on this Cloke *et al.*, *Approaching Human Geography*, pp. 17–18.
40. In the 1980s realist analyses of space informed a number of valuable contributions among geographers and social scientists alike. See, among others, D. Gregory and J. Urry, *Social Relations and Spatial Structures*, London: Macmillan, 1985; N. Thrift, 'On the determination of social action in space and time', *Environment and Planning D: Society and Space*, 1 (1983); E. W. Soja, 'The socio-spatial dialectic', *Annals of the Association of American Geographers*, 70 (1980).
41. For these distinctions, see A. Sayer, 'The difference that space makes', in Gregory and Urry, *Social Relations*. For Sayer's version of realism (explicitly influenced by Bhaskar's and Harré's views) and its relation to social science see Sayer, *Method in Social Science*, and his more recent *Realism and Social Science*, London: Sage, 2000, where he specifically discusses the case of geographical space.
42. Sayer, *Method in Social Science*, p. 89.
43. Ibid., p. 91.
44. Sayer, 'The difference that space makes', p. 50.
45. Ibid, p. 49.
46. Sayer, *Method in Social Science*, p. 92.
47. For this reason concrete research is not to be confused with empirical generalization, which is part of the positivistic method of establishing event-regularities. See on this Cloke *et al.*, *Approaching Human Geography*, p. 154.
48. Extensive methods study large numbers of individuals according to a limited number of properties used to define them. Intensive methods study a large

number of properties in a small sample of individuals. See R. Harré, *Social Being*, Oxford: Blackwell, 1979, pp. 132–4.

49. Sayer, 'The difference that space makes', p. 51.

50. See J. Blaut, 'Space and process', *Professional Geographer*, 13 (1963); quoted in Sayer, *Realism and Social Science*, p. 11.

51. This has been called 'spatial fetishism or separatism'. See Sayer, *Realism and Social Science*, p. 112.

52. Ibid.

53. Ibid.

54. Sayer, *Method in Social Science*, p. 116.

55. Sayer, *Realism and Social Science*, p. 112.

56. Ibid., pp. 122–3.

57. Ibid., pp. 109–110.

58. Ibid., p. 124.

59. A. C. Pratt, 'Putting critical realism to work: the practical implications for geographical research', *Progress in Human Geography*, 19 (1995).

60. This perspective is taken from various positions: Bhaskar, Harré, Outhwaite, and Sayer.

61. A. C. Pratt, *Uneven Re-production. Industry, Space and Society*, Oxford: Pergamon, 1994, pp. xi–xii. Andy Pratt explained to me that focusing on the social production of the built environment was part of his attempt to denaturalise the concept of space. His further research on rurality expands on this idea that space is 'constituted', and shows how an analysis of social practices and relations is able to explain that this is the case. See H. Jarvis, A. C. Pratt and C. C. Wu, *The Secret Life of Cities: The Social Reproduction of Everyday Life*, London: Pearson, 2001; and A. C. Pratt and J. Murdoch, 'From the power of topography to the topography of power', in P. Cloke and J. Little (eds), *Contested Countryside Cultures: Rurality and Socio-cultural Maginalization*, London: Routledge, 1997.

62. Pratt, *Uneven Re-production*, p. 78. Pratt's reference is to Urry's position as outlined in J. Urry, 'Social relations, space and time', in Gregory and Urry, *Social Relations*.

63. Pratt, *Uneven Re-production*, p. 78

64. Ibid., p. 83.

65. Pratt, 'Putting critical realism to work', p. 72.

66. R. G. Golledge, 'Fundamental conflicts and the search for geographical knowledge', in P. Gould and G. Ollson (eds), *A Search for Common Ground*, London: Pion, 1982, p. 21.

67. Fenland (or 'the Fens') is a lowland covered wholly or partially with shallow water, or frequently inundated. It refers to the low-lying districts in Cambridgeshire, Lincolnshire and adjoining counties.

68. D. I. Scargill, 'Space, place and region: towards a transformed regional geography', *Geography*, 70 (1985), pp. 140–41.

69. As Haggett puts it, maps are the geographers' 'mirrors', but the images seen in these mirrors are 'symbolic reflections' of the global reality captured by them. See Haggett, *The Geographer's Art*, p. 5.

70. Holt-Jensen, *Geography*, p. 114.

71. J. B. Harley, 'Maps, knowledge and power', in D. Cosgrove and S. Daniels (eds),

The Iconography of Landscape, Cambridge: Cambridge University Press, 1988; and J. B. Harley, 'Deconstructing the map', *Cartographica*, 26 (1989).

72. See for example, B. Axelsen and M. Jones, 'Are all maps mental maps?', *Geo-Journal*, 14 (1987). Here it is asked, even more radically, whether there even are any maps other than *mental* maps.

73. Darby pointed out how, despite overall agreement on the fact that geography must concern itself, among other things, with the description of the Earth's surface, what counts as 'description' faces several problems and difficulties in geography. In particular, description as the result of the ability to represent objectively all the various elements of, say, a landscape, is a highly controversial claim. There is no such a thing as 'mere' description. Geographical descriptions are constantly on the verge of becoming 'something different' (explanations, historical narratives, etc.). See H. C. Darby, 'The problem of geographical description', *Transactions. Institute of British Geographers*, 30 (1962).

74. On this, see the Introduction to this volume, sect. 4.

75. This is a consequence of Kant's transcendental perspective: 'I entitle *transcendental* all knowledge which is occupied not so much with objects as with the mode of our knowledge of objects.' I. Kant, 'Introduction', *Critique of Pure Reason*, London: Macmillan, 1933, p. 59 (A12). In particular, it is transcendental logic which, for Kant, correctly deals with the relation (or 'synthetic' agreement) between experience and those 'principles without which no object can be thought'. Kant, 'Transcendental Logic', ibid., p. 100 (B87).

76. The constructive function of these procedures of inquiry are taken as the equivalent of the constructive function of the Kantian categories of the human intellect. It is, nonetheless, the neo-Kantian interpretation of this function as being cultural and historical (rather than a priori) which allows us to make sense of this equivalence, and make a substantial analytic use of it, especially in view of assessing the notion of objectivity. For the neo-Kantian interpretation see Cassirer, E. (1929) *The Philosophy of Symbolic Forms: The Phenomenology of Knowledge*, Vol III, Oxford: Oxford University Press, 1957; also the introduction to this book, pp. 19–20 and especially n69.

Bibliography

Arnold, K. (1996), 'Time heals: making history in medical museums', in G. Kavanagh (ed.), *Making Histories in Museums*, London: Leicester University Press.

Ashman, K. M. and Baringer, P. S. (eds) (2001), *After the Science Wars*, London: Routledge.

Astuti, R. (2000), 'Are we all Natural Dualists? A Cognitive Developmental Approach', The Malinowski Memorial Lecture, London School of Economics, London: Mimeo.

Atkinson, J. (1978), *Discovering Suicide: Studies in the Social Organization of Sudden Death*, London: Macmillan.

Austin, J. L. (1955), *How to Do Things with Words*, Cambridge: Harvard University Press (revised from 1962 edn, Oxford: Clarendon Press).

Axelsen, B. and Jones, M. (1987), 'Are all maps mental maps?', *GeoJournal*, 14.

Barnes, B. (2001), 'Searle on social reality: process is prior to product', in G. Grewendorf and G. Meggle (eds) *Speech, Acts, Mind and Social Reality*, Dordrecht: Kluwer.

Barnes, B., Bloor, D. and Henry, J. (1996), *Scientific Knowledge: A Sociological Analysis*, London: Athlone Press.

Barrett, W. (1979), *The Illusion of Technique: A Search for Meaning in a Technological Civilization*, Garden City, NY: Anchor.

Barzun, J. and Graff, H. F. (1992), *The Modern Researcher*, 5th edn, Fort Worth: Harcourt Brace Jovanovich College Publishers.

Bavetta, S. (2001), 'Measuring Freedom: a review of the axiomatic and the statistical approaches', London: Mimeo.

Bazerman, C. (1988), *Shaping Written Knowledge*, Madison: University of Wisconsin Press.

Bennett, T. (1998), 'Speaking to the eyes. Museums, legibility and the social order', in S. Macdonald (ed.), *The Politics of Display*, London/New York: Routledge.

Benton, T. (1981), 'Realism and social science. Some comments on Roy Bhaskar's "The Possibility of Naturalism"', *Radical Philosophy*, 27.

Berry, B. J. L. and Parr, J. B. (1988), *Geography of Market Centres and Retail Distribution*, 2nd edn, Englewood Cliffs: Prentice Hall.

Bhaskar, R. (1975), *A Realist Theory of Science*, York: Alma Book Company.

Bhaskar, R. (1979), *The Possibility of Naturalism*, Brighton: The Harvester Press (2nd edn with new Introduction 1989, London: Harvester Wheatsheaf).

Black, T. R. (1998), *Doing Quantitative Research in the Social Sciences: An Integrated Approach to Research Design, Measurement and Statistics*, London: Sage.

Blaug, M. (1992), *The Methodology of Economics or How Economists Explain*, Cambridge: Cambridge University Press.

Blaut, J. (1961), 'Space and process', *Professional Geographer*, 13.

Bloch, M. (1961), *Feudal Society*, Engl. trans., London: Routledge and Kegan Paul.

Bloch, M. E. F. (1998), *How we Think they Think*, Oxford: Westview Press.

Bloor, D. (1976), *Knowledge and Social Imagery*, London: Routledge and Kegan Paul.

Blumer, M. (1984), 'Why don't sociologists make more use of official statistics?', in M. Blumer (ed.), *Sociological Research Methods*, 2nd edn, London: Macmillan.

Bohemer, H. (1930), *Luther and the Reformation in the Light of Modern Research*, Engl. trans., New York: The Dial Press.

Bohman, J. (1991), *New Philosophy of Social Science*, Cambridge: Polity Press.

Borutti, S. (1999), *Filosofia delle scienze umane. Le categorie dell'Antropologia e della Sociologia*, Milan: B. Mondadori.

Brandt, W. J. (1966), *The Shape of Medieval History: Studies in Modes of Perception*, New Haven: Yale University Press.

Broome, J. (1999), 'Qalys', in J. Broome, *Ethics out of Economics*, Cambridge: Cambridge University Press

Bullock, A. and Trombley, S. (1988), *The Fontana Dictionary of Modern Thought*, London: Fontana Press.

Burke, P. (1990), *The French Historical Revolution: The Annales School 1929–1989*, Cambridge: Polity Press.

Burke, P. (1999), 'Reflections on the historical revolution in France: The Annales School and British Social History', in S. Clark (ed.), *The Annales School. Critical Assessments*, vol. II, London: Routledge.

Button, G. (ed.) (1991), *Ethnomethodology and the Human Sciences*, Cambridge: Cambridge University Press.

Callinicos, A. (1995), *Theories as Narratives: Reflections on the Philosophy of History*, Cambridge: Polity Press.

Carter, H. (1988), *The Study of Urban Geography*, London: Arnold.

Cartwright, N. (1999), *The Dappled World*, Cambridge: Cambridge University Press.

Cassirer, E. (1929), *The Philosophy of Symbolic Forms: The Phenomenology of Knowledge*, vol. III, R. Manheim edn 1957, Oxford: Oxford University Press.

Christaller, W. (1966), *Central Places in Southern Germany*, Engl. trans., Englewood Cliffs: Prentice Hall.

Cicourel, A. (1964), *Method and Measurement in Sociology*, New York: The Free Press.

Clifford, J. (1988), *The Predicament of Culture: Twentieth-century Ethnography, Literature and Art*, Cambridge MA/London: Harvard University Press.

Clifford, J. and Marcus, G. (eds) (1986), *Writing Culture: The Poetics and Politics of Ethnography*, Berkeley: University of California Press.

Cloke, P., Philo, C. and Sadler, D. (1991), *Approaching Human Geography*, London: Paul Chapman.

Collingwood, R. G. (1946), *The Idea of History*, Oxford: Oxford University Press.

Comte, A. (1853), *The Positive Philosophy*, Engl. abridged edn, London: Paul Chapman, 2 vols.

Couclelis, H. and Golledge, R. (1983), 'Analytic research, positivism and behavioural geography', *Annals of the Association of American Geographers*, 73.

Craib, I. (1992), *Modern Social Theory*, 2nd edn, New York/London: Harvester Wheatsheaf.

Cunningham, F. (1973), *Objectivity in Social Science*, Toronto: University of Toronto Press.

D'Andrade, R. (1995), *The Development of Cognitive Anthropology*, Cambridge: Cambridge University Press.

Danto, A. C. (1965), *Analytic Philosophy of History*, Cambridge: Cambridge University Press.

Darby, H. C. (1962), 'The problem of geographical description', *Transactions, Institute of British Geographers*, 30.

Daston, L. (1992), 'Objectivity and the escape from perspective', *Social Studies of Science*, 22.

Daston, L. and Galison, P. (1992), 'The image of objectivity', *Representations*, 40.

Dicken, P. (1978), *Location in Space*, London: Harper & Row.

Douglas, J. D. (1967), *The Social Meanings of Suicide*, Princeton: Princeton University Press.

Dray, W. (1957), *Laws and Explanation in History*, Oxford: Clarendon Press.

Dray, W. (1959), 'Explaining "what" in history', in P. L. Gardiner (ed.), *Theories of History*, New York: The Free Press.

Droysen, G. (1875), *Grundriss der Historik*, Leipzig: Veit.

Dupré, J. (2001), *Human Nature and the Limits of Science*, Oxford: Oxford University Press.

Durkheim, E. (1952), *Suicide: A Study in Sociology*, Engl. trans. J. A. S. Spaulding and G. Simpson, London: Routledge.

Durkheim, E. (1982a), 'Debate on the relationship between ethnology and sociology', in S. Lukes (ed.), *Durkheim, The Rules of Sociological Method and Selected Texts on Sociology and its Method*, London: Macmillan.

Durkheim, E. (1982b), 'The Rules of Sociological Method', in S. Lukes (ed.), *Durkheim, The Rules of Sociological Method and Selected Texts on Sociology and its Method*, London: Macmillan.

Dwyer, K. (1982), *Moroccan Dialogues. Anthropology in Question*, Baltimore: The Johns Hopkins University Press.

Edgar, A. (1996), 'Measuring the quality of life', in P. Badham and P. Ballard (eds), *Facing Death: An Interdisciplinary Approach*, Cardiff: University of Wales Press.

Entrikin, J. N. (1976), 'Contemporary humanism in geography', *Annals of the Association of American Geographers*, 66.

Erickson, P. A. (1998), *A History of Anthropological Theory*, Peterborough: Broadview Press.

Evans-Pritchard, E. E. (1956), *Nuer Religion*, Oxford: Oxford University Press.

Eyles, J. (1985), *Senses of Place*, Warrington: Silverbrook Press.

Fabian, J. (1992), *Time and the Work of Anthropology: Critical Essays 1971–1991*, Amsterdam: Harwood Academic Publishers.

Favret-Sadat, J. (1980), *Deadly Words: Witchcraft in the Bocage*, Engl. trans., Cambridge: Cambridge University Press.

Febvre, L. (1985), *The Problem of Unbelief in the Sixteenth Century, The Religion of Rabelais*, Engl. trans., Cambridge MA: Harvard University Press.

Feyerabend, P. (1975), *Against Method*, London: New Left Books.

Findlen, P. (1994), *Possessing Nature: Museums, Collecting and Scientific Culture in Early Modern Italy*, Berkeley: University of California Press.

Flick, U. (1998), *An Introduction to Qualitative Research*, London: Sage.

Flyvbjerg, B. (2001), *Making Social Science Matter. Why Social Inquiry Fails and How it Can Succeed Again*, Cambridge: Cambridge University Press.

Forcese, D. P. and Richer, S. (eds) (1970), *Stages of Social Research*, Englewood Cliffs: Prentice Hall.

Foucault, M. (1982), *The Archeology of Knowledge*, Engl. trans., New York: Pantheon.

Fox-Keller, E. (1985), *Reflections on Gender and Science*, New Haven: Yale University Press.

Friedman, M. (1953), 'The methodology of positive economics', in M. Friedman, *Essays in Positive Economics*, Chicago/London: Chicago University Press.

Furet, F. (1981), *Interpreting the French Revolution*, Engl. trans., Cambridge: Cambridge University Press.

Furet, F. (1985), 'Quantitative methods in history', in J. Le Goff and P. Nora (eds), *Constructing the Past: Essays in Historical Methodology*, Engl. trans., Cambridge: Cambridge University Press.

Furet, F. and Ozouf, J. (1982), *Reading and Writing: Literacy in France from Calvin to Jules Ferry*, Engl. trans., Cambridge: Cambridge University Press.

Gallie, W. B. (1956), 'Essentially contested concepts', *Proceedings of the Aristotelian Society.*, LVI, New Series.

Garfinkel, H. (1967), *Studies in Ethnomethodology*, Englewood Cliffs: Prentice Hall.

Garfinkel, H. and Sacks, H. (1970), 'On Formal Structures of Practical Actions', in J. C. McKinney and E. A. Tiryakian (eds), *Theoretical Sociology*, New York: Appleton-Century-Crofts.

Geertz, C. (1973), *The Interpretation of Cultures*, New York: Basic Books.

Geertz, C. (1983), *Local Knowledge*, New York: Basic Books.

Geertz, C. (1988), *Works and Lives: The Anthropologist as Author*, Cambridge: Polity Press.

Genberg, A. H. (1976), 'Aspects of the monetary approach to the balance-of-payments theory: an empirical study', in J. A. Frenkel and H. G. Johnson (eds), *The Monetary Approach to the Balance of Payments*, London: Allen and Unwin.

Giddens, A. (1976), *New Rules of Sociological Method: A Positive Critique of Interpretativist Sociologies*, London: Hutchinson (revised version 1993, Cambridge: Polity Press).

Gilbert, N. (1993), *Researching Social Life*, London: Sage.

Goffman, E. (1969), *The Presentation of Self in Everyday Life*, London: Penguin.

Goffman, E. (1974), *Frame Analysis*, Cambridge MA: Harvard University Press.

Golledge, R. G. (1982), 'Fundamental conflicts and the search for geographical knowledge', in P. Gould and G. Ollson (eds), *A Search for Common Ground*, London: Pion.

Goodman, N. (1978), *Ways of Worldmaking*, Indianapolis: Hackett.

Gould, J. and Kolb, W. L. (eds) (1964), *A Dictionary of the Social Sciences*, London: Tavistock.

Gregory, D. and Urry, J. (1985), *Social Relations and Spatial Structures*, London: Macmillan.

Guelke, L. (1981), 'Idealism', in M. E. Harvey and B. P. Hollis (eds), *Themes in Geographic Thought*, London: Croom Helm.

Guelke, L. (1982), *Historical Understanding in Geography: An Idealistic Approach*, Cambridge: Cambridge University Press.

Haac, O. A. (1995), *The Correspondence of John Stuart Mill and Auguste Comte*, New Brunswick: Transaction Publications.

Hacking, I. (1997), 'Searle, reality and the social', *History of the Human Sciences*, 10:4.

Hacking, I. (1999), *The Social Construction of What?*, Cambridge MA: Harvard University Press.

Haggett, P. (1965), *Locational Analysis in Human Geography*, London: Arnold.

Haggett, P. (1990), *The Geographer's Art*, Oxford: Blackwell.

Haggett, P. (1994), 'Geography', in R. J. Johnston, D. Gregory and D. M. Smith, *The Dictionary of Human Geography*, Oxford: Blackwell.

Haggett, P., Cliff, A. D. and Frey, A. (1977), *Locational Analysis in Human Geography*, London: Arnold.

Hahn, F. (1992), 'Answer to Backhouse: Yes', *Royal Economics Society Newsletter*, 78.

Hahn, H., Neurath, O. and Carnap, R. (1973), 'The scientific conception of the world: The Vienna Circle', in O. Neurath and R. S. Cohen (eds), *Empiricism and Sociology*, Dordrecht: D. Reidel.

Hard, G. (1973), *Die Geographie, Eine Wissenschafttheoretische Einfurung*, Berlin: De Greuyter.

Harding, S. (1987), *Feminism and Methodology*, Bloomington, IN: Indiana University Press.

Harley, J. B. (1988), 'Maps, knowledge and power', in D. Cosgrove and S. Daniels (eds), *The Iconography of Landscape*, Cambridge: Cambridge University Press.

Harley, J. B. (1989), 'Deconstructing the map', *Cartographica*, 26.

Harré, R. (1979), *Social Being*, Oxford: Blackwell (revised edn 1993, Oxford: Blackwell).

Harris, C. (1978), 'The historical mind and the practice of geography', in D. Ley and M. S. Samuels (eds), *Humanistic Geography*, London: Croom Helm.

Hartshorne, R. (1959), *Perspectives on the Nature of Geography*, Chicago: Rand McNally.

Harvey, D. (1969), *Explanation in Geography*, London: Arnold.

Harvey, D. (1973), *Social Justice and the City*, London: Arnold.

Hempel, C. (1962), 'Explanation in science and history', in R. G. Colodny (ed.), *Frontiers of Science and Philosophy*, Pittsburgh: University of Pittsburgh Press.

Hempel, C. (1965), *Aspects of Scientific Explanation*, New York: The Free Press.

Hesse, M. (1980), 'The strong thesis of sociology of science', in M. Hesse, *Revolutions and Reconstructions in the Philosophy of Science*, Brighton: Harvester Press.

Hill, M. R. (1981), 'Positivism: a "hidden" philosophy in geography', in M. E. Harvey and B. P. Holly (eds.), *Themes in Geographic Thought*, London: Croom Helm.

Hindess, B. (1973), *The Use of Official Statistics in Sociology*, London: Macmillan.

Holt-Jensen, A. (1999), *Geography. History and Concepts*, London: Sage.

Holy, L. (1987), *Comparative Anthropology*, Oxford: Blackwell.

Hooper-Greenhill, E. (2000), *Museums and the Interpretation of Visual Culture*, London: Routledge.

Houghton, W. E. (1957), *The Victorian Frame of Mind*, New Haven: Yale University Press.

Howe, M. J. A. (1997), *I. Q. in Question*, London: Sage.

Jacoby, R. and Glauberman, N. (1995), *The Bell Curve Debate*, New York: Times Books.

James, P. E. (1952), 'Towards a fuller understanding of the regional concept', *Annals of the Association of American Geographers*, 42.

Jarvis, H., Pratt, A. C. and Wu, C. C. (2001), *The Secret Life of Cities: The Social Reproduction of Everyday Life*, London: Pearson.

Johnston, R. J. (1984), *City and Society: An Outline for Urban Geography*, London: Hutchinson.

Johnston, R. J. (1986), *Philosophy and Human Geography*, London: Arnold.

Johnston, R. J. (1988), 'Writing geographically', in J. Eyles (ed.), *Research in Human Geography*, Oxford: Blackwell.

Johnston, R. J. (1994), 'Central place theory', in R. J. Johnston, D. Gregory and D. M. Smith, *The Dictionary of Human Geography*, Oxford: Blackwell.

Johnston, R. J. (1997), *Geographers and Geography: Anglo-American Human Geography Since 1945*, 5th edn, London: Arnold.

Jordanova, L. (1989), 'Objects of knowledge: A historical perspective on museums', in P. Vergo (ed.), *The New Museology*, London: Reaktion Books.

Kant, I., *Critique of Pure Reason*, N. Kemp Smith edn 1933, London: Macmillan.

Kavanagh, G. (1996), 'Making histories, making memories', in G. Kavanagh (ed.), *Making Histories in Museums*, London: Leicester University Press.

Kennedy, P. (1993), 'British economic decline: bourgeois methodology versus Marxism', Glasgow: Mimeo.

Kind, P., Rosser, R. and Williams, A. (1982), 'Valuation of quality of life: some psychometric evidence', in M.W. Jones-Lee (ed.), *The Value of Life and Safety*, Leiden: North Holland Publishing.

King, G., Keohane, R. O. and Verba, S. (1994), *Designing Social Inquiry: Scientific Inference in Qualitative Research*, Princeton: Princeton University Press.

Kirby, M. W. (1992), 'Institutional rigidities and economic decline: reflections on the British experience', *Economic History Review*, XLV:4.

Kirk, W. (1951), 'Historical geography and the concept of behavioural environment', *Indian Geographical Journal*, 25.

Koertge, N. (1998), *A House Built on Sand*, Oxford: Oxford University Press.

Kuhn, T. (1962), *The Structure of Scientific Revolutions*, Chicago: Chicago University Press.

Kuhn, T. (1977), *The Essential Tension*, Chicago: Chicago University Press.

Kukla, A. (2000), *Social Constructivism and the Philosophy of Science*, London/New York: Routledge.

Lakatos, I. (1970), 'Falsification and the methodology of scientific research programmes', in I. Lakatos and A. Musgrave (eds), *Criticism and the Growth of Knowledge*, Cambridge: Cambridge University Press.

Lassman, P. (ed.) (2000), *Peter Winch and 'The Idea of a Social Science'*, special double issue of *The History of the Human Sciences*, 13:1/13:2.

Lawson, T. (1997a), *Economics and Reality*, London/New York: Routledge.

Lawson, T. (1997b), 'Economics as a distinct social science: on the nature, scope and method of economics', *Economie Appliquée*, L:2.

Lawson, T. and Kilpatrick, A. (1980), 'On the nature of industrial decline in the UK', *Cambridge Journal of Economics*, 4 (reprinted in D. Coates and J. Hillard (eds) (1986), *The Economic Decline of Modern Britain*, London: Harvester Press.

Le Goff, J. (1984), *The Birth of Purgatory*, Engl. trans., London: Scolar Press.

Le Goff, J. and Nora, P. (eds) (1995), *Constructing the Past: Essays in Historical Methodology*, Engl. trans., Cambridge: Cambridge University Press.

Lewis-Beck, M. S. (1993), *Experimental Design and Methods*, International Handbooks of Quantitative Applications in the Social Sciences, vol. 3, London: Sage.

Lizza, J. (1993), 'Persons and death: what's metaphysically wrong with our current statutory definition of death?', *Journal of Medicine and Philosophy*, 18:4.

Longino, H. (1990), *Science as Social Knowledge: Values and Objectivity in Scientific Inquiry*, Princeton: Princeton University Press.

Lukes, S. (1992), *Émile Durkheim, His Life and Work*, London: Penguin Books.

Lyas, C. (1999), *Peter Winch*, Teddington: Acumen.

McCloskey, D. (1986), *The Rhetoric of Economics*, Brighton: Harvester Press (revised edn 1998), Madison/London: The University of Wisconsin Press.

McCloskey, D. (1990), *If You're so Smart. The Narrative of Economic Expertise*, Chicago/London: The University of Chicago Press.

McCloskey, D. (1994), *Knowledge and Persuasion in Economics*, Cambridge: Cambridge University Press.

McCloskey, D. and Zecher, J. R. (1976), 'How the gold standard worked, 1880–1913.' in J. A. Frenkel and H. G. Johnson (eds), *The Monetary Approach to the Balance of Payments*, London: Allen and Unwin.

Malinowski, B. (1922), *Argonauts of the Western Pacific: An Account of Native Enterprise and Adventure in the Archipelagoes of Melanesian New Guinea*, London: Rouledge and Kegan Paul.

Mannheim, K. (1936), *Ideology and Utopia*, London: Routledge (2nd edn 1991, Routledge).

Marcus, G. E. and Fisher, M. M. J. (1986), *Anthropology as Cultural Critique*, Chicago: Chicago University Press.

Megill, A. (ed.) (1994), *Rethinking Objectivity*, Durham/London: Duke University Press.

Menget, P. (1982), 'Time of birth, time of being: the couvade', in M. Izard and P. Smith (eds), *Between Belief and Transgression: Structuralist Essays in Religion, History and Myth*, Chicago: Chicago University Press.

Milgram, S. (1974), *Obedience to Authority: An Experimental View*, London: Tavistock.

Mill, J. S. (1881), 'On the logic of the moral sciences', in J. S. Mill, *A System of Logic*, BK VI, in J. M. Robson and R. F. McRae (ed) (1974), *Collected Works of J. S. Mill*, vol. VIII, Toronto: University of Toronto Press.

Montuschi, E. (1993), 'Rhetorical aspects of scientific arguments', in R. Harré (ed.), *Reason and Rhetoric*, Lewiston: The Mellen Press.

Montuschi, E. (1994), 'Persuading science: the art of scientific rhetoric', *The British Journal for the Philosophy of Science*, 45.

Montuschi, E. (1996), 'Metaphor in social science', *Theoria*, 25.

Montuschi, E. (1999), 'Sociologia', in S. Borutti *Filosofia delle scienze umane. Le categorie dell'Antropologia e della Sociologia*, Milan: B. Mondadori.

Montuschi, E. (2000), 'Measuring life and choosing death: moral, empirical and social aspects of euthanasia', London: Mimeo.

Morgenbesser, S. (1966), 'Is it a science?', in D. Emmet and A. MacIntyre (eds), *Sociological Theory and Philosophical Analysis*, London: Macmillan.

Myrdal, G. (1958), *Value in Social Theory*, London: Routledge and Kegan Paul.

Myrdal, G. (1970), *Objectivity in Social Research*, London: Duckworth.

Myrdal, G. (1971), 'How scientific are the social sciences?', The Gordon Allport Memorial Lecture, Harvard University, Folio, LSE Library.

Nagel, E. (1961), *The Structure of Science: Problems in the Logic of Scientific Explanation*, London: Routledge and Kegan Paul.

Neurath, O. (1973), 'Empirical Sociology', in O. Neurath and R. S. Cohen (eds), *Empiricism and Sociology*, Dordrecht: D. Reidel.

Outhwaite, W. (1987), *New Philosophies of Social Science: Realism, Hermeneutics and Critical Theory*, Basingstoke: Macmillan.

Outhwaite, W. (2000), 'The philosophy of social science', in B. S. Turner (ed.), *The Blackwell Companion to Social Theory*, 2nd edn, Oxford: Blackwell.

Outhwaite, W. and Bottomore, T. (1992), *The Blackwell Dictionary of Twentieth-Century Social Thought*, Oxford/Cambridge MA: Blackwell.

Pocock, D. C. D. (1981), 'Place and the novelist', in *Transactions, Institute of British Geographers*, NS6.

Pratt, A. C. (1994), *Uneven Re-production. Industry, Space and Society*, Oxford: Pergamon.

Pratt, A. C. (1995), 'Putting critical realism to work: the practical implications for geographical research', *Progress in Human Geography*, 19.

Prat, A. C. and Murdoch, J. (1997), 'From the power of topography to the topography of power', in P. Cloke and J. Little (eds), *Contested Countryside Cultures: Rurality and Socio-cultural Marginalization*, London: Routledge.

Pred, A. (1984), 'Place as historically-contingent process: structuration and the time-geography of becoming places', *Annals of the Association of American Geographers*, 74.

Raging, C. (1987), *The Comparative Method: Moving Beyond Qualitative and Quantitative Strategies*, Berkeley: University of California Press.

Relph, E. (1976), *Place and Placelessness*, London: Pion.

Riviere, P. (1974), 'The Couvade: a problem reborn', *Man*, 9:3.

Robson, C. (1993), *Real World Research*, Oxford: Blackwell.

Root, M. (1993), *Philosophy of Social Science*, Oxford: Blackwell.

Rorty, R. (1980), *Philosophy and the Mirror of Nature*, Oxford: Blackwell.

Rosenberg, A. (1988), *Philosophy of Social Science*, Oxford: Clarendon Press.

Ross, A. (ed.) (1996), *Science Wars*, Durham NC/London: Duke University Press.

Rosser, R. and Kind, P. (1978), 'A scale of valuations of states of illness: is there a social consensus?', *International Journal of Epidemiology*, 7:4.

Roth, J. (1965), 'Hired hand research', *American Sociologist*, I.

Roth, P. A. (1994), 'Narrative explanations: the case of history', in M. Martin and L. C. McIntyre (eds), *Readings in the Philosophy of Social Science*, Cambridge MA/London: The MIT Press.

Runciman, W. G. (1972), *A Critique of Max Weber's Philosophy of Social Science*, London: Cambridge University Press.

Ryle, G. (1971), *Collected Papers*, London: Hutchinson.

Sack, R. D. (1980a), *Conceptions of Space in Social Thought*, London: Macmillan.

Sack, R. D. (1980b), 'Conceptions of geographic space', *Progress in Human Geography*, 4.

Sacks, H. (1963), 'Sociological description', *Berkeley Journal of Sociology*, 8.

Sayer, A. (1985), 'The difference that space makes', in D. Gregory and J. Urry (eds), *Social Relations and Spatial Structures*, London: Macmillan.

Sayer, A. (1992), *Method in Social Science. A Realist Approach*, 2nd edn, London: Routledge.

Sayer, A. (2000), *Realism and Social Science*, London: Sage.

Scargill, D. I. (1985), 'Space, place and region: towards a transformed regional geography', *Geography*, 70.

Schaffer, S. (2000), 'Object lessons', in S. Lindqvist (ed.), *Museums of Modern Science*, New York: Science History Publications.

Schutz, A. (1990), *Collected Papers I: The Problem of Social Reality*, 6th edn, Dordrecht/Boston/London: Kluwer.

Scriven, M. (1959), 'Truisms and the grounds for historical explanation', in P. L. Gardiner (ed.), *Theories of History*, New York: The Free Press.

Searle, J. (1995), *The Construction of Social Reality*, London: Penguin.

Searle, J. (1997), 'Replies to critics of *The Construction of Social Reality*', *History of the Human Sciences*, 4.

Sharrock, W. and Button, G. (1991), 'The social actor: social action in real time', in G. Button (ed.), *Ethnomethodology and the Human Sciences*, Cambridge: Cambridge University Press.

Silverman, D. (1993), *Interpreting Qualitative Data*, London: Sage.

Smith, D. M. (1981), *Industrial Location: An Economic Geographical Analysis*, New York: John Wiley.

Soja, E. W. (1980), 'The socio-spatial dialectic', *Annals of the Association of American Geographers*, 70.

Sperber, D. (1985), *On Anthropological Knowledge: Three Essays*, Engl. trans., Cambridge: Cambridge University Press.

Sperber, D. (1996), *Explaining Culture: a Naturalistic Approach*, Oxford: Blackwell.

Stafford, B. (1983), 'The class struggle, the multiplier and the alternative economic strategy', in M. Sawyer and K. Schott (eds), *Socialist Economic Review*, London: Merlin Press.

Taylor, T. G. (1946), *Urban Geography*, New York: E. P. Dutton.

Thompson, K. (1976), *Auguste Comte. The Foundation of Sociology*, London: Nelson.

Thrift, N. (1983), 'On the determination of social action in space and time', *Environment and Planning D: Society and Space*, 1.

Timms, D. W. G. (1971), *The Urban Mosaic*, Cambridge: Cambridge University Press.

Tuan, Y-F. (1974), 'Space and place: humanistic perspectives', *Progress in Geography*, 6.

Tuan, Y-F. (1976), 'Humanistic geography', *Annals of the Association of American Geographers*, 66.

Tuan, Y-F. (1977), *Space and Place: The Perspectives of Experience*, London: Arnold.

Tuan, Y-F. (1978), 'Literature and geography: implications for geographical research', in D. Ley and M. S. Samuels (eds), *Humanistic Geography: Prospects and Problems*, London: Croom Helm.

Turner, S. (1986), *The Search for a Methodology of Social Science*, Dordrecht/Boston MA: Reidel.

Tylor, E. (1929), *Primitive Cultures*, 5th edn, London: John Murray, 2 vols.

Urry, J. (1985), 'Social relations, space and time', in D. Gregory and J. Urry, *Social Relations and Spatial Structures*, London: Macmillan.

Van Langenhove, L. and Harré, R. (1993), 'Positioning in scientific discourse', in R. Harré (ed.), *Science and Rhetoric, Anglo-Ukranian Studies in the Analysis of Scientific Discourse*, Lampeter: The Edwin Mellen Press.

Vidal de la Blanche, P. (1926), *Principles of Human Geography*, Engl. trans., London: Constable.

Von Wright, G. H. (1971), *Explanation and Understanding*, London: Routledge and Kegan Paul.

Vovelle, M. (1973), *Piété baroque et déchristianisation en Provence au XVIIIe siècle*, Paris: Plon.

Weber, M. (1949), *The Methodology of the Social Sciences*, Engl. trans., New York: The Free Press.

Winch, P. (1990), *The Idea of a Social Science and its Relation to Philosophy*, 2nd edn, London: Routledge.

Windelband, W. (1914), 'Geschichte und Naturwissenschaft. Strasburger Rektorat-srede', in W. Windelband, *Präludien. Aufsätze und Reden zur Philosophie und ihrer Geschichte*, 5th edn, vol. 2, Tübingen: Mohr.

Wittgenstein, L. (1967), *Philosophical Investigations*, ed. G. E. M. Anscombe, 3rd edn, Oxford: Blackwell.

Wittlin, A. S. (1949), *The Museum: Its History and its Tasks in Education*, London: Routledge and Kegan Paul.

Wooldridge, S. W. (1936), 'The Anglo-Saxon settlement', in H. D. Darby (ed.), *An Historical Geography in England before 1500*, Cambridge: Cambridge University Press.

Woolgar, S. (1988), *Science: The Very Idea*, Chichester: Ellis Horwood and Tavistock.

Yin, R. K. (1994), *Case Study Research. Design and Method*, 2nd edn, Beverly Hills: Sage.

Zeller, R. A. and Carmines, E. G. (1980), *Measurement in the Social Sciences: The Link Between Theory and Data*, Cambridge: Cambridge University Press.

Index